S0-ADU-357

Houses of the Founding Fathers

OTHER BOOKS BY HUGH HOWARD AND ROGER STRAUS III

Writers of the American South

Natchez

Thomas Jefferson, Architect

Wright for Wright

OTHER BOOKS BY HUGH HOWARD

Dr. Kimball and Mr. Jefferson

Colonial Houses

House-Dreams

The Preservationist's Progress

How Old Is This House?

OTHER BOOKS BY ROGER STRAUS III

Modernism Reborn: Mid-Century American Houses (with Michael Webb)

U.S. 1: America's Original Main Street (with Andrew H. Malcolm)

Mississippi Currents (with Andrew H. Malcolm)

Houses of the Founding Fathers

HUGH HOWARD

Original Photography by

ROGER STRAUS III

ARTISAN

New York

Text copyright © 2007 by Hugh Howard
Original photography copyright © 2007 by Roger Straus III

For additional illustration credits, see page 354,
which constitutes an extension of this page.

All rights reserved.
No portion of this book may be reproduced—mechanically,
electronically, or by any other means, including photocopying—
without written permission of the publisher.

Published by Artisan
A Division of Workman Publishing Company, Inc.
225 Varick Street
New York, NY 10014-4381
www.artisanbooks.com

✤

Library of Congress Cataloging-in-Publication Data
Howard, Hugh, 1952–
Houses of the founding fathers / by Hugh Howard ;
original photography by Roger Straus III.
p. cm.
ISBN-13: 978-1-57965-275-3
1. Statesmen—Homes and haunts—United States. 2. Politicians—Homes
and haunts—United States. 3. Historic buildings—United States.
4. Dwellings—United States. 5. United States—History, Local.
6. Statesmen—United States—Biography. 7. Politicians—United States—Biography.
8. Statesmen—United States—Family relationships. 9. Politicians—
United States—Family relationships. 10. United States—Biography.
I. Straus, Roger. II. Title.
E176.H866 2007
973.3092'2—dc22
2006048015

✤

Design by Nicholas Caruso and Vivian Ghazarian

Printed in China

First printing, September 2007

1 3 5 9 7 10 8 6 4 2

To the conservators of the homes of the Founding Fathers: Because of their stewardship, we can glimpse the American past

MAINE
Thomaston: *Montpelier*

NEW HAMPSHIRE
Portsmouth: *Whipple and Langdon Houses*

MASSACHUSETTS
Cambridge: *Vassall-Craigie-Longfellow House*
Marblehead: *Jeremiah Lee Mansion*
Quincy: *Old House*

RHODE ISLAND
Providence: *Hopkins House*

CONNECTICUT
Wethersfield: *Deane and Webb Houses*

NEW YORK
Albany: *Schuyler Mansion*
Katonah: *Jay Homestead*
New York: *The Grange*
Schuylerville: *Schuyler Farm*

NEW JERSEY
Morristown: *Ford Mansion*
Princeton: *Morven*
Union: *Liberty Hall*

PENNSYLVANIA
Germantown: *Cliveden, Deshler-Morris House*

DELAWARE
Dover: *Poplar Hall*
New Castle: *Amstel House*

MARYLAND
Annapolis: *Hammond House, Paca House*

VIRGINIA
Charlottesville: *Monticello*
Mason's Neck: *Gunston Hall*
Stratford: *Stratford Hall*
Williamsburg: *Randolph House, Wythe House*

NORTH CAROLINA
Edenton: *Iredell House*

SOUTH CAROLINA
Charleston: *Drayton Hall, Heyward-Washington House, Middleton Place*

GEORGIA
Savannah: *Owens-Thomas House*

0   100   200 MILES

THE HOUSES OF THE FOUNDING FATHERS

Contents

Preface

The revolutionary generation has reengaged America's interest over the last decade. Today's scholars, readers, and students alike think of the Founding Fathers less as heroes than as men. Recent biographies of Washington, Jefferson, Franklin, and Hamilton have climbed bestseller lists; those books offer new insights, looking beyond the political to the personal and the prosaic.

In *Houses of the Founding Fathers,* we seek to revisit major figures and lesser ones in their own private worlds. As the book's title suggests, the emphasis is on the domestic aspects of their lives, on the places where leaders of the revolutionary generation lived with their wives and families. In order to understand better these Founding Fathers—and Founding Mothers—we visit them in circumstances of their own making, and we see them in the intimate context of their very different era. It was a time of achingly slow communications and travel, primitive and wrongheaded medical care, a moral code that had only begun to condemn slavery, and lifestyles that seem to us an odd mixture of the charming, the crude, and the peculiar. But to understand something of the private lives of the Signers, Framers, and Patriots is to glean a new appreciation of what produced these men of great courage, character, and vision.

In the pages that follow, you will encounter some fifty notable Founding Fathers, along with more than forty of their homes. Represented are roughly a third of the Signers, together with a range of military men, diplomats, jurists, politicians, and other Patriots. The narrative arc of the book spans more than a half century of American history, extending from prerevolutionary days into the Federal era. Each chapter opens with a revealing moment in the life of its Founding Father; taken together, these stories constitute stepping-stones to carry the reader along the historic course these men traveled.

The chapters also contain brief biographies of the Founding Fathers, along with stories of Founding Mothers and of many peripheral characters, including architects, builders, artists, slaves, and others. There are visits to towns and streetscapes as well as individual homes, along with interiors (and decorative arts) and exteriors (and gardens). More than one hundred freestanding essays in these pages offer details about life in the revolutionary era, the ways of birthing, dying, eating, cooking, building, reading, celebrating, and governing.

To ease access to this complex tale and its many players, you will find a Cast of Characters with thumbnail biographies of the Founding Fathers and a number of the Founding Mothers. A time line opens each of the three sections of the book to help locate the players amid the key moments of their era. At the close of the book is a Glossary of military, historical, architectural, cultural, and social terms of the time; an appendix provides visitor information, should you wish to journey to any of the historic sites illustrated in this volume, all of which are open to the public. Notes, acknowledgments, and a bibliography round out the volume.

I would like to think that the reader of this book—even the casual one who merely peruses some of its pages—will come away better informed not only about the founding men and women of our nation, but also about their lives, passions, culture, families, and aspirations.

Hugh Howard
Hayes Hill, New York

Cast of Characters

Abigail Smith Adams (1744–1818) of Massachusetts. During her marriage to John Adams, Abigail was her husband's chief confidante and partner. Their son John Quincy Adams became the nation's sixth president.

John Adams (1735–1826) of Massachusetts. A coauthor and Signer of the Declaration of Independence, Adams went on to become the nation's first vice president and second president.

Aaron Burr (1756–1836) of New Jersey and, later, New York. Burr served with distinction during the Revolutionary War, as a U.S. senator, and as vice president, but he is best remembered for his deadly duel with Alexander Hamilton.

Samuel Chase (1741–1811) of Maryland. A Signer of the Declaration of Independence, Chase later served as an associate justice of the Supreme Court.

Benjamin Chew (1722–1810) of Pennsylvania. Although reluctant to take sides early in the Revolution, Chew later rehabilitated his reputation and became president of Pennsylvania's High Court of Errors and Appeals. His country home, Cliveden, was the site of a dramatic confrontation during the Battle of Germantown, in 1777.

Hannah Lee Corbin (1728–1782) of Virginia. Sister of the Signers Richard Henry Lee and Francis Lightfoot Lee, and of Arthur Lee, who represented the new nation abroad. Hannah complained to Richard Henry about the failure of the Founding Fathers to permit Founding Mothers like herself to vote.

Silas Deane (1737–1789) of Connecticut. A delegate to the Continental Congress, Deane became the first American representative abroad and a secret agent.

John Dickinson (1732–1808) of Delaware. Author of the influential *Letters from a Farmer,* Dickinson later served as a delegate to the Continental Congress (where in 1776 he declined to sign the Declaration of Independence) and in 1787 helped draft the Constitution, which does bear his signature.

William Henry Drayton (1742–1779) of South Carolina. Before his premature death, Drayton was a pamphleteer and a delegate to the Continental Congress.

Benjamin Franklin (1706–1790) of Pennsylvania. A man of remarkably diverse accomplishments, Franklin participated in the Continental Congress and was a delegate to the Constitutional Convention. He made perhaps his signal contribution to the American cause in his long service abroad, where he played an essential role in securing French assistance in the Revolutionary War.

Catherine Littlefield Greene (1755–1814) of Rhode Island. Wife of General Nathanael Greene, Catherine was a friend and confidante of Martha Washington and, after her husband's death, sponsor of the schoolteacher turned inventor Eli Whitney.

Nathanael Greene (1742–1786) of Rhode Island and Georgia. A private in his colony's militia in 1774, by the close of the Revolutionary War, Greene was a major general and among George Washington's most trusted and valuable officers.

Alexander Hamilton (1755–1804) of New York. After serving as a trusted aide-de-camp and secretary to George Washington, he became a delegate to the Constitutional Convention, played an important role in the ratification of the Constitution as a principal author of the Federalist Papers, and served as the nation's first secretary of the treasury.

Elizabeth Schuyler Hamilton (1757–1854) of New York. The daughter of Philip Schuyler, Betsy married Alexander Hamilton in 1780. Her social cachet and financial stability, as well as her steadying influence on the passionate Hamilton, enabled him to emerge as a force with which to be reckoned in the Federalist era.

Matthias Hammond (1748–1786) of Maryland. A planter and member of his colony's Committees of Correspondence and Safety, Hammond was quartermaster of his local militia. Apparently for nonpolitical reasons, he withdrew from public life in 1776.

Patrick Henry (1736–1799) of Virginia. A legendary orator, Henry galvanized fellow members of the Virginia House of Burgesses to oppose the Stamp Act (1765) and to support military action against the British (1775).

Thomas Heyward, Jr. (1746–1809), of South Carolina. A Patriot in the years leading up to the Revolutionary War, Heyward was a member of the Continental Congress and signed both the Declaration of Independence and the Articles of Confederation.

Stephen Hopkins (1707–1785) of Rhode Island. A prominent governor, legislator, and jurist before the Revolution, Hopkins was a delegate to the Continental Congress and a Signer of the Declaration of Independence.

James Iredell (1751–1799) of North Carolina. An influential pamphleteer before the Revolutionary War, Iredell was a vigorous supporter of the Constitution. After ratification, George Washington named him one of the original associate justices on the Supreme Court.

John Jay (1745–1829) of New York. A member of the Continental Congress, chief negotiator of the Treaty of Paris, which ended the Revolutionary War, and author of five of the papers published in *The Federalist,* which proved essential to ratification of the Constitution, Jay became the first chief justice of the United States and later minister plenipotentiary to England.

Sarah Livingston Jay (1756–1802) of New Jersey and New York. Daughter of the longtime New Jersey governor and Continental Congress delegate William Livingston, Sally married John Jay and became one of the premier hostesses of the Federalist era.

Thomas Jefferson (1743–1826) of Virginia. Principal author and Signer of the Declaration of Independence, Jefferson was the nation's first secretary of state, second vice president, and third president.

Henry Knox (1750–1806) of Massachusetts. A Boston bookseller and student of artillery tactics, Knox was one of George Washington's most trusted advisers, becoming a major general during the Revolutionary War and serving as secretary of war under the Articles of Confederation and during Washington's presidency.

Lucy Flucker Knox (1756–1824) of Massachusetts. The daughter of Thomas Flucker, a wealthy Tory and secretary of the province of Massachusetts, Lucy married Henry Knox, then a Boston bookseller. During numerous winter encampments while her husband was one of George Washington's generals, she gained the friendship of Martha Washington.

The Marquis de Lafayette (1757–1834) of France. A wealthy aristocrat, Marie-Joseph-Paul-Yves-Roch-Gilbert du Motier volunteered to aid the American cause, arriving in the colonies at age nineteen. Lafayette provided military, monetary, and diplomatic assistance and became an intimate friend of George Washington.

He was widely feted as the "Nation's Friend" on his return to America in 1824–25.

John Langdon (1741–1819) of New Hampshire. A delegate to the Second Continental Congress, Langdon later served two terms as one of his state's original U.S. senators. As president pro tempore of the Senate, he sent official word to George Washington of his election as president in April 1789.

Benjamin Henry Latrobe (1764–1820) of England. America's first professional architect, Latrobe emigrated in 1796 and won the trust of Thomas Jefferson, who appointed him the nation's surveyor of public buildings. He would make major contributions to the evolution of the Capitol and the President's House between 1803 and 1817.

Arthur Lee (1740–1792) of Virginia. As a diplomatic representative of the new nation, Lee served with Benjamin Franklin and Silas Deane in Paris during the Revolutionary War and, upon his return to the United States, became a delegate to the Continental Congress.

Francis Lightfoot Lee (1734–1797) of Virginia. An early opponent of the Stamp Act, Lee called for the Virginia convention of 1774, and as a delegate to the Continental Congress, he signed the Declaration of Independence.

Henry Lee (1756–1818) of Virginia. Known as Light-Horse Harry, a cousin of the Signers Francis Lightfoot Lee and Richard Henry Lee, Henry Lee served with distinction in the Southern Department of George Washington's Continental Army.

Jeremiah Lee (1721–1775) of Massachusetts. A member of the Massachusetts Provincial Congress and Committee of Supplies,

Colonel Lee died of a fever in the weeks after the Battles of Lexington and Concord.

Richard Henry Lee (1733–1794) of Virginia. An original delegate to the Continental Congress and later its president, Lee would also serve as one of Virginia's first U.S. senators.

William Livingston (1723–1790) of New Jersey. A delegate to the Second Continental Congress, a brigadier general of the New Jersey militia, and governor of his state, Livingston was an effective voice for compromise as a delegate to the Constitutional Convention.

Edward Lloyd IV (1767–1825) of Maryland. A wealthy planter, Lloyd was a delegate to the Continental Congress after the Revolutionary War.

Thomas Lynch, Jr. (1749–1779), and *Thomas Lynch, Sr.* (1727–1776), of South Carolina. During his service in the Continental Congress, the elder Lynch fell ill. His colony's provincial congress dispatched his son to Philadelphia, where he would sign the Declaration of Independence after his father's death.

James Madison (1751–1836) of Virginia. A primary author of the Constitution, Madison became the fourth president of the United States.

George Mason (1725–1792) of Virginia. After helping draft Virginia's state constitution, Mason helped write the U.S. Constitution. His Virginia Declaration of Rights is often cited as a precursor to the U.S. Bill of Rights.

Henry Middleton (1717–1784) and *Arthur Middleton* (1742–1787) of South Carolina. When Henry resigned from the

Continental Congress, his son Arthur assumed his seat and subsequently signed the Declaration of Independence and the Articles of Confederation.

James Monroe (1758–1831) of Virginia. A veteran of the Revolutionary War and member of the Congress of the Confederation, Monroe because the nation's fifth president.

William Paca (1740–1799) of Maryland. A delegate to the Continental Congress and later a governor and chief justice of Maryland, Paca was a Signer of the Declaration of Independence.

Charles Willson Peale (1741–1827) of Maryland and Pennsylvania. Portraitist of and correspondent with many of the Founding Fathers, Peale served in the Continental Army and later founded the nation's first history and natural history museum.

Edmund Randolph (1753–1813) of Virginia. A delegate to the Continental Congress, Randolph served as the nation's first attorney general and succeeded Thomas Jefferson as secretary of state.

Elizabeth Harrison Randolph (1725?–1783) of Virginia. The daughter of Benjamin Harrison of Berkeley Plantation, Betty married Peyton Randolph, first president of the Continental Congress.

Peyton Randolph (1721–1775) of Virginia. The longtime speaker of the House of Burgesses in his home state, "Mr. Attorney" was unanimously elected first president of the Continental Congress in 1774.

Paul Revere (1734–1818) of Massachusetts. A metal worker by vocation, Revere was an early Patriot who played an active role in prerevolutionary Boston. He is best remembered for his "Midnight Ride" in the hours before the Battles of Lexington and Concord.

Benjamin Rush (1745–1813) of Pennsylvania. Trained in Edinburgh, Rush was early America's most celebrated physician, as well as a Signer of the Declaration of Independence. He was a friend of John Adams, Thomas Jefferson, and many others of the revolutionary generation, and treasurer of the U.S. Mint. His wife, Julia, was the daughter of Richard Stockton and Annis Boudinot Stockton.

John Rutledge (1739–1800) and *Edward Rutledge* (1749–1800) of South Carolina. These brothers were both delegates to the Continental Congress. Edward was a Signer of the Declaration of Independence. John attended the Constitutional Convention and served as chief justice of the United States.

Philip Schuyler (1733–1804) of New York. A member of the Continental Congress, Schuyler served as a major general in the Continental Army and later was one of the first U.S. senators.

Annis Boudinot Stockton (1736–1801) of Pennsylvania and New Jersey. Wife and widow of the Signer Richard Stockton, Annis was a poet of note and a friend to George Washington and other Founding Fathers.

Richard Stockton (1730–1781) of New Jersey. A delegate to the Continental Congress, Stockton was a Signer of the Declaration of Independence.

Nicholas Van Dyke (1738–1789) of Delaware. A delegate to the Continental Congress, Van Dyke signed the Articles of Confederation for Delaware and was later president (governor) of the state.

George Washington (1732–1799) of Virginia. A veteran of the French and Indian War, Washington was named commander in chief of the Continental Army. He would later serve as the first president of the United States.

Martha Dandridge Custis Washington (1731–1802) of Virginia. After her first husband died, leaving her with two young children, Martha married George Washington in 1759. The wealth, strength of character, and instincts she brought to their partnership helped shape the early days of the nation.

William Whipple (1730–1785) of New Hampshire. A Signer of the Declaration of Independence and brigadier general of the New Hampshire militia, Whipple led a brigade at the Battle of Saratoga.

George Wythe (1726–1806) of Virginia. Wythe was a member of the Continental Congress, a Signer of the Declaration of Independence, and mentor to Thomas Jefferson, James Monroe, and Chief Justice of the United States John Marshall.

SIGNERS, FRAMERS, AND FOUNDING FATHERS

The Signers were the fifty-six delegates to the Second Continental Congress who signed the Declaration of Independence in 1776. John Trumbull's painting *The Declaration of Independence, July 4, 1776* (see page 5), portrays most of them, although he painted several figures who did not sign the document and omitted a number of others who did.

The Framers were the fifty-five delegates to the 1787 Constitutional Convention who drafted the Constitution, the document that, upon its ratification in 1789, succeeded the Articles of Confederation as the legal instrument that codifies American governance.

The broader term *Founders*— that is, the Founding Fathers or Founding Brothers, since women were allowed no official role in the proceedings—includes the Signers, Framers, military men, and other Patriots who played prominent roles in the drama that led to the founding of the United States of America. Most of them served on one or more of the committees of safety, supply, or correspondence that colonies and municipalities established at the behest of the Continental Congress to manage local affairs.

Many of the Founders appeared in several guises: the rosters of the Signers and the Framers, for example, contain a number of the same names. Virtually all the essential players served in one or more of the new nation's early legislative bodies (there were three: the First Continental Congress, 1774; the Second Continental Congress, 1775–1781; and the United States in Congress Assembled, also called the Confederation Congress, 1781–1789). Some would survive to play crucial roles in the U.S. Congress, the Supreme Court, and the executive branch after the ratification of the Constitution in 1789.

PART ONE

The Colonies Unite

The British Parliament passes the Sugar and Currency Acts on April 5 and 9 to help defray costs of the war.

The First Committee of Correspondence is established in Boston to maintain communication with other colonies in the face of a growing antagonism to Great Britain; New York follows suit in 1765.

John Adams marries Abigail Smith. She will bear six children, including the future president, John Quincy Adams.

Parliament repeals the Stamp Act on March 18.

On March 30, Parliament passes the New England Trade and Fisheries Act, better known as the Restraining Act.

On June 29, Parliament passes the Townshend Acts, which include the New York Restraining Act, the Customs Service Reforms, and the Townshend Duty Act.

The first of John Dickinson's *Letters from a Farmer* is published in the December 2 edition of the *Pennsylvania Chronicle*.

TIMELINE **1763** **1764** **1765** **1766** **1767**

The Treaty of Paris is signed on February 10, ending the French and Indian War (known in Europe as the Seven Years' War).

On March 22, Parliament enacts the Duties in American Colonies Act of 1765 (the Stamp Act), establishing the first direct tax on the colonists.

On May 30, Patrick Henry proposes his resolutions in defiance of the Stamp Act to the House of Burgesses.

The Stamp Act Congress in New York approves the declaration of grievances on October 19 and sends it to King George III.

Thomas Jefferson becomes a member of the bar at Virginia's General Court, having read law for two years with George Wythe.

Parliament approves the Quartering Act on March 24, requiring colonists to put up British soldiers.

On June 13, Rhode Island becomes the first American colony to ban the importation of the enslaved; also this year, the Rhode Island Quaker Stephen Hopkins frees his slaves.

On September 5, the First Continental Congress convenes at Philadelphia.

Fifty-one North Carolinian women sign a petition on October 25 resolving to cease drinking tea and stop wearing British cloth. Decades later, the act of defiance will be called the Edenton Tea Party.

In the spring, Charles Willson Peale paints a portrait of the Annapolis worthy William Paca; later that year he journeys to Mount Vernon to paint Colonel George Washington's picture.

1770

1772

1773

1774

1775

Surrounded by a hostile mob, seven British grenadiers fire into a crowd on March 5, killing five and wounding six. Samuel Adams and his Whig colleagues call the event the Boston Massacre. Months later, a young attorney named John Adams wins acquittal for all but two of the soldiers.

Parliament passes the Tea Act on May 10 to enable the East India Company to dispose of a vast inventory of unsold tea. In Boston and New York, angry colonists turn away British ships carrying the tea, but on December 16 three companies of Patriots dressed as Indians toss the cargo into Boston Harbor, an event that will come to be known as the Boston Tea Party.

On March 23, Patrick Henry delivers his "Give me liberty or give me death" speech to the Virginia House of Burgesses.

On the evening of April 18, Paul Revere takes his midnight ride, which is followed in the morning by the Battles of Lexington and Concord. Chilled after escaping a British search party dressed only in his nightclothes, Colonel Jeremiah Lee contracts the fever that will end his life.

American military forces capture Fort Ticonderoga on the New York shore of Lake Champlain and on the same day—May 10— the Second Continental Congress convenes in Philadelphia.

George Washington is named commander in chief of the Continental Army on June 15.

In one of the bloodiest battles of the war, the British take Bunker Hill in Charlestown, Massachusetts, on June 17 but suffer more than one thousand casualties.

On August 23, King George III declares the colonies in open rebellion.

After eating Sunday dinner on October 22, Virginia's Peyton Randolph, first president of the Continental Congress, dies in Philadelphia of an "apoplectic stroke."

The Declaration of Independence

Thomas Jefferson towers over John Adams, Benjamin Franklin, and the other members of the Committee of Five. The Virginian places the document they have drafted before John Hancock, the sitting president of the Continental Congress. Forty-two other delegates look on. Among them is Jefferson's mentor, George Wythe, standing on the far left, rubbing shoulders with New Hampshire's William Whipple. Standing behind them are the Marylanders William Paca and Samuel Chase, together with Richard Stockton, the New Jerseyan who, just five months later, would be captured and imprisoned by the British. The man in the Quaker hat? That's Stephen Hopkins of Rhode Island.

The Moment was "recorded" by John Trumbull, the Connecticut artist who traveled widely in the years after the Revolution to collect the countenances of the Founding Fathers. With canvas in tow, he visited Jefferson in Paris and Adams in London. He toured the American colonies from South Carolina to New Hampshire. The modest-size painting he produced—it's 21⅛ by 31⅛ inches—required more than twenty years to complete and might have seemed anticlimactic, given his time and travels. But President

The Connecticut-born soldier, diplomat, and portraitist John Trumbull (1756–1843) determined after the Revolution to create a body of what he called "national work," a series of paintings that recorded important revolutionary events. The best known of them would prove to be his Declaration of Independence, July 4, 1776, *hung in the Capitol's rotunda in 1826. Since 1976 the image has also been engraved on the obverse of the two-dollar bill.*

James Madison and the House of Representatives soon rewarded Trumbull's efforts, commissioning him in 1817 to enlarge the work into a twelve-by-eighteen-foot canvas for which the federal treasury paid him the generous fee of eight thousand dollars.

Trumbull's life-size rendering, titled *The Declaration of Independence, July 4, 1776,* was installed in the Capitol rotunda in 1826. Admittedly, it has its inaccuracies (for example, the submission of the document actually occurred on June 28 and was accompanied by little fanfare). Trumbull quite evidently planned his work with an artificiality akin to today's photo ops, cleverly arranging the players into a conjectural tableau unlike any they assumed in life. (He could hardly have been expected to do otherwise—he hadn't been in Philadelphia to witness the events that summer.) He was forced to make compromises, since some of the Signers were already dead when he embarked on his quest to paint them. Hopkins's son, for instance, is believed to have stood in for his late father. Still, most of the likenesses were painted from life.

Trumbull conceived the painting in a conversation with Thomas Jefferson, and he discussed its details with dozens of the participants. As a result, the work portrays the setting, circumstances, clothing, and something of the collective spirit of the undertaking with a proximate fidelity. In the early nineteenth century, the work quickly assumed the status of certifiable icon and helped establish the event portrayed as The Moment.

By any measure, then, Trumbull's *Declaration* is the single best visual record of the Founding Fathers we have, and as such, it is the point of departure for our journey to revisit the lives, times, and homes of the Founding Fathers.

ENGLISHMEN BECOMING AMERICANS

The Founding Fathers were not bred to pursue independence. When most of them were born, in the second quarter of the eighteenth century, the notion of separating from England had virtually no adherents. Most colonists considered themselves Englishmen and were content with an ancestral allegiance to the British Crown.

In the years that followed, some of these men gradually began to think of themselves as "Americans." That usage came of age dur-

ing the French and Indian War (1756–1763), but the undercurrent of dissatisfaction with the British Crown did not appear until Parliament decided to demand that the colonists pay a share of the cost of their defense. Thus, the groundswell advocating change truly began in 1765, with the passage of the Duties in American Colonies Act (the Stamp Act), which amounted to the first direct tax on the colonists. Even then, most of the men we now call the Founding Fathers wished to repair the rift with England rather than sever the connection. The passage of the Townshend Acts (1767), the Boston Massacre (1770), and the Tea Act (1773), led to more calls for independence. Symbolically, the colonies were becoming a place where the New World custom of the handshake made more sense than the bow and bended knee.

The eighteenth century was a time of more than political change. Colonial America was far from classless. The society was divisible into the landless tenants at the bottom, the gentry—the upper class of professionals, landowners, and wealthy gentlemen—at the top, and the largest group, the so-called middling sort, in between. Unprecedented growth and prosperity had begun to transform everyday life for most Americans, but especially for those in the middle. Trade, technology, and agricultural advances made it possible for an ever increasing number of colonists to see beyond the basics. Life became less a matter of subsistence as people could begin to take for granted an adequate supply of food, decent clothing, and shelter. The middle class started to yearn for the refinements found in the mother country, and by mid-century, successful tradesmen and industrious farmers had the wherewithal to sit in their parlors and drink Chinese tea from cups made at English potteries.

These freemen of growing social status heard the call clearly in 1767, when the most effective of the early propagandists, John Dickinson, began his plea to his countrymen with the words "I am a Farmer." His tone was pitch-perfect, but ironically, he was not of the middling sort: Dickinson was a London-trained lawyer and the son of a plantation holder with properties in two colonies that amounted to more than ten thousand acres. Along with most of the other key players in the revolutionary generation, Dickinson was of the "better sort," a member of the gentry, which the economist Adam Smith described as "those few, who being attached to no particular occupations themselves, have leisure and inclination to examine the occupations of other people."

Certainly several of the Founding Fathers climbed the social ladder, especially in New England. They included Henry Knox (a fatherless lad who apprenticed as a bookbinder), Major General Nathanael Greene (the son of a blacksmith), and John Adams (whose father, Deacon John, was a shoemaker). Benjamin Franklin, once a printer's apprentice, was happy to describe himself as "an ordinary Mechanick." But these men were the exceptions. The large majority of the Founding Fathers were members of the landed gentry, who earned college degrees, many of them in England, and who understood from an early age that they belonged to the ruling class. In contrast, the majority of the soldiers in the Continental Army would be middling men.

The shared experiences of the Stamp Act Congress in New York and the Continental Congress in Philadelphia became the basis of hundreds of relationships among these men. The delegates were a diverse group, from large colonies and small, from the North and the South, some oriented to agricultural matters and others to commercial considerations. But they read one another's pamphlets and listened to the same speeches. They knew at first hand their colleagues' faces, voices, and moods; they shared bitter debates, countless committee meetings, and long nights in taverns.

THE WORLD OF THE FOUNDING FATHERS

As Trumbull's painting suggests, the Founding Fathers shared a remarkably small and interconnected world, one that extended to their personal as well as their public lives. Consider some of the multiple threads that bound them together.

When the delegate William Livingston of New Jersey rode to Philadelphia for the First Continental Congress, he traveled with his new son-in-law, John Jay. The president of that First Continental Congress was Peyton Randolph, a cousin of Jefferson and mentor of Washington; another Virginia delegate, the Signer George Wythe, had been Jefferson's "faithful Mentor in youth." John Adams and Thomas Jefferson first met at the second Philadelphia congress in 1775; a half century later, after both had lived long and colorful polit-

How Different Was Life in the Eighteenth Century?

In the world the Founding Fathers knew:

❧ the average child had a roughly 50 percent chance of surviving to adulthood;

❧ slavery was legal in all thirteen colonies;

❧ all cooking was done in or around the fireplace;

❧ men and women were not equal: women could not vote, hold public office, and unless widowed could not own property in most colonies;

❧ travel was slow and uncertain: by water, ships relied upon the wind for locomotion; by land, a rider might hope to cover thirty miles in a day, the passenger in a coach just twenty;

❧ aside from sunlight, the sole source of heat was fire, usually in an open fireplace; after sunset, illumination was by either moonlight or candlelight;

❧ there was no indoor plumbing: the flush toilet, the bathroom, and the kitchen faucet would be nineteenth-century innovations—meaning chamber pots, outhouses, and buckets were a way of life;

❧ privacy was a rare privilege for most: people, including children at home and strangers at inns, routinely shared beds;

❧ aside from a minority of city dwellers, everybody was a farmer;

❧ there was no anesthesia for surgery or childbirth;

❧ every household produced some, and in many cases all, of the candles, soap, foodstuffs, and clothing it required;

❧ the medieval notion of the four humors still dominated medical theory, so bloodletting and purging were employed to restore the balance of black and yellow bile, blood, and phlegm, and thus, presumably, good health.

Life, in short, was hard in the time of the Founding Fathers.

A great man represents . . . a strategic point in the campaign of history, and part of his greatness consists in his being there.

—Oliver Wendell Holmes, Jr., speaking on the one hundredth anniversary of John Marshall's becoming chief justice (1901)

ical lives, they were still thinking and talking together in their great correspondence. Both men penned innumerable letters to the Philadelphia Signer Benjamin Rush, who had married the daughter of another New Jersey Signer, Richard Stockton.

The ties were personal, intimate, and familial. The Signer John Dickinson was educated with a member of the Chew family; the Signer William Paca (of Maryland) married another Chew; a third Chew built a fine mansion outside Philadelphia that would be a focal point of the Battle of Germantown. Samuel Adams of Massachusetts was John Adams's cousin. In South Carolina, the world was even smaller. Two Pinckney brothers, Charles and Thomas, served in Washington's army; Charles Cotesworth Pinckney married Sarah Middleton, sister of the Signer Arthur Middleton, while various other sisters married into other powerful clans. The result was that the Middletons, Draytons, Rutledges, and Pinckneys became a formidable power bloc in the colony's—and later the nation's—politics. Members of each family served in the Continental Congress.

The name that opens the most portals to the Founding Fathers' network is, of course, George Washington. Although notably missing from Trumbull's great painting (he was otherwise engaged after June 15, 1775, the day John Adams proposed him for commander in chief of the Continental Army), General Washington was indisputably the most essential figure of the era. His adjutants included the painter (and sometime colonel) John Trumbull; the Marquis de Lafayette, whom he regarded as almost an adopted son; James Monroe (he's the one holding the flag in the famous painting *Washington Crossing the Delaware*); and his chief of staff, the precociously effective Alexander Hamilton. His generals included Philip Schuyler of New York and Henry Knox of Massachusetts. Years later, after ratification of the Constitution, Washington's first cabinet would include Secretary of War Knox, Secretary of the Treasury

Hamilton (by then married to Philip Schuyler's daughter Betsy, whom he met during the war at Washington's winter encampment). The rest of the cabinet consisted of Secretary of State Thomas Jefferson and Attorney General Edmund Randolph, another of Jefferson's cousins. Washington appointed John Jay the first chief justice of the United States, and John Adams served as his vice president.

The reserved Virginian was at the nexus of a world characterized by enduring ties of blood, marriage, and political kinship. When we look back at the historic homes of the Founding Fathers, Washington once more stands taller than the rest, like an accidental gatekeeper. His paramount role would outlive him; the conservation of his home by the Mount Vernon Ladies' Association in the years before the Civil War launched the historic preservation movement.

Making this book required a series of journeys, many of which followed the very paths that John Trumbull traveled. Sadly, more than a few of Trumbull's destinations are now gone, since most of the Founding Fathers are no longer survived by the domiciles they called home.

Fire and development account for most of the losses, but the Civil War, changing tastes, and the ravages of time also led to the disappearance of historic houses. Some sites that do stand were unavailable, including the home of the last surviving Signer, Charles Carroll of Maryland (he died in 1832); his Baltimore mansion is no longer open to the public. As this book goes to press, James and Dolley Madison's Montpelier is in a chrysalis stage, soon to reemerge as a premier historic site, restored to the house that the Madisons knew in the 1820s. But for our purposes, it offered no chance to photograph because it was under construction and empty of artifacts.

Founding Mothers

For the Founding Fathers, a woman's "department in life" was the domestic. Women were wives who bore children until they no longer could (if they didn't die first). They carried the responsibility for running their households, but married women could neither own property nor vote. Under English law, men legally *owned* their wives.

Most gentry women received rudimentary education in reading, writing, and arithmetic at home. In contrast, their brothers and husbands were likely to be taught Latin, Greek, and advanced grammar, and might attend Harvard, Yale, the College of New Jersey (later Princeton), or William and Mary. Girls seeking to further their education had few options other than ornamental accomplishments, such as dancing, drawing, and music, or skills such as needlework.

Ironically, some of these officially powerless women actually made their husbands powerful, because marriage was a means of advancement in the Founding Fathers' world. George Washington married a wealthy widow, and her fortune made him solvent while her social connections raised him in the status-conscious world of Virginia planters. Alexander Hamilton's marriage to Betsy Schuyler gave him a social acceptability far above his dubious origins.

Despite their overwhelming limitations, the Founding Mothers played large roles in the revolutionary era. If Abigail Smith, Elizabeth Schuyler, and Martha Dandridge had never been born, American history would have been different. In theirs and many other cases, women whose lives remained confined to the domestic sphere managed to transcend the societal limitations to become partners and even advocates in their own right.

Abigail Smith Adams, wife of John and mother of John Quincy Adams, wrote with remarkable candor, wit, and intelligence. In 1776 she warned her husband, then a delegate in Philadelphia to the Continental Congress, "If particular care and attention is not paid to the ladies we are determined to foment a rebellion, and will not hold ourselves bound by any laws in which we have no voice or representation." If her tone was teasing, her intent was true. Abigail posed for Gilbert Stuart as her husband was nearing the end of his presidency, in 1800, although the portrait was not completed until about 1815.

TOP: *The study of George Wythe, whom Jefferson regarded as his mentor.*

ABOVE: *Benjamin Henry Latrobe sketched his memory of Washington's home at Mount Vernon after a 1796 visit.*

RIGHT: *The front entrance of the home of the Chase-Lloyd House, in Annapolis, Maryland.*

Yet the chapters that follow are filled with a fine variety of houses from all thirteen colonies, along with one reconstructed house (Henry Knox's Montpelier) in the Massachusetts territory that became the state of Maine. All are museum homes and open to the public, though some, such as Jefferson's Monticello and Washington's Mount Vernon, are better known than others. Certain houses memorialize lesser-known figures, like America's first spy, Silas Deane of Connecticut, and the man who proposed the resolutions for independence at the Second Continental Congress, Richard Henry Lee, in Stratford, Virginia. If he had not caught cold on the night of Paul Revere's ride (and died soon thereafter), Jeremiah Lee might have been the banker of the Revolution; but his mansion still stands in Marblehead, Massachusetts, and its

collections and original paperhangings represent the elegant style of the wealthy merchant-Patriot in the years before the Revolution. The homes of John Adams, John Dickinson, Stephen Hopkins, George Wythe, Philip Schuyler, John Jay, Arthur Middleton, Alexander Hamilton, and some two dozen others are recorded here. Several of the dwellings are included here because Washington slept in them—in Massachusetts, New Jersey, Pennsylvania, and South Carolina, historic buildings have been conserved to commemorate their famous visitor.

We live in a time when the Founding Fathers are being demystified (for example, in Henry Wiencek's *An Imperfect God* and Joseph J. Ellis's *American Sphinx*). While not all of them have been knocked off their pedestals, most people today are more comfortable with less than heroic portrayals. And in looking at their domestic lives, one realizes that the Founders were the rich and famous of their time, so the homes seen here do not represent the lesser or middling sorts. Yet the wealth and status of these men meant that at most sites there is a shadowy but unavoidable presence—namely, the specter of slavery. (If the subject lingers over our society like a low-lying fog on an overcast day, in the late eighteenth century the morality was more ambiguous and at the essence of the historic paradigm.) Slavery shows its faceted face repeatedly in the pages that follow.

By some mix of inclination and an accident of timing, the Founding Fathers shaped one of the most dramatic stories in recorded history, transforming a baker's dozen of obscure colonies into an emergent nation whose political principles would become a worldwide wave of change. This book is an attempt to cast a softer, domestic light on the Founding Fathers, as well as to see each of them in events from the historic narrative that was their time. So let us journey to the homes of many of the Signers John Trumbull limned in his *Declaration,* as well as others who fill the ranks of Founding Fathers, including Framers, generals, jurists, and Patriots. After all, these were the men who, in a remarkable act of courage, embraced liberty, freedom, and the paradox of democracy—its basis being the understanding that the citizenry must agree to disagree—and then shaped a government around them.

Richard Henry Lee of Virginia.

The George Wythe House

The Governor's Palace was perhaps the grandest house in the colonies. The Palace Green lay like an immense natural carpet at the center of Williamsburg. Two rows of catalpa trees lined its sides, framing the vista of the elegant palace, which was shielded by its iron gate at the northern end of the lawn. The landscape and architecture had been artfully arranged to bespeak the power of King George III. The royal governor, Francis Fauquier, the king's official representative, called the place home.

Two doors away stood a lesser but still imposing dwelling. George Wythe lived there. During Governor Fauquier's tenure in Virginia, Wythe often dined at the palace, together with the men's mutual friends William Small, professor of natural philosophy at the College of William and Mary, and Wythe's law clerk, Thomas Jefferson. Fauquier held weekly concerts, in which he himself would often play, and guests at his table enjoyed discussions of literature, architecture, and in particular, scientific observations; Fauquier, like Small, was a natural philosopher as well as a member of London's prestigious Royal Society. Jefferson later recalled those evenings as filled with "more good sense, more rational and philosophical conversations, than in my life beside."

The rear elevation closely resembles the front but overlooks an orchard and kitchen garden as well as a pleasure garden, where Wythe and his guests could stroll. Beyond the shrubbery that bounded the garden stood two facing rows of dependencies. These wood-frame outbuildings included a smokehouse, a kitchen, a laundry, a lumber house, a poultry house, a well, a stable, and two "necessaries."

Although owned by his father-in-law, the fine brick manse (left) on Palace Street was inhabited by George Wythe for more than thirty years. Wythe arrived in 1755 and remained in residence until his move in 1791 to Richmond. Unlike those of many of his peers, Wythe's principal residence was within the city limits of Williamsburg; Thomas Jefferson, Wythe's next-door neighbor Robert Carter, and most other members of the Virginia gentry lived primarily on their plantations.

The Georgian Plan

A man of average height with a memorable aquiline nose, the courtly George Wythe was known for his deep bow—although with the advent of the Stamp Act, his willingness to bow obediently to his English rulers seemed suddenly to evaporate.

When constructed in the 1750s, the Wythe House was a model of the so-called Georgian plan, named after the Hanoverian kings who ruled England for much of the eighteenth century. The configuration was derived from gentry housing commonly found in English towns of the period.

The footprint of the Georgian house is rectangular, and each floor contains four more or less square rooms, one in each of the four corners, along with two chimneys and a center passage. In Wythe House, the passage is flanked on the left by the parlor (front) and the study, on the right by the dining room (front) and a bed chamber. The second floor has a similar arrangement, with a central stair passage and four chambers.

Well-to-do Americans who wanted to impress their friends with their status and refinement would mime this architectural model for decades to come.

The floor plan of the Wythe House features a parlor (front, left), dining room (front, right), bed chamber (rear, right), and Wythe's office.

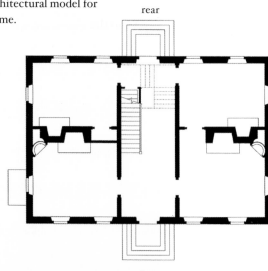

rear

front

Today a reproduction of the Governor's Palace dominates the Palace Green. Colonial Williamsburg opened the palace to the public in 1934; the original building was destroyed by fire in 1781.

Ironically, though, it was George Wythe—the man who lived and even sat literally at his right hand—from whom Governor Fauquier heard strident and rebellious words about the outrage that was the Stamp Act in the days after its passage in 1765.

Although born in Virginia, George Wythe, like most colonists of his time, grew up thinking himself very much an Englishman. Wythe (pronounced to rhyme with *Smith*) was a classicist who learned Latin and the rudiments of Greek under his mother's tutelage. He was orphaned before reaching adulthood, so he was not educated in England, as was his Williamsburg neighbor and fellow lawyer, Peyton Randolph (see "The Peyton Randolph House," page 66). But diligence in mastering the law earned Wythe the respect of his peers. Elected to represent Williamsburg in the Virginia House of Burgesses, he also served as the colony's attorney general, in effect putting him on the King's payroll.

George Wythe (1726–1806) also saw himself as a Virginian, so when word of the proposal before Parliament to impose a stamp tax reached his ears, he remonstrated with his fellow burgesses, objecting that Virginia's liberties were being violated. He drafted a resolution objecting to the taxation on both practical and legal grounds. His colleagues softened Wythe's outraged tone, but even Fauquier, as he himself observed, was not unsympathetic to the Virginians' pleas "to be permitted to tax themselves." However, the king and both houses of Parliament chose to ignore the letters of protest from the Virginia assembly.

The hated Stamp Act did not go into effect until November 1765, but its passage engendered in Wythe, Jefferson, and others a disquiet that superseded what Jefferson called "the dull monotony of . . . colonial subservience." Revolution was still years off, but Wythe's outrage helped set in motion forces that led to war in the years to come.

The central passage appears to be a corridor and stair hall providing access to the living spaces; in practice, however, the passage also limited access to the rooms on either side. Social status was important in the eighteenth century, and floor plans in Williamsburg reflected the social hierarchy. While social inferiors might gain entrée to the passage, only the privileged few would penetrate to the private spaces, where the finest finishes (for example, wallpapers) and objects (such as china and furniture) would be on display.

THE MENTOR'S MANSE

Long regarded as the finest private dwelling in Williamsburg, George Wythe's house is also the epitome of the eighteenth-century gentry house. *And* it is a model for what later generations came to call the classic colonial.

The mass of the house consists of a slightly elongated box that stands two stories tall, with a façade punctuated by five sets of vertical openings. In architectural terms, that makes it a five-bay house. The main entrance is at the center, with a window above; two matching, vertical pairs of windows fill the bays on either side. From the hip roof rise two massive chimneys.

Unlike many earlier houses in Williamsburg and elsewhere, the Wythe House was conceived and constructed as a whole. Each side is symmetrical; the whole is balanced and thoughtfully proportioned.

The floor plan echoes the generous and imposing appearance of the exterior. A visitor to George Wythe's household would first have entered the spacious passage that runs the full depth of the house. If the guest's station warranted, he or she might have been invited into the parlor or the dining room. A client, student, or confidant of Wythe might have been ushered into his study to the rear, with its entrance beneath the stair landing. The fourth room on the first floor, a bed chamber, was reached through the dining room.

The dignified brick block that was Wythe's house actually belonged to his wife's father, Richard Taliaferro (pronounced as if it were spelled *Toliver*). Taliaferro constructed the house between 1752 and 1754, while he was also renovating the Governor's Palace. He was both a planter (the owner of a substantial tract of cultivated land, or plantation) and a sometime undertaker (in the eighteenth-century sense, meaning contractor).

The house he built became his son-in-law's home after Elizabeth Taliaferro and George Wythe married, in 1755. The couple were granted life tenancy at Taliaferro's death, in 1779. Elizabeth lived out her life in the house (she died in 1787). The Wythes' only child died in infancy, and George moved to Richmond in 1791 to serve a judgeship on the commonwealth's court of chancery. Subsequent owners made minor modifications before 1939, when the house was restored to the form and appearance that George and Elizabeth Wythe had known.

A RESTRAINED ELEGANCE

Many Virginia houses are distinguished by the appealing contrast of warm, red-brick hues with white wooden trim. But the masons who built the Wythe House used brick—which consists of "fired" (baked) clay, sand, and water—for maximum expressiveness.

On first glance, the Wythe House seems understated. Its shape is its most obvious characteristic, since its brick mass is relieved only by simple window moldings and a modest cornice in the shadows of the eaves. On closer examination, one's attention is drawn to the windows, which are framed by "rubbed" bricks. To produce the effect, the masons selected bricks of a soft, rosy shade, then abraded one side against a stone or another brick to produce a smooth surface of uniform color. Rubbed bricks were used around door and window openings and in the decorative string course, the three horizontal rows of bricks just above the first-floor openings. Wedge-shaped (gauged) bricks were used to form the flattened arches over the openings. The result was a subtle architectural emphasis.

Other masonry techniques were also employed. Thin mortar joints distinguish some details, and the broader field of the house was laid up in Flemish bond, in which the ends (headers) and sides (stretchers) of the bricks alternate and the pattern is offset from one course to the next. Note, too, the beveled water-table brick at the level of the first floor and the tall, capped chimneys. By articulating key elements, these masonry devices transform a plain stack of bricks into an austere yet surprisingly expressive building.

In the photo above, note as well the geometric sophistication of the house design. The windows on the second floor are smaller than those on the first floor, the chimneys stand tall, and the hip roof crowns yet flattens the structure. The net effect is to make the house seem large and imposing.

MURDER?!?

The accomplishments of Wythe's life stand for themselves. He served in the Continental Congress in 1775 and signed the Declaration of Independence in 1776. He collaborated with Thomas Jefferson and Edmund Pendleton on a vast rewrite of Virginia's legal code, adapting the outdated English and colonial laws to the new revolutionary realities. For a time he served as speaker of the Virginia House of Delegates, the forerunner of the House of Burgesses.

His enduring fame is linked to Thomas Jefferson, who read law under Wythe's guidance between the ages of nineteen and twenty-one. Jefferson's respect and affection for Wythe surfaced in 1779, when he and the other members of the Board of Visitors created the professorship of law and police at the College of William and Mary. The chair was the first in the study of law at an American college; in assuming it, Wythe would be at the vanguard of the nation's move to establish its own legal traditions.

Wythe attended the Constitutional Convention, and subsequently the Virginia ratifying convention, and he spent many years as chancellor of his state's judicial system. When he left Williamsburg, in 1791, he resigned his professorship to preside over the

ABOVE: *On display in the parlor are a range of imported goods, including creamware cups and teapot, tricolor Chinese export porcelains, and glass tumblers, all framed by the molded and arched joinery of a built-in china cabinet called a buffet (pronounced BOW-fat).*

RIGHT: *The Wythe House has been restored to its appearance circa 1770, when it was repainted and wallpaper was installed in many of the principal rooms. The parlor features a crimson paper that imitates silk damask.*

LEFT: *Atop the sideboard in the dining room are a pair of knife boxes, four wineglasses with "air twist" stems (in which the glassmaker captured air bubbles), two wine bottles, and silver salvers, each of which suggests the Wythes' gentry status.*

BELOW: *The dining room at George and Elizabeth Wythe's house, set for a dinner that included fish, chicken, and sweet potatoes served on stylish creamware china.*

TOP AND ABOVE: *Thomas Jefferson described Wythe as "My faithful Mentor in youth, and my most affectionate friend through life." The intellectual passions the two men shared are reflected in this room (Wythe's study) and its objects, which include the optical viewer standing on the table, the terrestrial globe, and a bookcase chockablock with books. In his will, Wythe bequeathed Jefferson his "books and small philosophical apparatus."*

Richmond judicial district, but never tiring of teaching, he founded a small law school of his own. His Williamsburg students Thomas Jefferson, James Monroe, and John Marshall were strongly influenced by him, as was Henry Clay in Richmond. Monroe went on to be the nation's fifth president, and Marshall, as chief justice of the United States, established the doctrine of judicial review in the landmark case *Marbury v. Madison.*

As a Kentucky politician in the next generation, Henry Clay would play an important role in the Missouri Compromise (earning himself the sobriquet The Great Pacificator). Clay found that he and Wythe shared a strong antipathy to slavery, and he worked to abolish the practice throughout his long legislative career. Wythe himself was born into a slaveholding society, but he would free some of his slaves during his lifetime, teach at least two of them to read, and make the rest freemen in his will.

Both race and law played roles in Wythe's death; the circumstances of his end were these: When he rose on Sunday morning, May 25, 1806, Wythe bathed as usual in cold water drawn from his well. He dressed and rang for his breakfast. His devoted servant Lydia Broadnax, one of the slaves he had freed, brought him his eggs, toast, and coffee. Unbeknownst to them, the coffee was laced with yellow arsenic, a poison widely available for agricultural uses.

Later that morning, Wythe was stricken with intense abdominal pains, diarrhea, and vomiting. Soon both Lydia and a second former slave who resided in the household, a mulatto boy named Michael Brown, were seized by what was termed at the time *cholera morbus.* On June 1, Michael died, but somehow the elderly Wythe held on, despite being in great agony from the corrosive effects of the arsenic. Wythe's mind continued to function, and on June 5 he called out to those assembled around his bed, "I am murdered." Three days later he was dead.

Wythe solved the mystery, but it was Lydia who survived to tell the tale. She recalled that another member of the household, George Wythe Sweeney, had entered the kitchen early on the morning of the poisoning. Sweeney, Wythe's grandnephew, had taken the coffeepot to the table, professing to be in a great hurry. As Lydia prepared his toast, she saw Sweeney toss a small piece of white paper into the fire after pouring himself a cup of coffee.

ABOVE LEFT AND LEFT: *In her bed chamber, Mrs. Wythe would often have engaged in sewing projects. That's an embroidery stand in front of her chair, and a knitting basket on the table. This colorful room features striped wallpaper, Wilton carpeting (made in Wiltshire, England), and chintz bed hangings.*

ABOVE: *On the dressing table are two gentlemen's wigs of the sort most men of the gentry class—including George Wythe— wore in the prerevolutionary era.*

THE GEORGE WYTHE HOUSE   21

Et Tu, Patrick Henry?

From London, the logic of the bill seemed reasonable enough. The Seven Years' War (in America, the French and Indian War) had left England with an enormous national debt. His Majesty's government decided the colonists should pay for their own defense, particularly because British troops still guarded the American frontier. A tax was levied on printed matter, including court documents, ships' papers, licenses, almanacs, newspapers, and even playing cards.

The Stamp Act of 1765 was one of several legislative irritants imposed from London (others included the Sugar and Currency Acts). Though its fees were not outrageous, the Stamp Act loomed large because, with it, for the first time, a tax was being imposed *without* the colonists' consent. They felt this undermined the autonomy of their own legislatures and threatened their liberty.

That year a freshman member in the Virginia House of Burgesses, twenty-nine-year-old Patrick Henry, rose to speak against the act. He boldly suggested that those who had imposed it might encounter a brave opponent, just as Caesar had met up with Brutus and King Charles I had been confronted by Oliver Cromwell. Outrage against the Stamp Act spread, and nine colonies dispatched delegates to the Stamp Act Congress in New York, where declarations and petitions were approved. Mob violence broke out in Massachusetts. There, tradesmen and farmers of the middling sort formed groups called the Sons of Liberty. They burned effigies of royal officials and interfered with the imposition of the tax.

Although Parliament repealed the Stamp Act in 1766, the damage done to relations between England and her American colonies proved irreversible.

A Virginia radical best remembered for his oratory, Patrick Henry reportedly closed an impassioned speech on March 23, 1774, with the now immortal words, "As for me, give me liberty or give me death." However, historians today are uncertain whether he uttered the words (they may have been a dramatic paraphrase contributed by an early-nineteenth-century biographer).

Further facts had emerged during the Wythe deathwatch. Sweeney had already been accused of forgery and stealing the old man's law books. He also knew the contents of Wythe's will, which specified, first, that upon his death a substantial legacy was to go to Michael Brown and, second, that if the boy were to die before reaching his majority, the bequest would revert to George Wythe Sweeney.

A quantity of yellow arsenic was found in Sweeney's room, but a jury convicted him only of "counterfeiting his uncle's name to checks drawn upon the Virginia Bank." He was acquitted on charges of poisoning Wythe because the jury was not privy to Lydia Broadnax's testimony: under Virginia law, Negroes were not permitted to testify against white men. Sweeney went unpunished, having "sought refuge in the West" while an appeal on his forgery conviction was pending.

Even from the grave, however, the old jurist was able to ensure that one injustice was avoided. After solving the mystery of his ailment in the hours before his death, he signed a codicil to his will. As revised, that document left no legacy to George Wythe Sweeney.

Wythe possessed an orderly and disciplined mind; his house and his life seem a suitable reflection of the man.

In a guest chamber, the visitor today finds a tricorn hatbox, buckle shoes, a dressing glass (mirror), and a white lace lady's cap.

John Dickinson's Poplar Hall

On December 2, 1767, the first letter appeared in the *Pennsylvania Chronicle*. Although its author chose to remain anonymous, this public letter and eleven similar ones that followed it would soon make John Dickinson famous.

The letter began this way:

> *My dear Countrymen,* I am a *Farmer,* settled after a variety of fortunes, near the banks of the River *Delaware,* in the province of *Pennsylvania.* I received a liberal education, and have been engaged in the busy scenes of life; but am now convinced that a man may be as happy without bustle, as with it. My farm is small; my servants are few, and good; I have a little money at interest; I wish for no more . . . and with a contented, grateful mind . . . I am completing the number of days allotted to me by divine goodness.

The thirty-five-year-old Dickinson was everything he said he was—but he was also a London-trained lawyer. No country bumpkin, he served in both the Pennsylvania and Delaware assemblies (originally Pennsylvania's "Three Lower Counties," Delaware would achieve full autonomy only in 1776, just in time to be one of the thirteen colonies). Dickinson brought to his *Letters from a Farmer* a sense of the world, but his straightforward message immediately attracted the average colonist.

A 1797 appraisal described Dickinson's Kent County property as consisting of "A Spacious Dwelling house and Every other building that is Needful for a Farm."

Early historians of the republic honored John Dickinson's literary contributions, dubbing him the "penman of the American Revolution."

Along with the Stamp Act, Parliament had passed in 1765 the Quartering Act, requiring Americans to provide housing and supplies for British soldiers. When colonists in New York objected to the cost of stationing the soldiers, Parliament retaliated with the New York Restraining Act, which suspended that colony's assembly. It was part of a larger body of legislation called the Townshend Acts, which imposed duties on glass, tea, lead, paints, and paper. Most infuriating of all, Parliament passed these laws without consulting the elected bodies of its American constituents.

"From infancy I was taught to love humanity and liberty," wrote Dickinson in his first letter. And the recent acts of Parliament, he argued, ran counter to those principles. "An act of parliament commanding us to do a certain thing, if it has any validity, is a tax upon us for the expense that accrues in complying with it." In the interests of liberty and American rights, Dickinson went on, "a firm, modest exertion of a free spirit" would be appropriate. He proposed not "inflammatory measures" but advocated raised voices in "testimony" against the unfair legislation.

Within days of publication of the first letter in the *Chronicle,* other Pennsylvania papers reprinted it. Soon the editors of nineteen colonial newspapers (out of twenty-three then publishing) published Dickinson's letters, too. All twelve of the letters were then collected in a pamphlet called *Letters from a Farmer in Pennsylvania, to the Inhabitants of the British Colonies.* British and French editions soon followed, with glowing introductions by Benjamin Franklin.

Dickinson's message and common-man manner rang true to an eager and growing readership. When he concluded his first letter, "Small things grow great by concord," he could hardly have known how prescient these words would be. Dickinson's *Letters* quickly became the most acclaimed and best-known document of the emerging revolutionary movement.

POPLAR HALL

John Dickinson (1732–1808) was eight years old when his family moved to the six-square-mile plantation of fertile fields and marshlands along the St. Jones River in Kent County, Delaware. For three generations, the Dickinsons had lived on Maryland's Eastern Shore, but on January 29, 1741, his father, Samuel, led an orderly caravan of wagons, slaves, and men on horseback on a seventy-mile journey across the peninsula. When they arrived at the flat, sandy site of their new home, some three hundred yards from the river and six miles southeast of Dover, Samuel recorded the event in the family Bible.

Samuel had ordered construction of a "Homeplace" for himself; his second wife, Mary Cadwalader, daughter of a prominent Philadelphia family; and their firstborn son, John. The Maryland properties remained in the care of a grown son from Samuel's first marriage.

The Dickinsons called their new home Poplar Hall. While the Maryland plantations continued to produce tobacco, the crops of choice in Delaware were wheat and corn. Once harvested, the grains would be loaded onto open, two-masted boats called shallops from the family's private pier, bound upstream for Philadelphia to be ground into flour. On one journey in 1745, the Dickinsons' boat returned with an Irish tutor named James Orr. For three years Orr would instruct John; his younger brother, Philemon; and the child of a physician neighbor. When he turned eighteen, having added the study of Latin and history to his mastery of reading, writing, and arithmetic, John was ready to leave home for the Quaker city. For three years he read law with one of Philadelphia's leading practitioners; then he traveled to London to continue his legal studies.

When he came back to America, in 1757, John found his father aging and ill. Upon his arrival, the members of the household, black and white, surrounded him "like a flock of blackbirds," welcoming him as the returning heir. The children dressed in their best clothes to honor him, and Old Pompey, the personal servant of Samuel Dickinson, bent to kiss John's hand. John formally greeted each child, and then cakes were passed around. In a time when the rituals of daily life varied little, the son's homecoming was an event that those in attendance would remember many years later.

SLAVE OR SERVANT?

Colonial America was a slaveholding society, in which African-Americans and their children were regarded as the chattel (property) of their owners. A slave had no prospect of freedom unless manumitted (freed) by his or her owner. *Manumission* could be the result of purchase or an act of humanity by the slaveholder. George Washington, for example, instructed in his will that his slaves were to be freed upon the death of his widow, Martha.

Many white laborers and tradesmen arrived in America as indentured servants. Typically in return for the cost of passage and room and board, these individuals signed a contract by which they were bound, often as apprentices, to a period of service. After completing the agreed-upon term (four or seven years was usual), the indentured servant became a freeman.

Upon being manumitted, some slaves remained with their former masters as indentured servants. Some white and black freemen worked as servants bound only by mutually agreed upon terms with their employer.

Although the original outbuildings at the Dickinson Plantation are gone, archaeological investigations and the examination of surviving structures on other Delaware properties have made possible a reconstruction of several service buildings, among them the corncrib, the feed barn, and the smokehouse (left to right) pictured here.

After his time in England, John viewed his family property through very different eyes. The farm was productive, its fields an expanse of waving grains, but from the north windows of the house he could see the plantation's working buildings, among them the slave quarter, which still housed most of Samuel Dickinson's seventy-odd slaves. In London, John had come to think of slavery not as a social norm but as an evil that debased those who owned other men. He could take no action on his father's lands, but in the years that followed, like some others of his generation, he would begin to change the old ways.

The Dickinson Plantation was a long journey from any metropolis, and John had many large ideas that could not be acted upon on St. Jones Neck. After passing the summer with his family, the twenty-five-year-old lawyer returned to Philadelphia, where he could practice law and join friends and other members of his family, including Philemon, who had gone there to study at the College of Philadelphia. John rose quickly in his profession, and he soon argued cases before the colonial supreme court. In October 1759, he was elected a member of the Delaware Assembly, and a year later its speaker. In 1760 his father died, and John became executor of the estate. Although he inherited his father's Delaware plantation, John chose to remain in Philadelphia, and in 1762 he was elected to the Pennsylvania Assembly.

Pictured here is a reconstruction of a "log'd dwelling," a one-room domicile like those used by the slaves and tenant farmers, black and white, who worked the fields in Delaware's Kent County in the revolutionary era.

At the Dickinson Plantation today, the fireplace in the logged dwelling is used to demonstrate hearth cooking.

The "Log'd Dwelling"

In 1777, Dickinson acted upon his long dormant desire to free his slaves, manumitting all those "old Black folks" who remained in his possession. The law required security be provided for freed blacks, so initially four of the slaves were indentured to him, while two remained as servants. In 1785, he freed them all unconditionally.

Many of the former slaves remained as free tenants on Dickinson's properties. Typically they lived in dwellings like this one, small structures with footprints roughly sixteen by twenty feet. The walls were clapboarded with local pine or oak, the chimneys were of brick, the floors dirt. Dickinson's tenant farmers maintained small gardens and their own livestock (cattle, oxen, horses, pigs, and sheep), but their humble dwellings contained little more than beds, a chest, a table, kitchen and gardening implements, a chair or two, and rudimentary cooking apparatus.

Dickinson attempted to persuade his brother, the legislators in Delaware, and the other delegates at the Constitutional Convention to free their slaves, too. He believed that slavery was inconsistent with the sentiments expressed in the Declaration of Independence. He wrote that, by his interpretation, slaves *"could not afterward be imported into these states.* The Sanctions of Law, the most solemn rational acts, and the eternal Distinctions between right and Wrong, all forbid property to spring from such a source [as slavery]." His desire to end slavery proved unsuccessful, but Dickinson did help to shape the compromise that was adopted at the Constitutional Convention, which permitted the slave trade to be continued only until 1808.

John Adams, writing of John Dickinson at the First Continental Congress in August 1774, described him this way: "He is a shadow—tall, but slender as a reed—pale as ashes. One would think at first sight that he could not live a month. Yet upon a more attentive inspection, he looks as if the strings of life were strong enough to last many years." A 1768 engraving by James Smither.

THE RELUCTANT REVOLUTIONARY

John Dickinson was not an imposing man. Never physically strong, he suffered prolonged bouts of bronchitis and colds throughout his life. He had been constantly seasick in traveling to England and often ill during his years abroad. He'd also inherited his father's tendency to gout. But Dickinson's persuasiveness as a writer and public speaker gained him wide influence.

A key figure in Pennsylvania politics during the revolutionary era, Dickinson was chosen to represent the colony at the Stamp Act Congress in New York in 1765. By then he was thirty-three and an experienced lawyer and legislator. In 1770 he married Mary (Polly) Norris, a devoted Quaker. With their combined fortunes, John and Mary Dickinson were among the wealthiest couples in Philadelphia, and Dickinson embarked on a major updating of Fairhill, the Norrises' estate in Germantown, outside Philadelphia. He also built a new house downtown on Chestnut Street, but Mary would not leave Fairhill, so the Dickinsons never moved in. The couple would have two daughters who survived to adulthood.

When he was appointed to serve in the Continental Congress in 1774, John Dickinson's name was recognized by more Americans than any but Benjamin Franklin's. Dickinson called for moderation, not violence; he wanted to seek redress of the colonists' grievances through traditional legal means, such as petition. Even after the publication of Thomas Paine's *Common Sense,* in January 1776, Dickinson sought conciliation with the British rather than independence. But Paine's radical call to action better suited the changing temper of the time.

In July 1776, Dickinson abstained in the vote for the Declaration of Independence. As he had said in *Letters from a Farmer,* "The Cause of Liberty is a cause of too much dignity to be sullied by turbulence and tumult." In following his conscience, he found himself out of touch.

Despite his reluctance to seek independence, John Dickinson knew which side he was on. During the Revolution, he took up arms in support of the new country and helped write the first draft of the Articles of Confederation. He served as president (governor) of Delaware and later of Pennsylvania. His last public office was as a delegate to the Constitutional Convention, where he voted for ratification of the finished document. After retiring from public life, he managed his estates, published an edition of his papers, and periodically offered advice and comment as a respected elder statesman.

For most of his married life, Dickinson lived in Germantown and, later, Wilmington, because both locales offered access to his business and political interests. He had an enduring affection for his Delaware plantation, and he visited Poplar Hall in mid-May each year; during the Revolution, he and his family took refuge there and added a four-horse stable, a shed with a corncrib and mangers, a henhouse, a bathhouse, a distillery, and a pigeon house. Dickinson tried on more than one occasion to persuade his wife of the virtues of his Kent County estate. "Our place affords a luxuriant Prospect of Plenty," he wrote her in 1780, "the clover lawns as green as a favorable Season can make it—About twenty head of cattle grazing and gambling [*sic*] over the verdure—The trees bending down to the grass with red and reddening apples—peaches & damascenes without number." Nevertheless, he was never able to persuade Mary to abandon her ties to her family and her Quaker meeting, so she spent little time at Poplar Hall.

After retiring from public life, in 1793, Dickinson himself spent more time at Poplar Hall. Like virtually all the Founding Fathers, he was a farmer; in eighteenth-century America, most people kept at least a kitchen garden and a few animals, even if they practiced a trade or a profession. But it was Dickinson who addressed his fellow farmers in such a way that the plainest and the most refined all felt as if he spoke for them. Voltaire would compare him with Cicero. Jefferson was among his admirers, the two men

In the early twentieth century, restorers of Dickinson's home added a Colonial Revival–style formal garden to his plantation.

Dickinson's brick mansion at Poplar Hall from the rear; his "new room" (originally built in 1793 and after, restored in 2005–2006) is attached to the gable end of the main block.

This was Dickinson's parlor chamber (that is, the bedroom over his parlor). In the eighteenth century, gauze mosquito netting was used not only around the beds but on looking glasses, chandeliers, and portraits, to protect both the people and their valuable objects. Screening wouldn't be introduced until the Civil War era.

having collaborated on important resolutions in the Continental Congress before the Revolution.

Perhaps a letter John Dickinson, Farmer, squire of Poplar Hill, wrote his wife leaves the clearest sense of the property that grounded him:

> I always feel a melancholy kind of pleasure in being at this place where I have spent so many happy days with those that were so justly dear to me. Some of their previous remains rest in the garden. I walk, I ride, I read, I think of thee and our dear children, and humbly implore your happiness. All nature is blooming around me, and the fields are full of promises. It is surprising, how I am serenaded by heaven-taught songsters, morning and evening constantly, frequently in the day. I observed and listened yesterday for some time to a lark warbling his delight from the large Mulberry tree before the door. There is a great variety of birds and therefore of notes. A charming mocking bird every morning initiates them all. I enjoy these amusements, for I am very well.

When Dickinson died, in 1808, his old colleague in arms President Jefferson, along with a unanimous House and Senate, resolved to wear black crepe armbands in his honor.

"THE LIBERTY SONG"

In his *Letters,* John Dickinson found a large audience of disgruntled colonists. But his 1768 composition "The Liberty Song" gave people a way to sing about their dreams.

Writing to James Otis, a Boston friend from the Stamp Act Congress, Dickinson sent along a string of couplets he had composed to the tune of a well-known English patriotic song of the day. The first verse goes:

> *Come, join hand in hand, brave Americans all,*
> *And rouse your bold hearts at fair Liberty's call;*
> *No tyrannous acts shall suppress your just claim,*
> *Or stain with dishonor America's name.*

Otis submitted the song to the *Boston Gazette.* It was also published in Philadelphia and New York papers, as well as in two Boston almanacs. The chorus became a rousing call to join the cause:

> *In Freedom we're born and in Freedom we'll live.*
> *Our purses are ready. Steady, friends, steady;*
> *Not as slaves, but as Freemen our money we'll give.*

Dickinson once again expressed sentiments in a way that many colonists felt rang true. The words *Freedom* and *Liberty* stand out from the lyrics, as does the earliest expression of a phrase that would become an American standard:

> *Then join hand in hand, brave Americans all,*
> *By uniting we stand, by dividing we fall.*

"The Liberty Song" proved widely popular and became, as Dickinson himself termed it, "a song for American freedom."

Laundry Day

In the eighteenth century, at least one day a week was devoted to washing clothes, bedding, and table linens. The process was labor-intensive. Water drawn from the well was carried to the kitchen or, if there was one, the washhouse. A brass or copper caldron was heated in a fireplace, where the clothes were soaked and soaped. A second kettle would be on hand for wringing, bleaching, and rinsing.

The clothes were stirred with a clothes stick (with the kettle positioned over the fire, the clothes needed to be agitated so they didn't get burned). They were then transferred by hand from one container to the other. The entire process might involve as many as five immersions in kettles and washtubs and great volumes of water, much of it heated, all of it carried and poured by hand. The clothes were then hung out on lines to dry—if the weather allowed. In times of uncooperative weather, clothes could be damp for months.

Laundry day was dreaded as hard, tiring, and messy. Ironing was a great deal of work, too, with flat and cylindrical irons, heated over open fires, applied to clothes on large ironing boards.

ABOVE: *Food was prepared in this basement kitchen.*

FACING PAGE, TOP: *During his retirement, Dickinson constructed what he called the "New Room Addition." Built between 1793 and 1796, it consisted of this dining room as well as a pantry and a farm office. The paneled structure in the far corner contains both a cupboard and stairs to the loft space above. Dickinson, a forward-thinking householder, added an early ten-plate stove near the end of his life.*

FACING PAGE, BOTTOM: *Restorers of the house installed paneling salvaged from another eighteenth-century home, in nearby Little Creek, which had been demolished. Over the fireplace hangs a copy of Charles Willson Peale's 1780 portrait of John Dickinson.*

Fire!

I n March 1804, a chimney fire ignited the wooden frame of Poplar Hall. Dickinson learned from one of his tenants that, fanned by a northwest wind, the fire had gutted the house. A kitchen ell he had constructed shortly after his retirement from public life was saved, along with some of the furniture. But the rest of the house was a ruin.

Dickinson ordered reconstruction of the house, and the job was completed in 1806. The roofline was changed (a simple gable roof rose in place of the old hipped shape), and the main staircase was modeled on the stair in his Wilmington house. The old floor plan was largely retained, and Dickinson specified paint colors (three coats, he demanded, "of a handsome stone color"), with the doors and balustrade painted in imitation of mahogany and the baseboards a dark brown. What survives today is John Dickinson's redesigned 1806 house.

The William Paca House

The gentry in Maryland's capital aspired
to the refinements of high English culture. Ships departed for
England, their holds heavy with hogsheads of tobacco grown on
nearby plantations, the major source of the Annapolitans' wealth;
when they returned, they carried luxury goods such as fine china,
the latest fashions, spices, mirrors, tea and tea services, and books.
The wealth and opulence of Annapolis led one English visitor to call
it "the genteelest town in North America."

By the 1770s, some of the finest houses in the colonies lined
the town's streetscapes. In building their homes, gentlemen planters
of the Chesapeake sought to outdo their neighbors to the south, in
Mr. Wythe's Williamsburg, and to compete with the colonies' most
sophisticated city, Philadelphia, to the north. It was in Annapolis
that Charles Carroll, barrister, European-educated and one of the
richest men in Maryland, and his friend Horatio Sharpe, proprietary
governor of the colony, determined to raise the artistic standard.

Carroll, Sharpe, and nine others of the highest political and
social caste raised the princely sum of eighty-five guineas to fund
a term of study in London for a Mr. Charles Willson Peale. The
twenty-five-year-old Maryland native was earning a name for himself

*The parlor at the Paca House has been returned to its original Prussian blue. At the
time the color was fresh (though developed in Berlin in 1704, the formula, a
mixture of white lead and a blue pigment made from a salt compound of iron and
potassium, was kept secret for some years). The woodwork is a stone color
fashionable in the 1770s.*

as a portraitist, having already worked at the trades of saddler, silversmith, upholsterer, and even clock maker and watchmaker before deciding that painting was his true calling. He quickly distinguished himself from the itinerant artists of the time, but Sharpe, Carroll, and the rest had still higher expectations for Peale.

Their financial support enabled him to spend two years in London, much of it in the studio of Benjamin West, an American expatriate. On his return to Annapolis, Peale immediately began painting portraits of provincial aristocrats. His patrons were members of the nation's small elite—the merchants, the successful professionals, and the wealthy land and slave owners (roughly a third of Maryland's population was enslaved). Among those who could afford the luxury of a portrait were Farmer John Dickinson (see "John Dickinson's Poplar Hall," page 24) and George Washington.

Another who sat for Mr. Peale in 1772 was an Annapolis gentleman named William Paca (1740–1799). The thirty-one-year-old Paca (pronounced *PAY-ka*) had been schooled in Philadelphia and perhaps at London's Inns of Court before returning home to practice law in Maryland, where he became involved in the revolutionary cause.

REASSEMBLING A LIFE

Although none of William Paca's personal diaries and letters survive (family papers were lost in a fire in 1879), the outline of his public life can be sketched from other documents.

Paca helped lead the opposition to Parliament's hated taxes and other unwanted legislation in the 1760s as a founder of the local Sons of Liberty. He represented Maryland at the Continental Congress, signed the Declaration of Independence, and helped write the state constitution. During the Revolution, he served as a state senator and in peacetime was three times elected governor.

In 1787, Paca declined to serve as a delegate to the Constitutional Convention in Philadelphia. He objected to strengthening

ABOVE: *A game of cards in the Paca parlor.*

LEFT: *The decorative overmantel is surrounded by plaster garlands, which were restored on the basis of plaster "ghosting" uncovered during restoration.*

The Pacas and their guests took tea in the second-floor porch chamber, with its elevated view of the garden.

PEALE'S PORTRAIT OF PACA

Charles Willson Peale painted a large portrait (the canvas is almost seven and a half feet high) of a large man. The self-assured Paca is relaxed, his left arm akimbo, his right hand gracefully displayed on a plinth, and he looks thoughtfully into the distance. The bust is of Cicero and, along with the subject's clothes and portly physique, confirms Paca's status as a wealthy and erudite member of Annapolis's elite.

Fortunately for the restorers of the Paca House gardens, Peale portrayed his subject in his own backyard. The image of the pleasure garden depicts in particular the overall shape of the wilderness garden, which would be confirmed by archaeological evidence. Still more valuable was the presence of the summerhouse and the bridge, with its latticework railing. Both structures were entirely lost, but Peale's draftsmanship made possible a reconstruction of Paca's elaborate landscape.

A handsome man, more than 6 feet high, of portly appearance, being well educated and accustomed to the best company, [William Paca] was graceful in his movements and complaisant to everyone; in short his manners were of the first polish. In the early period, when the people's eyes first became opened to their rights, . . . [he] made the first stand for the independence of the People.

—Charles Willson Peale

The Carvel Hall Hotel

When completed in 1903, the Carvel Hall Hotel was the best accommodation in town, and its entrance was the former Paca House. But by 1965, the facility had become obsolete, poorly maintained, and damaged by three fires, and a plan was afoot to demolish the entire structure and replace it with a high-rise office and apartment complex.

Historic Annapolis Foundation raised $275,000 to purchase the house (and hotel); it also lobbied Maryland's General Assembly to acquire the acres that had been William Paca's garden. When the wrecking crews arrived, they were instructed to carefully preserve the remains of the Paca House. The workers stripped away the much larger hotel grafted to its rear, and subsequent archival, architectural, and archaeological studies made possible restoration of the house. The William Paca House opened to the public during the 1976 celebration of the nation's bicentennial.

In 1965, the façade of the William Paca House welcomed guests to the Carvel Hall Hotel; by 1966, the rear of the house was the site of a large demolition project that eventually uncovered the remains of the Pacas' fine landscape garden.

the national government, because he believed that to do so would pose a threat to the powers of the states and to individual liberties. The following year he devised his own means of addressing what he saw as a glaring omission from the draft document and sought to add twenty-two amendments to the Constitution at Maryland's Constitution ratification convention. Although his attempt failed, his advocacy helped draw attention to the need for a bill of rights. When the first federal Congress convened, in 1789, the Bill of Rights we know today was passed, and it was subsequently ratified by the states. Paca would spend the last ten years of his life serving as the first judge of the Federal District Court for Maryland, a position to which he was appointed by President Washington.

Though he was born into a prosperous planter family, as the second son, Paca had little fortune of his own. But in 1763 he married the heiress Mary Chew, daughter of one of the richest and most influential families in the colony. His marriage to Mary enabled the couple to shop for the finest items in the town's shops and attend the theater, and it provided Paca access to the most influential men in Maryland. Their marriage also made possible the couple's high-style new home, constructed between 1763 and 1765, for which Paca purchased land just four days after the wedding.

In the absence of Paca's personal papers, his elegant Annapolis mansion provides important clues to his life and times. When constructed, it was one of the most impressive houses in town, proving itself a harbinger of architectural experiments to come. Paca's was among the first five-part houses in Annapolis. This design incorporates a large central block flanked by matched pairs of support structures consisting of a pavilion and a connecting passageway. Other important five-part mansions would follow, notably the Hammond House (see "The Matthias Hammond House," page 182).

Paca probably played a role in the design of his house, after having studied architectural books in his library and seen stylish houses in Philadelphia and London. Undoubtedly he collaborated with a master builder, but the design itself suggests the work of amateurs. Attributes such as the sheer bulk of the house, its enclosed rear porch, and the forty-five-foot-tall chimneys that bookend the main block all echo medieval houses known to the builder and characteristic of the seventeenth century. At the same time, however,

From the street, the sheer bulk of the house, along with its lack of adornment, makes it seem almost fortresslike.

many of its interior details suggest Paca's interest in the Georgian style, coming into vogue in the cultural centers he had visited.

William Paca's marriage to Mary lasted just eleven years, ending with her death in 1774. Paca's later political obligations drew him often to Philadelphia, and there he met and married his second wife, Ann Harrison. In 1780 he sold his Annapolis home, choosing to reside at his country estate on Wye Island, east of Annapolis on the Wye River. In the nineteenth century, his house in town became a rental property and a rooming house; in the twentieth, Paca's once grand home became no more than the lobby for a two-hundred-room hotel.

HENRIETTA'S SICKROOM

In the eighteenth century, many people believed that reason, as distinct from superstition and tradition, offered the prospect of progress in human affairs. In this Age of Enlightenment, as the time is often called, people aspired to control their world. William Paca's fine garden suggested that nature had been tamed—but in reality, of course, that was little more than an illusion.

If on the one hand there was a manicured garden, on the other lurked the realization that illness and death were always nearby. During the Founding Fathers' era, medical care was primitive at best, infectious diseases spread unchecked, and infant mortality was high among the privileged as well as the poor.

Even by the standards of the time, young Henrietta Maria Dorsey saw more than her share of death and disease. In December 1765, not long after the Pacas moved into their grand new home, Mary Chew Paca's orphaned niece arrived on their doorstep. The girl's father had died five years earlier, followed by her sister and then her mother. Henny spent the next several years living with her grandmother before losing her, too, and moving in with Aunt Mary, her sole surviving relation.

The eight-year-old found refuge at the Paca House, where she was cared for by Bett, a slave some ten years her senior. The bedroom or chamber here is the sickroom where Bett may have watched over Henny. Charged with the girl's personal hygiene, Bett probably bathed her hands, neck, feet, and face daily, and changed her gown and bedclothes when they became soiled. Also, at Mary Paca's instruction, Bett would have brought Henny food and drink.

The administration of medicaments, too, would have fallen to Bett, but whatever measures were taken to care for Henny, she died ten months after coming to the Pacas' home. Barely eight years later, her aunt, aged thirty-eight, would die, too, probably after childbirth complications, leaving her husband a thirty-three-year-old widower.

As for Bett, her status as a personal slave to Henny had elevated her well above most other slaves in the household, though she would have become Henny's property on the girl's twenty-first birthday. Instead, she reverted to Mary and then to William Paca. Bett's fate is unknown; references to her cease in the records. Most likely she became no more than a nameless entry in Paca's slave inventory.

An upstairs bed chamber (opposite) is interpreted as Henrietta Maria Dorsey's sickroom, where the Pacas' ailing eight-year-old niece was tended by the slave Bett. On the dresser top (above) are two remedies common to the mid-eighteenth century. The pinkish fluid is tincture of rhubarb, a powerful emetic; the other liquid is tincture of Jesuit bark, a treatment for malarial fever we know today as quinine. The other accoutrements—the medicine chest, earthenware pots for ointments, and even a brass lancet, used to initiate bleeding—were commonplace medical paraphernalia of the time in well-to-do houses. "Curative" drugs of the era also included digitalis, laudanum, and licorice.

LEFT: *The garden façade of the massive Paca House.*

RIGHT: *The grand, formal garden descending from the rise on which the house stands. The parklike pleasure ground invites visitors to experience its varied spaces and plantings. The dome in the distance is the U.S. Naval Academy Chapel.*

FACING PAGE: *The picturesque summer house and the bridge to the wilderness garden, as reconstructed in the twentieth century.*

PACA'S PLEASURE GARDEN

Thomas Jefferson, who resided in Annapolis during the winter of 1783–84, noted that "the gardens [here] are better than those of Williamsburg." The best of these gardens was found behind the house built by Jefferson's fellow Signer William Paca.

Paca's pleasure garden encompassed two full acres bounded by a brick wall. A series of terraces descended the gentle slope from the rear of the house. When the Pacas and their guests took a walk around the garden, they regarded it as an extension of the home and were careful to comport themselves with proper grace, practicing the fine art of conversation. Those privileged to tarry there might have walked down limestone steps like those in place today and paused to admire one or more of the parterres, the formal, roomlike gardens laid out in geometric forms.

The upper terraces overlooked an ornamental pond in the shape of a fish and a stream that traversed the landscape at the foot of the garden. An arched bridge led to a "wilderness garden" containing densely planted thickets and penetrated by paths. Paca probably knew of such informal gardens from his travels; they represented a contemporary trend in English gardening. With the use of native plant materials—trees, shrubs, and blooming trillium and Virginia bluebells—the wilderness garden suggested wild nature captured, as distinct from the more artificial parterres. Visitors would also be drawn to the wilderness garden by architectural fea-tures such as a summerhouse, where they could rest for a time. At the farthest reaches were a spring house, the source of the house-hold's water, and a cold bathhouse, where members of the household bathed. Today two matching necessaries (outhouses) are also located at strategic—and symmetrical—spots in the garden.

Paca oversaw construction of his garden, the Enlightenment ideal of an earthly paradise, between 1763 and 1770, and it would remain an open space for more than a hundred years. In the twenti-eth century, however, it was entirely obliterated, with portions backfilled with up to twelve feet of soil, raising the ground level to accommodate the Carvel Hall Hotel as well as a gas station, parking lot, and bus station. After restorers decided to conserve the house, they elected to resurrect the landscape as well.

Archaeological excavations revealed the stone foundation of the enclosing wall; it, in turn, delineated the five terrace levels and four linking inclines. The foundations of the bridge and other build-ings were also uncovered in the wilderness area. Although the original design of the upper garden was lost, four parterres, as well as a physic (medicinal herb) garden and herb and vegetable gardens were planted in a manner consistent with eighteenth-century practice.

Since no other visual evidence survived, Mr. Peale's painting made possible the reconstruction of the bridge and, in particular, the summerhouse, with its ogee-shaped roof topped with an antique statue of Mercury.

The James Iredell House

In December 1773, Patriots masquerading as Mohawk Indians turned Boston Harbor into a great, churning basin of saltwater tea. While the Boston Tea Party famously galvanized public opinion, it was neatly counterbalanced some months later, when a group of North Carolina women further stirred the pot of public opinion in both America and England with another act of resistance.

Women had no official political status in revolutionary America. They lacked the right to vote and to hold public office; unless widowed, they couldn't even own property in most states. But those who gathered in Edenton, North Carolina, on October 25, 1774, found a way to add their voices to the cry of protest against Parliament's encroachments upon American liberties.

At least fifty-one women assembled. The exact location of their meeting is uncertain, though the second-floor assembly room in the Chowan County Courthouse is a likely location. One of the largest paneled rooms in the colonies, the elegant, thirty-five-by-forty-five-foot space would have accommodated the crowd, its stylish appointments appropriate for a meeting of the most prominent ladies in the district.

What is certain is that a petition was approved by those in attendance. According to a letter that accompanied the resolution,

The interior is surprisingly bright, in part because the one-room-deep floor plan means there are windows on two sides of the major rooms, including the parlor.

LEFT: *On the garden side, the northwest-facing porches are shielded from the sun and offer a view of the gardens and working buildings.*

RIGHT: *A nineteenth-century decorative porch railing on the house's street façade.*

"BLACK WATER"

Tea didn't *cause* the Revolution. Yet the dry, loose leaves that merchant ships brought all the way from Asia represented to the colonists money, power, and refinement. When Parliament imposed a tax on tea—without the Americans' agreement—the action carried enormous symbolic significance.

Dutch traders first called China tea "black water," but the habit of drinking it probably crossed the Channel to England from France in the seventeenth century. Initially confined to royals and the nobility, the practice descended the social ladder in England, then to wealthier colonists. Tea was exotic and expensive, as were the custom-made teapots, bowls, jars, and cups, but as the rumbles of revolution echoed in the 1770s, more than half of America's households of the middling sort owned tea equipment.

Serving tea became an essential social ritual. The mistress of the house typically kept the tea, often both green (hyson) and black (souchong), under lock and key in her personal closet, along with the precious cooking spices, such as cinnamon and nutmeg. When serving her guests, she measured out tea for the pot from her cache. Tea might be served to male and female guests at any time of day, but tea drinking was also common among women after the main meal, the midafternoon dinner, when the ladies "withdrew" to the parlor or drawing room, leaving the men to their smoking and wine.

Coffee was also a common household beverage among the gentry. They drank chocolate, too, consuming it scalding hot, usually with spices or sugar added, often at breakfast.

they resolved "not to drink any more tea, nor wear any more British Cloth." In so doing, "many ladies of this Province," the petition continued, "have determined to give a memorable proof of their patriotism, and have accordingly entered into [an] honorable and spirited association." The women, who hailed from five counties, then signed the document. Nine days later the *Williamsburg Gazette* published the petition; after making its way across the Atlantic, it appeared in the *London Advertiser* and *Morning Chronicle* on January 16, 1775.

The London publication of the ladies' letter produced much commentary, not least in a satirical cartoon (see page 52). The gathering came to be celebrated as the Edenton Tea Party, and historians characterize the event as the earliest organized political activity of American women.

At the time, Arthur Iredell, a Londoner and Anglican clergyman, encountered the petition and wrote of it to his brother in America. He inquired of James Iredell, "Pray are you become patriotic?" In truth, James was betwixt and between, working both as a young lawyer in the independent-minded town and as the King's customs officer. Outwardly a servant of the Crown, he privately expressed an "impatient [desire] to be attached to my friends in the noblest of all causes, a struggle for freedom."

The house is finished to the period of the Iredells' habitation, from 1778 to 1826.

James Iredell, a lawyer and jurist of modest means, resided in Edenton in a comfortable but hardly grand home.

> [A]ll government was instituted for the good of the people, and . . . when it no longer answers this end, and they are in danger of slavery, or great oppression, they have a right to change it.
>
> —*James Iredell, 1777*

LEFT: *At the Iredell House, a two-story porch overlooks Church Street.*

RIGHT: *Although he had a speech impediment, James Iredell became a highly successful lawyer, advocate, and justice.*

Although he may not have said so to his Tory brother, young James undoubtedly took a certain pride in the ladies of his town, whom Arthur disparaged as the "female artillery of Edenton." In the several decades that followed, James Iredell proved to be a valuable member of the new country's legal establishment.

JAMES IREDELL: A BRIEF LIFE

James Iredell (1751–1799) arrived from England in 1768. The village of Edenton must have seemed tame to him after a childhood spent in the burgeoning port of Bristol in southwest England, but the young man came to the colonies to make a new start. After his father's merchant business had failed, some of his mother's connections secured him a post as customs agent for northeastern Carolina.

Within five years of arriving, Iredell (among North Carolinians, the name is pronounced *AHR-ah-dell*) completed a clerkship with one of the town's leading citizens and lawyers, Samuel Johnston. He also found a suitable bride in Johnston's sister, Hannah, and gained a license to practice law. He quickly earned a professional reputation in general practice: he made wills, administered estates, resolved property disputes, and litigated a variety of matters before the bar. His abilities were recognized, and as he put it in a letter to his wife, he was soon "a little in vogue."

For some years, Iredell remained a customs officer. Although those who knew him spoke of him as "being very warm" toward the Patriots, just a month before the Declaration of Independence was signed, Iredell asserted his hope that England and her American colonies might resolve their differences, writing that such a reconciliation was "the first and most earnest object of every man's wish and attention." In truth, the picture was more complicated, as he explained years later. "In regard to my official character, I was scrupulously careful, so long as the least vestige of a British government remained to do nothing inconsistent with it but afterward, I thought myself so much at liberty to choose my side as any man." Certainly he anticipated what was coming: he made his last entry as the port's collector in April 1776, noting in the account book, "No Duties in July 1776—accounts then to close."

Iredell gained a reputation for his anonymous essays (some he signed simply "A Planter"). In his writings, he disputed assertions of the King's rights over Americans, anticipating the Declaration of Independence. "Mankind were intended to be happy," he wrote in "The Principles of an American Whig." He went on to argue "that government being only the *means* of securing freedom and happiness to the people, whenever it deviates from this end, and their freedom and happiness are in great danger of being irrevocably lost, the government is no longer entitled to their allegiance."

This caricature, published by Sayer & Bennett of 53 Fleet Street, London, was labeled "A Society of Patriotic Ladies at Edenton, North Carlina."

The Edenton Tea Party

Parliament and Lord North's government chose to ignore many of the petitions sent to them by the colonists, but when a London printmaker started selling this caricature of the Edenton Tea Party, the Parliamentarians suddenly became the object of ridicule.

Look closely: Despite the words "We the ladies of Edenton" in a copperplate hand on the parchment, those are *not* the Carolina ladies. The bewigged mesdames in the cartoon are really men, many of them London notables of the day, whose faces were well known to readers of the popular press. The image was hardly complimentary, but in certain quarters, it was highly amusing. Note, as well, that even the canine in attendance got to offer a political commentary, leaving his message on the tea canisters by his feet.

Sugar with Your Tea?

Sugar arrived at the homes of the Founding Fathers not in spoonable granules but in solid loaves shaped like blunt-topped cones. The molded cones were wrapped in paper and typically weighed several pounds each (though they could weigh up to sixty-four pounds). The sugar itself was rock hard and had to be chipped off with a knife and mallet, then pounded into granules. Once powdered, the sugar was stored in a tightly lidded tin box.

Iredell would play a considerable role in the coming decades in North Carolina. During the Revolutionary War, his pamphleteering continued. After the peace, he was quick to recognize the weakness of the Articles of Confederation, and though he seems to have lacked the means to journey to Philadelphia for the Constitutional Convention, friends kept him abreast of progress there. Once the Constitution had been drafted and submitted to state conventions for ratification, Iredell's penchant for penning strong arguments came to the fore once again.

Writing under the pseudonym Marcus, he refuted the objections of George Mason (see "George Mason's Gunston Hall," page 218) and others with another published polemic, "Answers." At the North Carolina convention, his service on several committees demonstrated his skills as a debater, and he soon became the leader of his state's pro-Constitution forces. Initially he and the other Federalists failed to overcome objections concerning states' rights and the absence of a bill of rights, but North Carolina ratified the document in November 1789, the twelfth state to do so.

Iredell's skills caught the eye of George Washington, by then president of the new nation. His arguments for the Constitution not only had been persuasive, Washington saw, but also demonstrated a broad understanding of the document itself. The President invited Iredell to be one of the first interpreters of the Constitution, appointing him to the Supreme Court in 1790.

Iredell was thirty-eight and remained on the court until his death, just nine years later. Traveling the federal circuits, as Supreme Court justices were required to do in that era, took a toll on Iredell's the fragile health. By the time he died in 1799, he had won the respect and friendship of not only Washington but also his successor, John Adams.

FACING PAGE: *James Iredell worshipped at St. Paul's Episcopal Church. Begun in 1736 and completed in 1774, the church served both whites and their slaves. The slaves sat in the gallery until the African-American population formed its own congregations and built its own churches after emancipation.*

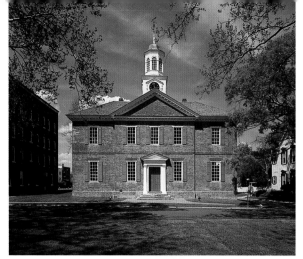

LEFT: *The Chowan County Courthouse, constructed 1767.*

BELOW LEFT: *The courtroom at the Chowan County Courthouse features a semicircular rear apse with the chief justice's chair at the center. The Greek Revival columns in the fore-ground were installed in the early nineteenth century to help support the floor above.*

ONE COLONIAL COURTHOUSE

Local historians believe the Edenton Tea Party took place here. Certainly James Iredell, Esquire, knew the building intimately as both judge and attorney.

Constructed in 1767, the Chowan County Courthouse on King Street is regarded as the finest and most intact colonial courthouse in America and as the earliest government building still standing in North Carolina. The pedimented pavilion at the center of the façade echoes the interior arrangement, fronting the two focal spaces of the building, the courtroom on the first floor and the assembly room above.

The building is Georgian in style, blending remnants of the Baroque (the cupola) with the Palladian.

Its designer undoubtedly knew buildings inspired by the Renaissance master Andrea Palladio; the publication of his book, *The Four Books of Architecture* (*I Quattro Libri dell'Architettura,* originally published in Venice in 1570) had led to a widespread revival of classical buildings in eighteenth-century England. The Chowan County Courthouse is an elegant but restrained example that, with a minimum of ornamentation, relies upon its shape and proportions to express the grand aspirations of its builders.

The courthouse remained in service for more than two hundred years, and today, after a recent eight-year restoration, it continues to be used for a range of public purposes.

EARLY EDENTON

In the time of Charles I (reigned 1625–1649), a few early European settlers arrived in the province of Carolana (Latin for "land of Charles"), but more permanent settlements developed after the Restoration in 1660. Charles II granted the Duke of Albemarle the lands of which Chowan County would be a part, and plantations were established along the Albemarle Sound. The locale's geographical advantages—all water and land routes in the area seemed to lead there—made the emerging little town at the fork of Queen Anne's Creek central to the developing colony. Edenton's grid of streets was laid out in 1712 and the town incorporated in 1722, taking its name from Charles Eden, the recently deceased colonial governor.

Early Edenton had a courthouse, a council chamber, and a jail. A town wharf, public warehouse, and the shops of various tradesmen lined the waterfront of what had become a bustling port town. Edenton was the seat of the colony's colonial government until 1743, and shipbuilding, mercantile interests, and politics made the town a prosperous place.

Today much early architectural fabric survives in Edenton, including its courthouse, the church where Iredell worshipped, and the Cupola House, a grand home constructed for another English administrator. Extensive trade was conducted in the town—some eight hundred ships cleared the port in the early 1770s—and these structures attest to the royal grandeur and wealth of Edenton in the mid-eighteenth century.

The home of James Iredell stands in humble contrast. He was never a wealthy man, having arrived in America in part because of his father's business failures. His decision to become a Patriot eventually cost him a share of the family legacy back in England, and his service as a judge never provided him with a substantial income.

He and his wife purchased a house in Edenton in 1778. The original structure, built in 1759, had two rooms on the ground floor

and two upstairs. The Iredells were planning an addition when James died (it was observed at the time of his death that the house "was very much out of repair"). His widow carried out their plans, with the addition completed in 1800, and remained in the house until her death, in 1826. In 1827, James Iredell, Jr., built a new structure to replace the earliest portion.

The restored house is a modest, comfortable dwelling of six rooms, but much larger than the average homestead of people of the middling sort in that era. The strongest impression left by a visit to the Iredell House is that it grew organically. The Cupola House makes a bold architectural statement; the charm of the Iredells' home is in its lack of presumption; it is a dwelling quite obviously the result of changing practical needs. In it Hannah and James raised their children (three of four reached adulthood, and James Iredell, Jr., became North Carolina's governor). Although his work as an associate justice often took him away, Iredell always returned to his home in Edenton. As he confided in a friend, "My heart will forever be among my friends in N.C., however painfully separated from it."

THE CUPOLA HOUSE

Francis Corbin had his instructions: His employer back in England had made clear the need for a proper office in Edenton "for the safe lodgement of my papers & records and for your transacting my business with decency and order." Corbin, himself a wealthy land agent, began construction of the home, now known as Cupola House, in 1757. It is a house that dispels any doubts about Corbin's—and Edenton's—prosperity in those years.

The roof is crowned with an octagonal cupola, an unusual architectural ornament in a colonial outpost such as North Carolina. The upper floor is jettied, meaning it overhangs the first story. This feature is more characteristic of the seventeenth than of the eighteenth century, but inside, the elaborate classical moldings, including tall cornices, fine pedimented doorways, and carved mantels, were derived from plates in contemporary English architectural books. The house is a mix of old and emerging architectural styles, with a floor plan that features a central hall and stair and generous parlors on either side of the entrance.

The cupola surveys the bay, but the elegance of the structure itself suggests that the builder intended the house itself to draw the eye. The cupola roof is bell-shaped and capped with a spherical finial. The siding of the cupola is of wood panels shaped to look like cut stone.

Corbin died in 1767. After his death, the house passed into Patriot hands.

The Jeremiah Lee Mansion

On the day before Paul Revere's ride,
Jeremiah Lee was a hero in the making. His peers—among them
John Hancock and the Adams cousins Samuel and John—saw him
as an essential player in the revolutionary movement. Yet in one of
history's unpredictable reversals, Lee died in the days after Revere
delivered his midnight message, and instead of gaining fame, Lee
faded into obscurity.

In the year leading up to the Revolution, Lee had been a leading citizen of Marblehead, described as a "Gentleman of trade, of
fortune, and of good character." He commanded the town's militia,
a regiment of veteran sailors that would later distinguish itself ferrying George Washington and the Continental Army across the
Delaware (see "Victory at Trenton," page 143). His prominence as a
member of the Massachusetts Provincial Congress led to his nomi-
nation to the Continental Congress as Marblehead's delegate. He
declined, but his townsman Eldridge Gerry, who went in his stead,
eventually signed the Declaration of Independence and served as
James Madison's vice president; his surname survives in the term for
congressional redistricting, *gerrymandering.*

Colonel Lee was also a key member of the Committee of
Supplies, charged with the clandestine purchase of cannons, gunpowder, munitions, and foodstuffs, including fish, flour, and salt.

*The stairway and raised-panel wainscoting are mahogany. Note that each stair has
three distinct twisting balusters, as well as a return consisting of a raised panel.*

In addition, he arranged for their delivery to inland towns for safekeeping.

On Monday, April 17, 1775, Lee journeyed to Concord, the temporary home of the Provincial Congress, to meet secretly with fellow members of the Committees of Safety and Supplies. The following day he and his revolutionary colleagues met once more, this time at Newell's Tavern in a nearby town. A third meeting was supposed to take place at Ethan Wetherby's Black Horse Tavern on Wednesday, but unexpected circumstances prevented Lee from attending.

Tensions were high all over the region. In February, Parliament had declared the American colonies to be in a state of rebellion; in March, Virginia's Patrick Henry, in support of the insurrectionists in New England, is said to have uttered his famous call to arm, "Give me liberty or give me death." The Patriots were fearful that the Redcoats might march on Concord at any time to arrest the rebel leaders, disperse their supporters, seize their supplies of arms, and thereby quash the rebellion. Parliament had just imposed another of its Restraining Acts, this one forbidding American vessels to fish off Newfoundland or trade with anyone but the English. That was the crowning blow for both Marbleheaders in general and Jeremiah Lee in particular, since their livelihoods came from the sea.

Thanks in part to the poet Henry Wadsworth Longfellow and his memorable "Paul Revere's Ride" (published much later, in 1863), part of the story of the night of April 18–19 is well known. The British general Thomas Gage issued the order to march "with utmost expedition and Secrecy to Concord." The two lanterns in the belfry of Boston's North Church alerted Revere that the Redcoats were moving by sea, and he rode into the night to warn the revolutionists (in fact, Revere didn't make it to Concord, but another rider, Dr. Samuel Prescott, did). At dawn, seventy-seven Minutemen confronted British troops in Lexington, and the "shot heard round the world" was fired (though by whom no one is certain). A series of skirmishes in Concord followed.

Colonel Jeremiah Lee wasn't there. In the predawn hours, Lee and two other Marblehead men had awakened to the sounds of British soldiers marching past the tavern where they slept. Knowing the Redcoats were looking for rebel leaders, they fled, barely escaping the raiding party that ransacked the tavern.

With so little warning, Lee was clad only in his nightclothes. He hid himself by lying in a field, barely obscured by the previous year's cornstalks. With no coat or blanket, he caught a chill. The severe fever that resulted killed him, and in the dramatic days to come, other heroes emerged. Jeremiah Lee was soon forgotten.

CODFISH ARISTOCRAT

For a hundred years, selling dried and salted fish had made people in coastal New England rich—but none of the so-called codfish aristocrats did it better than Jeremiah Lee (1721–1775). The third son of a merchant in nearby Manchester, Massachusetts, he moved at age twenty-one to Marblehead, then one of the ten largest cities in the colonies and a prosperous port. Its natural harbor was protected by the rocky headlands from which the town got its name.

Soon after his arrival, Lee married Martha Swett, a daughter of one of the town's wealthiest merchants. In the next decade, he accumulated more real estate, warehouses, wharf footage, and marketable goods than any other Massachusetts merchant, including those in Salem and Boston. At the time of his death, Lee owned outright twenty-one schooners, brigs, snows, and other vessels, as well as an inland farm and a variety of trade shops.

Although Jeremiah, Martha, and their growing family resided in a fine house before 1768, that year they moved into a new mansion, a bold expression of wealth and taste. After purchasing three adjoining parcels at the foot of the town common, Lee had demolished the existing buildings and started afresh. Over a period of two years, he watched as his mansion was framed and finished. From a cupola that sprang from the roof, the vista reached to the Atlantic, so Lee could observe the comings and goings of his ships.

In its time, the Lee Mansion was probably the largest dwelling in New England. Its fifteen generous rooms and ten thousand square feet of living space were home to the Lees and their six surviving children, as well as servants, slaves, and perhaps a clerk or apprentice or two. Lee probably based the place on a plate from an English architectural pattern book, *Select Architecture* (1755), by Robert Morris. But building such a house in America required significant adjustments.

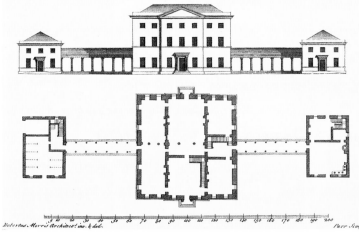

TOP: *The Lee Mansion stands a full three stories, with a habitable attic and crowning cupola. In the densely developed townscape of Marblehead, adding an extra story provided living space without enlarging the footprint.*

ABOVE: *The presumed source for the design of Colonel Lee's manse was* Select Architecture, *a book by the English architect and plan book author Robert Morris. This is Plate 11 from the 1757 edition.*

RUSTICATED SIDING

I n mid-eighteenth-century England, rustication was all the rage. The walls of the finest houses consisted of blocks of stone, typically of uniform size, laid up in horizontal courses. The deeply recessed joints between the chamfered edges of the stones produced a massive and substantial appearance. *That* was the look Jeremiah Lee wanted— although neither the materials nor the masons were at hand in Marblehead to accomplish it.

His solution was to use locally harvested white pine, shaping and finishing it so that it would resemble rusticated stone. To imitate cut ashlar stone, wide, matched planks were cut and their edges beveled before being nailed to the building's frame as exterior cladding.

A faux finish came next. After a layer of paint was applied, a fine, dry sand was dusted onto the tacky surface, perhaps with a bellows. Late-twentieth-century paint analysis revealed remnants of this mixture in a soft gray hue. The illusion of stone was enhanced by the wooden quoins at the corners and the keystoned jack arches over the windows.

The result then—and now, after a recent restoration—was the monumental look of a stolid stone mansion towering over the Marblehead streetscape of smaller, lower wood-frame structures.

The imposing entrance portico was shaped of wood. The siding was, too, although its long boards were beveled and finished to resemble dressed stone.

The first-floor stair hall (opposite), welcomes visitors in grand style. More than seven feet wide, the stairs seem an invitation to ascend to the second floor (above), where the Copley portrait of Jeremiah Lee watches over the landing and the generous upstairs hall, decorated with a range of scenic papers.

RIGHT: The largest room in the house was called the hall or best parlor, and its focus was the grandest chimneypiece. The mantel shelf and overmantel were richly decorated with carved flowers, fruit, and acanthus leaves. The dark wood finish came later, when the Marblehead Bank had the room painted faux boix, a simulated wood grain intended to resemble oak.

The parlor on the first floor would typically have been used by the family for modest entertainments. The chairs here were once part of a set of twenty-four and are among the few Lee pieces in the house, given by a descendant.

PAPERHANGING

In the time of the Founding Fathers, the new interior wall coverings of ornamental paper were termed paperhangings. The papers were usually English, printed on sheets glued into strips. But not all paperhangings were created equal. There were flocked and block-printed papers, with patterns that ranged from imitation chintz to stripes and florals. But the very fanciest were those that were not printed but hand-painted.

Those were the sorts of paperhangings that Jeremiah Lee chose for his house. His scenic papers illustrated classical themes and were surrounded by Rococo decorations. In Great Britain, the light and fanciful "frames" would have been made of delicate applied plasterwork, but since there was no *stuccodore* craft tradition in America, trompe l'oeil frills took their place.

Lee's mural papers were not colorful—the palette ranges from black to white, with shades of gray between (thus the French name, *grisaille*). When he ordered his papers, he would have sent the London paper-staining shop scale drawings of the rooms where they were to hang. Then the scenes were drawn and painted in tempera, copying French engravings of the time. That these elegant paperhangings still remain on the walls of the Lee Mansion is remarkable, since only one other set of *en grisaille* papers survives, preserved at the Metropolitan Museum of Art in New York.

In England, major houses were generally built of stone; in New England, wood structures were standard. Because more carpenters than masons were at hand and his older brother operated a lumber business (after fish, New England's second major export was timber), the Colonel found a way to give his impressive new dwelling the appearance of a stone house while building it of readily available wood. By chamfering and applying fine sand to the siding, the builders gave the exterior walls the look of cut ashlar stonework (see "Rusticated Siding," page 59).

Colonel Jeremiah Lee had a great deal of wealth—and no reluctance about showing it off in the building and decoration of his house. Mahogany wainscot lines the central halls; above the paneling, the walls are adorned with hand-painted scenic wallpapers that, in turn, are framed by trompe l'oeil scrolls and naturalistic Rococo motifs. The design of the staircase incorporates low-rise treads, assuring a genteel ascent. Hand-carved brackets decorate the stairs, while intricate carving makes the grandest chimneypiece in the house a Rococo showpiece. An inventory taken after Lee's death

RIGHT: *The Lee Mansion as the Marblehead Bank in a post-1871 photo. The house was then chocolate brown.*

BELOW: *The scenic wallpapers extend into the principal upstairs bed chambers. The canopied bedstead in the hall chamber (named for the room below) is hung with yellow silk damask bed curtains.*

enumerates a vast array of personal possessions, among them china, silk damask, mahogany furniture, looking glasses, carpets, and even a telescope—none of which most people in prerevolutionary New England would have been able to afford.

WASHINGTON COMES TO TOWN

Visiting on his presidential tour in 1789, years after Lee's death, George Washington remarked on Marblehead's desolate air. The town, he observed, had "the appearance of antiquity."

Washington knew the sailors of Marblehead well; they had served him honorably in the war. But the Revolution had taken a terrible toll, leaving the town with 459 widows and 865 orphaned children in a population of fewer than 5,000 people.

Although Jeremiah Lee did not survive the Revolution, his house, a symbol of Marblehead's once booming economy, did. By Martha Lee's death, in 1791, much of the estate had been liquidated, the assets sold to pay off creditors. Little besides the house and the John Singleton Copley portraits remained.

The boom in Asian and Pacific trade that brought wealth to nearby Salem simply sailed past Marblehead. But the new Marblehead Bank purchased the grand Lee Mansion in 1804 and occupied it for a century. After the bank closed, the house became headquarters of the Marblehead Historical Society, which purchased it in 1909.

Jeremiah Lee's lavish house survives as a testimony to his aristocratic pretensions. Ironically, he sought to imitate the great houses of England only a few years before he died pursuing independence from English rule.

JOHN SINGLETON COPLEY, AMERICAN MASTER

In the years before the Revolution, Jeremiah Lee assumed the air of an English lord and hired the one man in the northern colonies who could render him on canvas with consummate skill.

Born in Boston in 1738, John Singleton Copley was self-taught as a painter (in 1774 he would travel to Europe, where he would reside the rest of his life). In a distinguished American career before the Revolution, he found a ready market for his portraits thanks to the growing prosperity of the merchant class. Perhaps Copley's greatest achievement (a "miracle," the historian James Flexner has called it) was that he painted greater pictures than he had ever seen and did so before turning twenty-one.

Copley's English-born stepfather, Peter Pelham, taught classes in manners. Etiquette defined the genteel in that era: carriage, facial expression, and proper deportment were used to convey social status. In his pictures of Jeremiah and Martha Lee, Copley gave the sitters the grandiloquent portrayals they wanted; the pendant canvases became accessories in their grand house, hanging on either side of the immense staircase. Unlike virtually everything else Lee owned, the canvases remained in the family for generations, reminders of the wealth, power, and taste of the merchant and Patriot Jeremiah Lee.

Although this giant portrait (it's eight feet tall) offers a life-size portrayal of Jeremiah Lee in 1769, in truth it is a carefully elaborated fiction. The assemblage of clothes, furniture, and fabrics, and even the scenic backdrop, are pure stagecraft. Lee owned no such table as the one pictured; John Singleton Copley took it from an English mezzotint of the day.

The Peyton Randolph House

The cause, it was said, was an "apoplectic stroke." Unanimously elected president of the First Continental Congress a year earlier, Peyton Randolph (1721–1775) was dead, eight months before the signing of the Declaration of Independence.

On October 22, 1775, Peyton and Elizabeth, his wife, along with his younger cousin Thomas Jefferson, had been invited to have Sunday dinner with friends. After attending church, they left their lodgings in downtown Philadelphia and mounted a carriage for the three-mile journey. The ride that afternoon was a welcome respite from the pressures of the congress, where as John Adams had observed a few days earlier, the delegates felt "the spirit of war more intimately than they did before."

After their midafternoon dinner, the guests settled into conversation. Randolph was a good-tempered man of gentle humor, with a dimple in his chin and heavy jowls. His friends valued his company; Jefferson, for one, thought him "of the sweetest affability." Randolph was an excellent listener, a man who described himself as more interested in "the productions of any man's brain than those of my own."

His fellow Virginians bowed to his easy authority; he had served for more than twenty years in various public offices, including the preceding nine as Speaker of the House of Burgesses. While

The best bed chamber featured two high-post bedsteads. The bed curtains on one are of "Virginia Cloth" (likely the plain material was made locally); the other bed was more elaborately dressed with fancier fabric.

LEFT: *The largest room in the house, the dining room boasted a tall marble mantel and matching built-in cupboards. According to an inventory prepared after Randolph's death, the room contained a dozen mahogany chairs, as well as much china and a large quantity of silver.*

BELOW LEFT: *In the mid-1750s, Peyton Randolph updated his house. The original three bays of his parents' home (near corner) became seven. Behind the new center doorway stood an entrance hall and stair; to the right were two new major rooms, one for dining (on the ground floor) and a master chamber on the second floor. Like the man himself, the façade of Randolph's elongated house became a noteworthy presence on Nicholson Street. Its red-brown iron oxide paint contained red lead, giving it a richer hue and ensuring it would last longer.*

Designed by nature for the business, of an affable, open and majestic deportment, large in size, though not out of proportion, [Peyton Randolph] commands respect and esteem by his very aspect, independent of the high character he sustains.

—*Silas Deane, Connecticut delegate to the Continental Congress, 1774*

his abilities were also recognized by delegates from other states at the Philadelphia meetings, among them Benjamin Franklin and John Adams, age was catching up with Randolph. His movements were labored and slow, his legs so swollen with dropsy (edema) that they carried his ample girth only with difficulty.

Randolph's burdens were personal and political. His own family was a house divided, since his younger brother, John, had sided with the Crown and moved his family to England. Yet John's grown son, Edmund, much devoted to his uncle, entered the military on the Patriot side. The events at Lexington and Concord hung over all the Patriots, and as one of their most prominent leaders, Randolph was on the list of rebels subject to arrest and execution.

Two months earlier he had been "much indisposed" and relinquished his role as president of the Virginia revolutionary convention. But a week later the *Virginia Gazette* reported Randolph had "greatly recovered," and he traveled to Philadelphia with Elizabeth. While the company unwound after dinner that Sunday, however, his companions observed that Randolph seemed to be choking. One side of his face contorted, and his friends rushed to his aid. Despite their efforts, by eight o'clock that evening Peyton Randolph was dead, at age fifty-three.

Peyton Randolph was variously described by his contemporaries as "noble," "venerable," and "a true Roman spirit." Despite his early death, his influence lived on. He had befriended and advised both his cousin Thomas Jefferson and George Washington, who regarded him as his political mentor. Randolph signed Patrick Henry's license to practice law (despite concerns that Henry was "very ignorant of the law," Randolph "perceived that he was a man of genius").

MR. ATTORNEY'S HOUSE

Peyton Randolph's death deprived the Patriot cause of a sage man of steady calm; if Randolph had lived longer, he almost certainly would have been remembered for a larger role in the revolutionary drama. As it is, the man known to his neighbors as Mr. Attorney is survived by an invaluable architectural legacy.

The original structure on Williamsburg's Nicholson Street was built between 1715 and 1718 in the form of a two-story cube. The

THE SPEAKER'S MAN

Johnny was among the lucky slaves. He was taught to read and write. Since he dressed in an elaborate uniform, his clothes were clean and handsome. He slept in the house, probably on a pallet in a hall, rather than in an unheated stable or storage building. Peyton Randolph trusted him, dispatching him to buy supplies and deliver letters. Johnny saw something of the world beyond Williamsburg, too, traveling to Philadelphia in 1775.

As Randolph's personal servant, he was charged with shaving and dressing his master each morning. He had no choice but to do as he was told, tending to many duties around the house. Even after his owner died, Johnny's fate was determined by the dead man's will, which bequeathed his "man Johnny" to Edmund Randolph, his master's favorite nephew. Johnny's name appeared at the top of the list of Negroes in Randolph's inventory, value one hundred pounds.

Johnny soon resolved to take his own path, and in December 1777, his new master published a reward for his return. According to the advertisement Edmund Randolph placed in the *Virginia Gazette,* "Johnny, otherwise called John Harris, a mulatto man slave . . . is about five feet seven or eight inches high, wears straight hair, cut in his neck, is much addicted to drinking, has gray eyes . . . and may probably endeavor to pass for a freeman."

No evidence survives that Randolph's five-dollar bounty was ever awarded or that Johnny was captured.

main floor was divided into four rectangular spaces, with the entry in one corner offering access to the hall and dining room on either side. A bed chamber in the far corner completed the twenty-nine-foot-square footprint. Each of the three sizable rooms had its own fireplace, as did the three bedrooms above, which were reached by a stairway.

The house was grand for its place and time, since dwellings with dining rooms and two full stories were rare in early Virginia. But Peyton Randolph's father, Sir John Randolph, who purchased the property in 1724, was the only native-born Virginian to be knighted and the most distinguished lawyer in Virginia's capital. It was Sir John's wealth and influence that made possible Peyton's three years of law studies at London's Inns of Court and his appointment as the King's attorney general for Virginia at age twenty-two. Peyton himself improved his prospects by marrying Elizabeth Harrison of Berkeley Plantation.

By the time Peyton took title to the house after his father's death, he was a man of distinction in his own right. He and Betty, as his wife was known, moved in with Peyton's widowed mother in the early 1750s. They lived in a most desirable location, just a block east of the prestigious Palace Green and one block north of the courthouse where Randolph practiced law. He made his home a reflection of his growing prominence. He ordered the ceilings plastered and many of the walls paneled, and specified paperhangings for one room (wallpaper was an expensive rarity).

After his mother's death, Randolph transformed the house once more, adding a wing in 1754–55 to the east side, effectively doubling its volume. The childless Randolphs did not require numerous additional rooms, so the wing enclosed just two living spaces and a stair passage. The effect was to elongate the original box into a grand statement on the streetscape, with a center entrance flanked by symmetrical sets of windows. Inside, a grand entrance hall was lit by a tall window. The new dining room contained a large marble mantel and two built-in cupboards; it was the biggest room in the house, a reflection of the dining room's emergence as the primary entertainment space for the Virginia gentry. Upstairs, the personal quarters improved, too, with a new bed chamber and three closets, an extraordinary number for the time.

ABOVE: *The two-handled cup resting on the marble sideboard in the dining room belonged to Peyton's father, Sir John Randolph, the only Virginia-born colonial to be knighted.*

RIGHT: *The corner fireplace in the Randolph parlor, flanked by fire screens and decorated with an ornately carved looking glass. The mantel is lined with a set of ornamental china.*

The upstairs hall, overlooking the stairs. The shape of the round-headed window (called a compass window) is echoed by the pillar-and-arch motif of the architectural wallpaper.

Aunt Betty

Like other wives of the landed gentry in colonial Virginia, Elizabeth Randolph was charged with management of her husband's household and supervision of the slaves. Referred to as Aunt Betty by some of her younger friends and neighbors, Betty Randolph was rich, but she wasn't spoiled. During the Revolution she nursed a neighbor's child infected with smallpox even after most of Williamsburg's residents sought refuge elsewhere to avoid the disease. She also pitched in to help render salt from saline river water when the supply of that essential preservative ran low.

More than a year after Peyton's death, his body was interred in the family vault in Williamsburg. According to an account in the *Virginia Gazette,* "The remains of this worthy man were brought thither from Philadelphia by Edmund Randolph, Esq; at the earnest request of his uncle's afflicted and inconsolable widow." Peyton and Elizabeth Randolph were, the *Gazette* reported, "when united, a perfect pattern of friendship, complacency, and love. No wonder, then, when separated, that the survivor should deeply bewail her irreparable loss." Betty Randolph would live nine more years, dying in 1783.

"Aunt Betty," in a copy of her circa 1755 portrait painted by John Wollaston. She would leave her and her husband's portraits (she called them "the Family Pictures") to her nephew, Edmund, who became the nation's first attorney general.

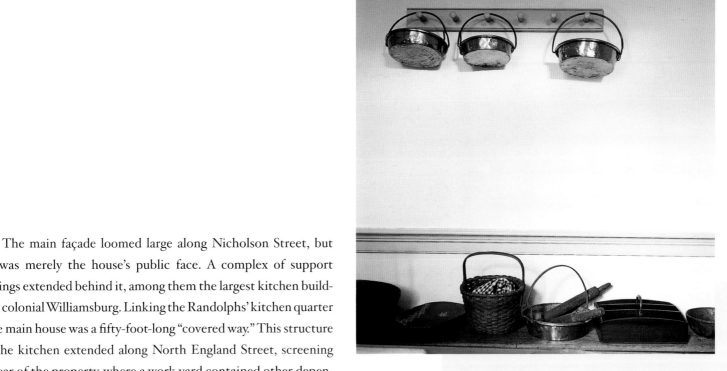

The main façade loomed large along Nicholson Street, but that was merely the house's public face. A complex of support buildings extended behind it, among them the largest kitchen building in colonial Williamsburg. Linking the Randolphs' kitchen quarter to the main house was a fifty-foot-long "covered way." This structure and the kitchen extended along North England Street, screening the rear of the property, where a work yard contained other dependencies, including a dairy, a smokehouse, a granary, and storage buildings. Farther back were kitchen gardens, stables to hold twelve horses and two carriages, and several acres of pasture ground.

The house today, as one of the most popular museum homes in Colonial Williamsburg, offers almost a million visitors a year a glimpse of Peyton Randolph's life.

A RESTORATION LABORATORY

The Randolph compound was home to both masters and slaves, reflecting the racial realities of Williamsburg's slaveholding culture. Half the town's population was enslaved, and according to an inventory prepared a few weeks after Peyton Randolph's death, his personal holdings in Williamsburg included twenty-seven slaves.

Though they shared the same address, the Randolphs and the enslaved lived utterly different lives in an era when class and racial differences defined and limited the prospects of all but a few. Social mobility was limited, but there was an interdependence; the Randolphs relied upon their slaves to grow and cook their food, wash their clothes, care for their animals, help them dress, and even powder Peyton's wig.

The Randolph property today is a mix of original (the house) and reproduction structures (the service buildings to the rear). The reconstruction was made possible by archaeologists who uncovered foundation remains and other evidence. Paleobotanists found seeds

WHAT'S FOR DINNER?

The extensive archaeology conducted at the Randolph House produced more than architectural data: zooarchaeological evidence—that is, bone fragments—made possible the identification of wild and domesticated animals cooked and served at the Randolph table.

A statistical analysis of the archaeological findings suggests that about half the meat consumed by the household was beef; another quarter was pork, and about 7 percent mutton. Chicken accounted for less than 1 percent, while wild game and fowl constituted another 5 percent, and fish about 3 percent. (For a contrast in foodstuffs, see "Cookery, Charleston Style," page 155).

One finding that may seem strange to twenty-first-century diners is that virtually all parts of the animals, including heads and feet, were consumed. Some cuts were more likely to be used in so-called made dishes (pies, hashes, and ragouts), but the calf head, for example, was valued for its flavor. It was used in the Randolph household, cooked whole, then carefully carved.

and other minute plant remains. Surviving elements in the house itself were dated and analyzed, and historians examined deeds, diaries, letters, and other documents that could be interpreted anew in light of the archaeological findings. Colonial Williamsburg craftsmen then constructed the reproduction buildings, using materials fabricated as they would have been in the eighteenth century. Timbers were hewn and sawn by hand, nails and hardware made in the blacksmith shop, and bricks fired nearby at the brick maker's yard.

Randolph's house has proved to be an enduring restoration laboratory for the study of early Virginia architecture, society, and material culture, with historians revisiting it over the years, most recently in the late 1990s, in attempts to interpret not only the lives of Peyton and Betty Randolph but those of their twenty-seven slaves.

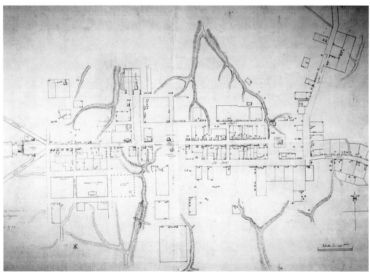

TOP: *The Randolph House was the subject of four restoration efforts in the twentieth century. The first was undertaken by a private owner; the second after Colonial Williamsburg acquired the property in 1938, when it emerged from behind its picket fence and two-story porch.*

ABOVE: *This map was found in 1927 in the library at the College of William and Mary. Known as the Frenchman's Map, it had been drawn by a French cartographer in 1782 in anticipation of the billeting of French soldiers in the town. It would prove an invaluable record of the appearance of Williamsburg's streetscapes in the late eighteenth century.*

At the time of Randolph's death, his library contained six mahogany book presses, a round table, and a clock—very much as it does today. The bookcases then contained a "library of books" that Thomas Jefferson purchased from Elizabeth Randolph.

Sharing a Bed

Judging from their household inventory, Peyton and Betty Randolph slept in separate beds. But that was far from the rule then, when many bed chambers had more than one bed—and each bed typically had more than one occupant.

The master bed chamber, the most private room in the house, was used for more than sleeping. It also served as a public space, to which social equals and friends might be invited to view a new baby, visit the sick, or take tea (inventories often listed side chairs and tea tables). New babies slept in their parents' bed or a cradle; upon the arrival of another baby, the next oldest child would be relegated to a nearby trundle bed.

For strangers in rooming houses, sharing a bed was also usual, as the story of a September 1776 diplomatic journey suggests.

Journeying to Staten Island to meet with Admiral Lord Howe, Ben Franklin and John Adams stopped for the night at an inn in New Brunswick, New Jersey. The only available accommodation was a small room with one bed. Neither man objected to sharing the bed—but deciding whether or not to keep the window open proved a problem. Adams moved to close it, whereupon Franklin, according to Adams's diary, called out, "Oh! Don't shut the window. We shall be suffocated." Franklin—one of the most respected scientists of his day—then expatiated on his theories regarding "air and cold and respiration and perspiration." Adams reported dryly, "I was so much amused that I soon fell asleep."

According to Peyton Randolph's inventory, the items in his bed chamber included "1 China Bason and Bottle."

PART TWO

A Time of War

On January 10, Thomas Paine publishes *Common Sense*.

On March 2, the Secret Committee of Congress (its members include Benjamin Franklin, John Dickinson, and John Jay) appoints Connecticut's Silas Deane as the nation's first spy.

With the guns Henry Knox brought from Fort Ticonderoga looming over the city, the British evacuate Boston on March 17, handing General Washington his first military triumph.

At the Second Continental Congress in Philadelphia on June 6, Richard Henry Lee introduces a motion for independence. Thomas Jefferson, John Adams, Benjamin Franklin, Robert R. Livingston of New York, and Roger Sherman of Connecticut are appointed to a committee to write the document that will become the Declaration of Independence.

In the days before the adoption of the Declaration, the South Carolina delegate Thomas Lynch falls ill; his son, Thomas Lynch, Jr., is summoned to Philadelphia.

Though the senior Lynch dies on his way home, his son returns to the congress and signs the Declaration of Independence.

On July 4, the Declaration of Independence is accepted, and John Hancock and Charles Thomson, president and secretary of the Continental Congress, affix their signatures.

John Hancock, Benjamin Franklin, and Stephen Hopkins, along with the other members of the Continental Congress, sign the official parchment of the Declaration of Independence on August 2.

On August 27, British troops rout American forces at the Battle of Long Island and take New York City.

On December 1, the Signer Richard Stockton of New Jersey is arrested by the British; a month later he is pardoned, having agreed to take no further revolutionary actions.

On Christmas night, George Washington, along with General Henry Knox, General Nathanael Greene, and a youthful James Monroe, leads the depleted Continental Army across the Delaware River and, the following morning, overwhelms Hessian troops at the Battle of Trenton.

In another surprise attack, the Continental Army overcomes British forces at the Battle of Princeton on January 3. During the winter months, American troops continue to harry and ambush British and Hessian troops.

On July 27, the Continental Congress names the French aristocrat the Marquis de Lafayette, age nineteen, a major general in the Continental Army.

British forces are victorious at the Battle of Brandywine on September 11; on September 26 they occupy Philadelphia.

After the tide of battle turns on October 4, the Continental Army retreats at the Battle of Germantown. Meanwhile, Benjamin Chew, owner of Cliveden mansion, where a key Germantown confrontation is fought, remains under house arrest as a suspected Royalist, confined in New Jersey with the royal governor, John Penn.

On October 17, at Saratoga, New York, General John Burgoyne surrenders his entire army to a force led by General Horatio Gates; among the other American officers present is William Whipple, brigadier general of the New Hampshire militia.

In the days after the battle, Philip Schuyler provides "Gentleman Johnny" Burgoyne and other British and Hessian officers accommodations at his Albany mansion.

Approved by Congress on November 15, the Articles of Confederation are sent to the states for ratification.

On December 19, the Continental Army begins its encampment at Valley Forge, a winter of legendary hardship but also a time when foreign arrivals, such as the Marquis de Lafayette and the Prussian Baron von Steuben, help transform the American volunteers into a unified fighting force.

In the early months of the year, the Continental Army encamps at Morristown, where George and Martha Washington are headquartered at the Ford House, along with the aide Alexander Hamilton. In May, the Marquis de Lafayette arrives, bringing news of French reinforcements.

The British commander Sir Henry Clinton uses Drayton Hall as his headquarters before the siege of Charles Towne; on May 12, the Americans surrender at Charles Towne, leading to a British occupation that will last two years. The captured

Signers Thomas Heyward, Jr., and Edward Rutledge are sent to St. Augustine, Florida, where they are imprisoned.

On August 16, British forces prevail in the Battle of Camden, South Carolina.

Benedict Arnold's treachery is revealed on September 25, after his escape across British lines.

Alexander Hamilton and Elizabeth Schuyler, daughter of General Philip Schuyler, take their wedding vows in the parlor at the Schuyler Mansion in Albany on December 14, 1780.

On February 6, France signs a treaty pledging military assistance.

Savannah falls to the British on December 29.

1778

1779

1780

1781

1782

1783

At the suggestion of William Henry Drayton of South Carolina, fireworks accompany the celebration of Independence Day in Philadelphia.

American troops are victorious at the Battle of Cowpens, South Carolina, on January 17.

On March 1, Maryland becomes the last of the thirteen states to ratify the Articles of Confederation, thereby establishing The United States in Congress Assembled or Confederation Congress.

Lord Cornwallis surrenders at Yorktown on October 19, ending the battle that effectively brings the war to a close.

On November 30, the preliminary articles of a peace treaty are agreed to in Paris.

On December 14, the citizens of Charles Towne, having watched British troops evacuate their city, welcome General Nathanael Greene and the Continental Army.

The Treaty of Paris ending the Revolution is signed on September 3. John Adams, Benjamin Franklin, and John Jay are signatories for the new nation.

On December 23, George Washington resigns his commission before Congress, then meeting at the Maryland State House in Annapolis.

The Vassall-Craigie-Longfellow House

Two days before the Battle of Bunker Hill, Congress appointed George Washington commander in chief of the Continental Army. Philadelphia was three hundred miles away, so he arrived in Boston too late to play any role in the battle, but on June 17, 1775, the Patriots fought bravely. They held out against two major British onslaughts before retreating from their hilltop fortifications overlooking Boston. For the British general William Howe, gaining control of the hill proved a bloody and hollow victory, with 1,054 of his soldiers left dead.

When Washington did arrive to assume command of the American troops, on July 2, he inherited a stalemate. The British held Boston and Charlestown, peninsulas that pincered the mouth of the Charles River. Through his field glasses, Washington could also see a veritable forest of softwood masts afloat in Boston Harbor, where the ships of the Royal Navy lay at anchor.

Yet the colonials held the mainland that surrounded the watery town and its harbor. Washington knew his military objective: he needed to blockade the city, to keep the British forces from moving inland. That would mean building barricades and fortifications, gathering intelligence, and perhaps most important of all, unifying his diverse soldiers into a single fighting force.

Carefully articulated architectural elements—the colossal Ionic pilasters, the cornice with its modillion blocks, the roof balustrade, and the tall chimneys—all contribute to the majestic appearance of the Vassall-Craigie-Longfellow House.

For some forty years before his death, in 1882, Longfellow used this room as his study. It was his inner sanctum, where he composed his poetry, wrote in his journal, corresponded with friends, and welcomed visitors and family members. During Washington's time at the Vassall House, this functioned as both a meeting and a dining room.

George Washington also needed to find a residence large enough to accommodate the needs of his military family. It would be his headquarters, and many of his aides would work, dine, and sleep there, too. He needed meeting rooms for councils of war with his generals as well as for more intimate strategy discussions with visitors and officers. Washington had no way of knowing how long he would remain in Boston, and writing home in August, the Virginian expressed his hope that he might return to Mount Vernon before the snow fell. But Vassall House, the elegant mansion where he made his quarters, would prove to be his home for the long winter to come.

TORY ROW

Major John Vassall was twenty-one in 1759. His maturity meant inheritance of a generous property on the King's Highway in Cambridge. He promptly demolished the existing dwelling and built a Georgian mansion, one of several on what came to be known as Tory Row. The pairs of colossal pilasters that frame the façade and the projecting pavilion at its center expressed his aristocratic pretensions.

Vassall married Elizabeth Oliver in 1761. She delivered seven children in the house, but as anti-Tory sentiment surged—Vassall was a proud Royalist and his brother-in-law, Thomas Oliver, the royal lieutenant governor of Massachusetts—the family took refuge in Boston in 1774. Soon afterward they sailed for England.

In the days after the events at Lexington and Concord in April 1775, Patriot forces used the abandoned Vassall House as a hospital. In June, Captain John Glover and 405 of his Marblehead Mariners made it their headquarters, pitching their sailcloth tents around the house. Forever sailors at heart, the Marbleheaders felt at home on a property whose generous acres rolled down to the tidal banks of the Charles River.

Ernest Longfellow painted the portrait of his father in 1876; the bust is of George Washington Greene, a contemporary of Longfellow's. He was a historian and grandson of General Nathanael Greene (see "Three Yankees Who Went Down to Georgia," page 313).

WASHINGTON'S MILITARY "FAMILY"

At his Vassall House quarters, the motley assemblage that George Washington referred to as his family included army staffers, relatives, and household servants. Ebenezer Austin, the man who managed his household, kept a running log of its membership.

Since Vassall House was the Continental Army's headquarters, the military men came first. Several aides-de-camp, including Colonel Robert H. Harrison, the general's private secretary, bunked in whatever space was available in the commander in chief's quarters.

When Martha Washington arrived, she brought with her Washington's nephew George Lewis and her own son, John (Jacky) Parke Custis, along with his wife, Eleanor. For Washington, who pined for Mount Vernon whenever he was away from it, the arrival of his wife and family signaled a welcome return of what he called "the softer domestic virtues" to his household.

Ebenezer Austin brought his wife and daughter. For their labors, the Austins were given room and board and paid seven pounds, ten shillings a month, at a time when a single pound would buy five or more bushels of corn. The cook had help in the scullery, and the household had a washerwoman. Washington soon added to his staff a tailor,

Giles Alexander, who would remain part of his retinue for the duration of the war.

Slaves also had roles in Washington's Cambridge headquarters. William (Billy) Lee was the general's body servant (Washington had acquired him seven years earlier for sixty-one pounds). While at Boston, Lee married Margaret Thomas, a free mulatto seamstress, who also became a fixture in Washington's mobile household. A number of slaves, among them Dinah, Peter, Servant Jack, and Sailor Jack, as well as Hannah, who was working to buy her freedom, performed various duties.

The additions the Craigies made to the basic box of the early house by adding rooms and porches are most apparent from the rear. Though today known as the Vassall-Craigie-Longfellow House, in the early nineteenth century the place was referred to as Castle Craigie.

On July 15, 1775, General George Washington took possession of the house, establishing his office and study in the dining room, to the right of the entry passage. His clerks wrote his orders in the room behind it and kept the accounts in good order. He slept in the bed chamber above the office, while his aides crowded several to a room in other chambers. When it appeared that the siege of Boston might take longer than her husband hoped, Martha Washington made the journey from Mount Vernon, arriving in December 1775. The parlor across the passage from her husband's office, still outfitted with the fine English-made furniture of the Vassalls, became her reception room.

The Washingtons were Southerners and at first felt like strangers in a foreign land, but the commander in chief quickly made an impression on his new troops. As one bystander noted, Washington astride his horse was "truly noble and majestic, being tall and well proportioned." According to the Bostonian Henry Knox, "General Washington fills his place with vast ease and dignity, and dispenses happiness around him." Knox soon emerged as one of Washington's most valuable military advisers (see "General Knox's Montpelier," page 250). A twenty-four-year-old bookseller turned soldier, Knox was eager for action, and he lived nearby with his wife of a year, Lucy Flucker Knox, the daughter of a prominent Tory whose family was among the Loyalists ensconced in Boston. Lucy, estranged from her family, became a fixture in Martha's company.

That first winter, Harry Knox demonstrated his military worth, proposing a strategy to drive the British from the city. Having been appointed head of artillery despite his youth, Knox volunteered to go to Fort Ticonderoga on Lake Champlain, where American troops had captured an array of British weaponry six months earlier. Few cannons were at hand in Cambridge, so Washington quickly approved Knox's plan to bring the guns back from upstate New York. After an arduous two-month journey, Knox returned with fifty-nine cannons, hauled some three hundred miles by oxen and horses over snowy and mountainous terrain.

Martha Washington held her sewing circles here. However, the flowered wallpaper, furnishings, rug, and upholstery are characteristic of a lady's taste circa 1845, since the room reflects Fanny Appleton Longfellow's time.

A Lovely Place for a Party

For over 150 years, the occupants of the Vassall House—the Vassalls, Washingtons, Craigies, and Longellows—entertained in grand style.

In the third quarter of the eighteenth century, the best room was the parlor, then the largest space in the house, with a large fireplace and grand overmantel. Mistress Vassall danced the minuet in the parlor, while the next lady of the house, Martha Washington, received many visitors there. Despite the state of war, she and her husband held a party to celebrate their seventeenth anniversary on Twelfth Night, January 6, 1776.

Mrs. Craigie welcomed the French diplomat Talleyrand and Prince Louis-Philippe. When the Craigies remodeled the rear of the house, the library became the largest room, and in 1876, the Longfellows celebrated the one hundredth anniversary of the Washingtons' Twelfth Night party. On that occasion the library became a theater, where a performance was attended by more than a hundred guests.

The room that saw the most distinguished list of guests was Longfellow's study, which had also been Washington's military office. Washington welcomed Benjamin Franklin, John and Abigail Adams, Benedict Arnold, his generals, and even the spy Dr. Benjamin Church (whom the general confronted there with evidence of his treachery). Longfellow's list of notable literary visitors included his colleagues Henry David Thoreau, Ralph Waldo Emerson, and Nathaniel Hawthorne, as well as the visitors Anthony Trollope, Charles Dickens, and Oscar Wilde.

Originally the kitchen, this space became a dining room after Andrew Craigie renovated the house. The eclectic array of furniture and decorative objects reflects the lengthy tenure of the Longfellow family in the house. Note the high chair to the left of the mantel; it belonged to Longfellow's wife, Fanny, as a child. The large painting on the left-hand wall portrays Longfellow's daughters.

All houses wherein men have lived and died are haunted houses.

—Henry Wadsworth Longfellow, "Haunted Houses," 1858

Colonel Knox—a promotion had come through from Philadelphia while he was away—then supervised the installation of the cannons in the dead of night behind portable ramparts of wooden frames (chandeliers) and bundles of sticks. In a few hours, the vantage atop the promontory of Dorchester Heights, a headland that overlooked Boston from two miles away, became a heavily armed bulwark.

When the British awoke on the morning of March 5, the sight of the guns atop Dorchester Heights was a stunning surprise. In the next few days, Washington and General Howe executed a few tentative military maneuvers, but on March 17, British ships, loaded with evacuated troops and a thousand Tory citizens, raised sail and headed for Halifax, Nova Scotia. The siege of Boston was over, and Washington and his army had won their first major victory. The Continental Army soon began the march to New York for its next military engagement.

LONGFELLOW LOOKS BACK

If history is memory—and, in part, it is—then at the Longfellow National Historic Site one cannot help but see the past from Henry Wadsworth Longfellow's point of view.

Longfellow was no Founding Father (he was born in 1807), but his maternal grandfather, Peleg Wadsworth, had been a general in Washington's army. On Longfellow's Grand Tour of Europe in 1826, he made the acquaintance of Washington's favorite foreign volunteer, the Marquis de Lafayette. Longfellow proved to be a man who recognized the echoes of history when he heard them—and hear them he did when he knocked at Mrs. Craigie's door in 1837.

Elizabeth Craigie and her late husband, Andrew, who had been the first apothecary general in the Continental Army, had acquired the Vassall House in 1791. They added porches to the sides, an extension to the rear, and elaborate gardens. After her husband's death, in 1819, Mrs. Craigie took in lodgers, often students from nearby Harvard University.

Although already a widower, Longfellow looked fresh-faced enough that Mrs. Craigie mistook him for a student. The thirty-year-old professor of modern languages (he spoke eight) moved into the room that had been Washington's upstairs quarters. He was still in residence when he married Fanny Appleton, the daughter of the Lowell industrialist Nathan Appleton, in 1843. His wealthy father-in-law purchased the house from Mrs. Craigie for the newlyweds.

From the start, the Longfellows planned to honor the property's most famous resident. As Fanny wrote to her brother after their wedding journey to New York and the Berkshires, "We have just returned to our home & are enraptured with its quiet & comfort. . . . [W]e are full of plans & projects with no desire, however, to change a feature of the old countenance which Washington has rendered sacred."

Longfellow bought a bust of Washington. It was a copy of the original that the French sculptor Jean-Antoine Houdon had traveled to Mount Vernon to model from life in 1785. Purchased from London, the sculpture assumed a place of honor in the entrance hall, where it remains today. For decades, Longfellow gave periodic tours of the house, indicating which rooms had been occupied by the great man. As America's national bard, Longfellow came to regard the American past as raw material for his poems.

After his death, in 1882, Longfellow's descendants conserved the house as a monument to the poet and established the Longfellow House Trust in 1913. In 1972 the house was given to the National Park Service, which administers it today as a house museum.

The place contains a mix of distinctly eighteenth-century architecture and high Victorian objects dating from the Longfellow ownership. Longfellow, a sociable man, surrounded himself with literary companions and an ample staff of servants, and enjoyed a well-stocked wine cellar. Washington had done the same (his accounts record the purchase of 217 bottles of Madeira in a single two-week period during his residence). The marriage of memories at the Vassall-Craigie-Longfellow House is appealing, informed as it is by the writings of America's first professional poet. Longfellow helped shape a nativist mythology in an era when Americans were just beginning to take an interest in their historical recollections.

From "To a Child"

Once, ah, once, within these walls,
One whom memory oft recalls,
The Father of his Country, dwelt.
And yonder meadows broad and damp
The fires of the besieging camp
Encircled with a burning belt.
Up and down these echoing stairs,
Heavy with the weight of cares,
Sounded his majestic tread;
Yes, within this very room
Sat he in those hours of gloom,
Weary both in heart and head.

—Henry Wadsworth Longfellow (1845)

As a reminder of the house's famous guest, Henry Wadsworth Longfellow purchased a bust of George Washington. His wife, Fanny, wrote in her journal on April 17, 1844, "Washington's bust, by Houdon, arrived from London! a cast that is—It has rather a heavy, sleepy look, but what a massive strength of feature & a noble dome-like head. It is strange to see this senseless clay looking forth into the room which its original once occupied so familiarly." Today the bust sits in the entry hall.

Phillis Wheatley, poet . . . and slave

Henry Wadsworth Longfellow was not the first poet linked to the Vassall House. In 1761, the slave ship *Phillis* delivered a young girl to the shores of Boston. Her owners found that the fragile child they had purchased possessed a gift for language. Phillis Wheatley soon read and wrote English; permitted to pursue her studies, Wheatley in her teens knew Latin poetry, history, and astronomy; her volume *Poems on Various Subjects, Religious and Moral*, appeared in England in 1773.

In 1775, Wheatley penned verses in praise of General Washington. They read, in part,

> *Proceed, great chief, with virtue on thy side,*
> *Thy every action let the Goddess guide.*
> *A crown, a mansion, and a throne that shine*
> *With gold unfading, WASHINGTON! Be thine.*

She sent the poem to Washington. He wrote to thank her "most sincerely for . . . the elegant lines you enclosed." He had one hesitation— "I would have published the poem, had I not been apprehensive that . . . I might have incurred the imputation of vanity." But the editor of the *Pennsylvania Magazine* published Wheatley's couplets two months later.

"If you should ever come to Cambridge," Washington wrote to her, "I shall be happy to see a person so favored by the Muses." Perhaps it is no coincidence that the general, a slave owner, extended the invitation as a debate raged about African-American troops serving in the Continental Army (eventually he endorsed the idea). The evolution of Washington's racial thinking culminated decades later when he inserted an instruction into his will to free his slaves at Martha's death.

Phillis Wheatley, from the frontispiece of her book.

The Lees' Stratford

The short-form history handed down over the centuries commemorates July 4, 1776, as the moment when thirteen of Britain's American colonies declared their independence. The document that expressed the will of the Continental Congress, the Declaration of Independence, has attained the status of holy writ and gained its principal author, Thomas Jefferson, an indisputable immortality. However, another day in 1776, just four weeks earlier, might also have been chosen as the nation's Independence Day.

On June 7, 1776, forty-three-year-old Richard Henry Lee rose from his seat in the State House in Philadelphia. Tall and slim, the third son of one of Virginia's wealthiest landowners, and a fourth-generation American, Lee had an aristocratic grandeur. His revolutionary zeal was a given. As a longtime member of the Virginia House of Burgesses, he had angrily opposed the Stamp and Townshend Acts. He penned a preface to the Williamsburg edition of John Dickinson's *Letters from a Farmer* (see "John Dickinson's Poplar Hall," page 24) and had been among the first to broach the notion that each colony ought to appoint select committees "for mutual information and correspondence between the lovers of liberty in every province."

The "Great House" at Stratford is unusual for its time in Colonial America, because of both its great scale and its unusual footprint, which is shaped like an **H**.

The dining room has a Colonial Revival character, with early Lee portraits, Oriental carpets, curtains, and a mix of tableware that echoes Philip Ludwell Lee's 1776 inventory.

THE WIDOW CORBIN

She was his big sister, after all, and Hannah Lee Corbin felt empowered to complain to Richard Henry Lee. Under the new government, a widow who owned property could be taxed, she pointed out, but that same widow was not permitted to vote. Was that not taxation without representation?

Hannah's complaint was a consequence of harsh personal experience. Her husband had died before the Revolution, leaving her his property—but only, the late Gawen Corbin II insisted from the grave, if she remained his widow. Should she remarry, she would forfeit his estate, except for her widow's third. When she learned that the property would be subject to tax but that she had no voice in the matter, she wrote to her brother to "complain that Widows are not represented."

In his reply in March 1778, he condescended to explain. "The doctrine of representation is a large subject," he began. He went on to wonder whether "Perhaps 'twas thought rather out of character for women to press into those tumultuous assemblages of men where the business of choosing representatives is conducted."

The spirited Hannah chose to keep her own counsel, and despite the strictures in Corbin's will, she and her late husband's physician lived together with their two children. Their union would, over time, gain acceptance.

An orator well known for his mellifluous voice and literate diction (he had been educated in England), Lee offered three resolutions, recorded in the official *Journals* of the Continental Congress:

Resolved, That these United Colonies are, and of right ought to be, free and independent States, that they are absolved from all allegiance to the British Crown, and that all political connection between them and the State of Great Britain is, and ought to be, totally dissolved.

That it is expedient forthwith to take the most effectual measures for forming foreign Alliances.

That a plan of confederation be prepared and transmitted to the respective Colonies for their consideration and approbation.

In three sentences, Lee proposed that a new and independent nation be established; that the new nation find a place for itself in world politics; and that a form of government be devised. "Let this day give birth to an American republic," he argued. As the first official move by the colonies toward independence, Lee's resolutions were critical; rather than being a band of rebels, the Continental Congress was about to claim status as an independent nation.

John Adams seconded the motion. Discussion followed, but a vote was postponed for three weeks so delegates could consult with their constituents. Anticipating approval, the members appointed a committee to ready a formal declaration.

Thomas Jefferson proved to be the most essential member of the Committee of Five, overshadowing the others (John Adams, Benjamin Franklin, Robert R. Livingston of New York, and Roger Sherman of Connecticut). As for Lee, upon learning that his wife had fallen ill, he hurriedly departed for Virginia but returned with his brother Francis Lightfoot Lee in time to sign the Declaration of Independence in August. In a quirk of fate, Richard Henry Lee is remembered more for being one of the only pair of brothers to sign the document than for his memorable speech on a warm June day in Philadelphia.

TOP: *Stratford's parlor, featuring a shield-back chair at the card table that belonged to Richard Henry Lee.*

ABOVE: *In the parlor, a painting of Henry (Light-Horse Harry) Lee hangs over the fireplace. The canvas has been attributed to Gilbert Stuart; the mantelpiece dates from a Federal era renovation Lee engineered between 1790 and 1800.*

By the twentieth century, the original entrance stairs were gone. Restorers interpreted architectural fragments found in archaeological digs at the site to re-create fan-shaped stairs.

Stratford, the seat of my forefathers, is a place of which too much cannot be said; whether you consider the venerable magnificence of its buildings, the happy disposition of its grounds, or the extent or variety of its prospects.

—*Thomas Lee Shippen, 1790*

BUILDING STRATFORD

They were only boys when Richard Henry Lee (1733–1794) and Francis Lightfoot Lee (1734–1797) moved into Stratford, along with their parents and siblings. The house and family were both unfinished, and the plantation complex approached completion as more brothers and another sister joined the household (eight of the eleven Lee children would live to adulthood).

The patriarch, Thomas Lee, built Stratford on a property he had coveted for many years. Called the Clifts, the 1,443-acre tract featured high bluffs and an expansive view of the Potomac River. Thomas had traveled to England in 1717 to acquire the land from its owner, but he embarked on his ambitious building program only after his nearby house burned in 1729. He named his new home after his grandfather's Sussex estate in Stratford Langdon.

Stratford Plantation was a grand undertaking (one visitor called it "[a] towne in itself"), with a deepwater harbor and a wharf at the foot of the cliffs. Blacksmiths, joiners, and wheelwrights worked on the property; at the docks, British teamsters off-loaded manufactured goods from arriving ships, then dispatched American agricultural products for the return journey. While tobacco would deplete the soil by the middle of the eighteenth century, grains and timber continued to be exported.

This structure isn't eighteenth-century Lee—it is 1930s Fiske Kimball. When archaeology revealed an octagonal foundation on the site, Kimball, an architect as well as an art historian, designed a garden folly just north of the east garden.

FISKE KIMBALL

When it was founded in 1929, the stated mission of the Robert E. Lee Memorial Foundation was "to acquire the estate known as 'Stratford Hall' in Westmoreland Co., Virginia, the birthplace of Robert E. Lee, and to restore, furnish, preserve, and maintain it as a national shrine in perpetual memory of Robert E. Lee." The model was the Mount Vernon Ladies' Association, which some seventy-five years earlier had preserved George Washington's home (see "Washington's Mount Vernon," page 260).

The fifty-five-member board soon found that the past at Stratford was actually a many-splendored thing, with a rich historical layering in which General Robert E. Lee had left only a late and rather minor imprint.

Enter the pioneer architectural historian Fiske Kimball, the consultant the Stratford ladies hired to advise them on what he already knew to be "a precious building." From the first, he made the case for the architectural importance of the eighteenth-century artifact and warned of the risks of "restoration" in order to return it to "the way it is supposed formerly to have been. More harm has perhaps been done to historic buildings," Kimball pointed out, "by ill-judged 'restoration' than by neglect, and such damage is really irreparable."

In practice, Kimball's principle proved difficult to adhere to, and the restored house has a parapetted staircase at each end and other elements that probably owe more to English architectural precedents than to the house that the eighteenth-century Lees inhabited. Yet Stratford is a unique and largely unspoiled eighteenth-century survivor.

When Stratford is viewed from the side (top), the entry stair and the subtler brickwork on the upper level suggest a one-story building—but there's actually a full story at grade in the raised basement. This lower level contains service rooms, kitchen, servants' hall, several bed chambers, and a schoolroom. From the building's front (above), the unusual and massive arrangement of chimneys contribute to the mansion's unique appearance. Consisting of four chimneys each and sixteen fireplaces total, each set of four chimneys is bound by arches and encloses a balustraded platform that may have functioned as a pavilion and been outfitted with louvered blinds for privacy. Architectural investigators have recently concluded there was also a walk with railings between the two chimney towers. This roof deck provided a vista of the Potomac roughly a mile away.

At the center of the plantation property stood the Great House and the complex of buildings surrounding it. Detached from the house but arranged symmetrically near its corners were four "out houses," service buildings that contained an office, kitchen, and servants' quarters. Other buildings on the property included a smokehouse, stables, barns, an icehouse, and an orangery. Kitchen and ornamental gardens grew near the manse, while farther afield were acreage in tillage, pastures, and peripheral buildings.

The sprawling mansion was a one-of-a-kind architectural experiment. It appears to be a one-story house, with the main floor well above grade, but a tall basement allowed for a full set of habitable rooms at ground level. The joiners built the frame of local timber, and the masons constructed the shell with brick fired on the site of local clay, bonding it with lime mortar made of ground oyster shells from the nearby river. Two massive chimney clusters surmount the hipped roof, each consisting of four chimneys connected by arches.

The crossbar in the unusual **H**-shaped floor plan contains the Great Hall, a twenty-nine-foot-square room with seventeen-foot ceilings. Today this public space is entered from grand exterior stairways looking north and south; the other rooms on the principal floor fill the structures on the east and west that form the legs of the **H**-plan.

A Virginian named William Walker probably built the house. The source of the plans is unknown, but the sophistication and originality suggest it was the work of a British-trained designer. Walker may have been influenced by Virginia's colonial capitol in Williamsburg, also constructed in an **H**-plan, and similar plans appear in eighteenth-century English architectural books.

An intriguing story suggests that the lady of the house, Hannah Lee, played a role in the evolution of the design. A visitor reported well after Stratford was completed that Philip Ludwell Lee, the son who inherited it, complained about his home. While brandishing a picture that portrayed an early drawing for Stratford, he declaimed, "See what it is to be ruled by a woman. I should have been now living in a house like this had not my father been persuaded by his wife to put up this very inferior dwelling over my head."

It appears, then, that the uniqueness of Stratford is the result of a coincidental collaboration involving a British designer, a Virginia master builder, and a lady who knew exactly what she wanted.

A VIRGINIA DYNASTY

Stratford was the childhood home of the Lees of the revolutionary generation, including the Signers Richard Henry Lee and Francis Lightfoot Lee. Arthur and William, the two youngest brothers, served the Patriot cause abroad, working in England and then on the continent as spies and diplomats.

The oldest, Philip Ludwell Lee, made modest changes to the estate in his quarter century of ownership. His daughter, Matilda, and her husband (and cousin), Henry Lee (1756–1818), next took title. Henry, known as Light-Horse Harry, was a military hero during the Revolutionary War (his nickname recognized his skillful horsemanship) as well as the wordsmith remembered for his eulogy of his friend George Washington. Harry immortalized Washington as "First in War, First in Peace, and First in the Hearts of his Countrymen."

When Matilda died, Harry continued to live at Stratford. Using the dowry of a new wife, Ann Hill Carter, he did some updating as the eighteenth century ended. But Harry proved less effective as a farmer than as a soldier and soon found himself in debtors' prison. He did, however, add to the Lee line. The fifth son of Harry and Ann was Robert Edward, born at Stratford in 1807. Later, partly because his family was unable to afford to send him to Harvard and because West Point was free, Robert E. Lee embarked on a military career and spent thirty-two years in the U.S. Army. He resigned his commission in 1861 and went on to become commander in chief of the Army of the Confederacy. The nineteenth-century General Lee could hardly be described as a Founding Father, but his enduring fame and symbolic importance led directly to the preservation of his birthplace.

Wes Payne worked for many years as an interpreter at Stratford's Old Kitchen.

A SON OF SLAVERY

His father experienced the radical social transformation that the Civil War wrought, but William Wesley Payne (1875–1954) witnessed firsthand the transition at Stratford from private home to public institution. When the Robert E. Lee Memorial Foundation was established, Wes Payne and his wife, Louise, chose to remain at the only home he had ever known. After Stratford was opened to the public as a house museum, in 1935, Payne became a memorable presence, demonstrating crafts and holding forth in the Old Kitchen.

Wesley Payne's long service to the property was honored by the construction of a cabin like the one in which he was born. It is a humble, one-room dwelling with a chimney made of logs, wood strips, and mud daubing. His presence at Stratford also made him a pioneer. He worked as an interpreter decades before other sites acknowledged the role of slaves (much of Virginia and the South would remain segregated into the 1950s and beyond, with many accommodations, restaurants, and public conveniences explicitly whites-only). Wesley Payne's presence reminded visitors that his enslaved ancestors had inhabited the immense plantation, too. Perhaps it is only appropriate that Payne played his pioneering role at Stratford, since Richard Henry Lee had been among the first Virginians to advocate the abolition of slavery.

Researchers suspect the Payne connection to the plantation extends back to 1782 and a slave named West. If so, then the African-American Paynes can claim a presence on the property of 216 years' duration, whereas the Lees inhabited Stratford for fewer than 90 years.

LEFT: *In the southwest chamber, a gentleman's toilet has been arranged, with a brass shaving bowl, a wig on a stand, and an adjustable looking glass.*

RIGHT: *A large bed chamber facing southeast with a view of the garden is believed to have been the birthplace of Harry Lee's son Robert in 1807. The walnut crib is hung with mosquito netting, which would have been loosely draped around the bed once the child was settled into it.*

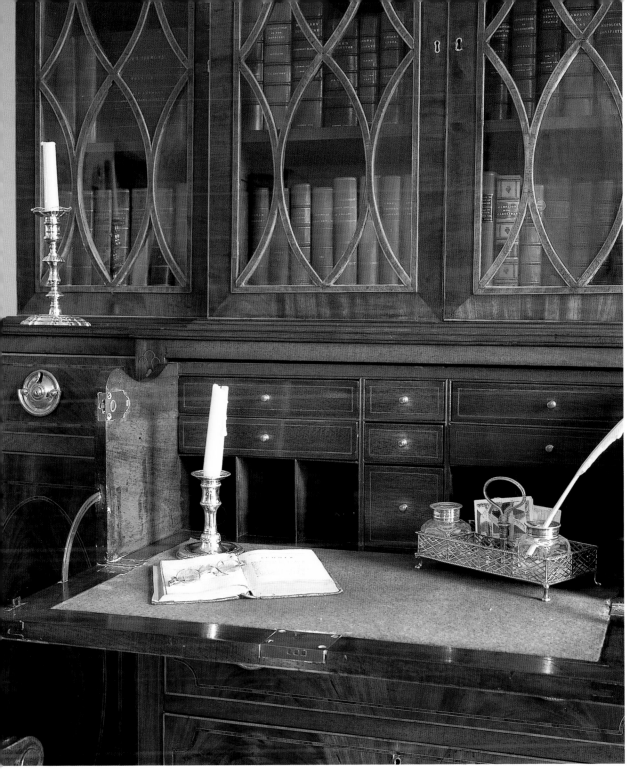

ABOVE: *Not many Lee family pieces survive at Stratford, but one that does is this Federal era secretary bookcase, which belonged to the family of Robert E. Lee's wife. It rests in the parlor.*

RIGHT AND TOP RIGHT: *Lined with pilasters to resemble a Roman atrium, the Great Hall is an enormous room (twenty-nine-feet square), which was used primarily in the summer (it has no fireplaces). Its tall ceilings, large windows, and generous north-south doorways enhanced ventilation. The lower image was taken in 1933 by Frances Benjamin Johnston, a pioneering woman photographer who recorded many historic Southern homes in the 1930s.*

Governor Hopkins House

The signature is abbreviated (it reads "Step. Hopkins"). The penmanship even now seems to quaver. Yet Stephen Hopkins harbored no doubts when he put his hand to the parchment before him in August 1776. On signing the Declaration of Independence, he remarked, "My hand trembles but my heart does not."

The delegates had voted their approval on the night of July 4, but only the president of the congress, John Hancock, and Secretary Charles Thomson signed the draft. Copies of the document were printed and distributed overnight, and in the days that followed, they were prominently posted in village squares. At the command of General George Washington, the Declaration was read to each brigade in the Continental Army on July 9. And three weeks later, Hopkins and the other delegates attended a formal ceremony to affix their signatures. By then the document had been "fairly engrossed on parchment" (that is, written in a large hand) by Timothy Matlack, a congressional assistant. It bore the title "The unanimous Declaration of the thirteen States of America."

Stephen Hopkins (1707–1785) suffered from shaking palsy, as it was called in his time, and relied upon a clerk to write for him in his mercantile business and in his various roles in Rhode Island public life. But he refused to let his infirmity slow him down.

The original house contained this "keeping room." As suggested by the cooking utensils in the fireplace, food would have been prepared here, though there is no bake oven.

ABOVE LEFT: *The relocated house on what has become Hopkins Street. The home of Stephen Hopkins is a simple structure but with some notable highlights, among them the tall, narrow windows, each capped with a molded headpiece.*

ABOVE RIGHT: *The entrance was designed in the early twentieth century, when caretakers hired the antiquarian and architect Norman Isham to create a doorway appropriate to the revolutionary era.*

LEFT: *An early-twentieth-century view of the Stephen Hopkins House before its relocation.*

He was an elder statesman at the Continental Congresses, both as the second oldest delegate and as an experienced public servant. He had been among the first to call for colonial unity, more than ten years earlier, and in many years of service to his native Rhode Island, he headed each branch of the government, as Speaker of the General Assembly, a ten-term governor, and despite having no formal training as a lawyer, chief justice of the Rhode Island Supreme Court. He helped establish the first college, newspaper, and bank in Providence. In sum, he was an inevitable choice as one of Rhode Island's delegates to the national gathering of Patriots.

Hopkins was sixty-nine when he, with his friend of more than twenty years, Benjamin Franklin, and fifty-four other men signed the document on August 2, 1776. Hopkins needed both hands to accomplish the small task, steadying his writing hand with his left.

A HUMBLE SURVIVOR

The Stephen Hopkins House still stands in bustling Providence. But the small dwelling, its clapboards painted Spanish brown, looks alien amid later governmental and college buildings (the house shares the streetscape with Brown University and the Rhode Island School of Design). Governor Hopkins's ghost would undoubtedly do a double take if it were to happen upon the corner of Benefit and Hopkins Streets today. The dwelling there, which Hopkins inhabited for more than forty years, wasn't on that spot at all in the eighteenth century.

Rather than see it demolished to make way for a new courthouse, the local chapter of the Daughters of the American Revolution saved the place in 1927. The women persuaded the state to move the house half a block (it had already been moved a similar distance in 1804). Devoted gardeners surrounded the dwelling with a pretty vest-pocket park, designed by Alden Hopkins, a descendant of Stephen, and, in later years, the resident landscape architect at Colonial Williamsburg. The caretakers saved the Hopkins home as the only surviving house museum for a Rhode Island Founding Father.

Built in 1707, the year of Hopkins's birth, the original house stood on the corner of Town Street (now South Main Street) and a

At Work in the Colonial Kitchen

Food preparation in the early American kitchen was backbreaking work. Tasks such as cutting and dough making could be done at a worktable, but the cooking was done near or on the floor, requiring constant bending and squatting. Overheated skin and smoke-filled eyes and lungs were givens, and the cook was at risk of setting her clothes on fire because her long skirts constantly brushed the coals at her feet. Many eighteenth-century women died of burns sustained in kitchen fires.

With no thermometer, the cook determined the readiness of the bake oven by inserting her arm into the oven cavity. If she had to remove her arm after counting to ten or fifteen, the temperature might be suitable for coarse breads, meats, or certain hardy pies; at milder temperatures, white breads or cakes could be prepared. Heat on the hearth was controlled by moving the cooking vessel closer to or farther away from the flames and using trivets of varying heights.

The culinary tastes of the time differed from ours. Raw foods were generally thought unappetizing, so fruits and vegetables were most often cooked. Nothing went to waste: organ meats such as brains and hearts were delicacies, and even fat was valued. Meals tended to be greasier than those we prepare today. Among the gentry, the cuisine was heavy in meats and spices (sugar, cinnamon, and nutmeg); people of lesser means ate plainer meals, with less meat and more grains.

A distinctive architectural feature found in a few prerevolutionary Rhode Island homes was the overmantel cupboard. This example has an arched top and flanking raised panels.

cart road, later named Hopkins Street, that climbed the hillside overlooking the town's natural harbor. It was a plain structure, typical of its time and place, with an end chimney, one room on the first floor, and a sleeping space above.

Hopkins arrived later, having been born in greater Providence (at that time, Providence encompassed virtually all of northern Rhode Island). His ancestors included members of three of the families who had been the colony's original European settlers. As a young man, Stephen Hopkins tilled the soil and harvested flax; at twenty-four he was elected town moderator when Providence was quartered and his outlying section became Scituate. Winning the trust of his neighbors, he soon added the job of town clerk, for which his training as a surveyor proved invaluable because it involved the registration of deeds. In 1742, he left Scituate for Providence, deciding that farming was less likely to provide for his wife and seven children than the commercial enterprises he might pursue in the port town.

The Providence of Hopkins's young manhood was home to some four thousand people. It consisted of modest dwellings, a shipyard, a mill, a row of wharves, three taverns, and four houses of worship; there was no customhouse, post office, or school. In the decades to come, the Hopkins family achieved a prosperity second only to that of their neighbors the Browns as owners and ship captains (two of Hopkins's brothers and three of his sons would die captaining their ships).

When he sold his upland farm and bought the house on Town Street, Hopkins set about adding a "big house" to the existing little house. The new structure was only one room deep but stylish for the time, with a center hall flanked by a study and parlor on the first floor, with two bed chambers above. The footprint of the combined structures was L-shaped. By the time Hopkins went to Philadelphia for the Continental Congress, the view from his home included the new customhouse and his own warehouses and wharves, where his ships docked. In his public life, he had pressed for construction of roads, bridges, and a public market. It was on his watch, as well, that a library was established and the town's first newspaper founded (the *Providence Gazette,* in 1762). Hopkins's writings—usually unsigned—appeared often in its pages, for he became an early and frequent

An inventory that survives from Hopkins's death, in 1785, has been the guide for furnishing this bed chamber. Among the objects are leather-covered trunks (there are no closets in the house), a tall-post maple bed covered in eighteenth-century fabric, and a portrait of George Washington by Gilbert Stuart's daughter, Jane. Washington himself is said to have slept here on a visit in 1781.

proponent of revolutionary notions. "British subjects," he wrote in *Rights of Colonies Examined,* published in November 1764, "are to be governed only agreeable to laws to which they themselves have in some way consented." It predated John Dickinson's more widely distributed *Letters from a Farmer* by some three years.

HOPKINS REMEMBERED

The self-taught Stephen Hopkins succeeded in business and government. He became an early member of the American Philosophical Society, an organization founded by Benjamin Franklin in 1743. The society was dedicated to the study of "natural philosophy," or nature, and implied the investigation of anything scientific or technological, including anthropology, botany, geology, and meteorology. Hopkins is remembered for his observations of the transit of Venus in 1769.

He married twice. His first wife, Sarah Scott, gave birth to all seven of his children. As a Quaker, Sarah undoubtedly contributed to Hopkins's gradual conversion to the principles of the Friends, which influenced him late in life (he publicly called for abolition and freed all his slaves in 1774, the same year he led the Rhode Island General Assembly to ban importation of the enslaved). After Sarah's death, Hopkins remarried, but he was destined to outlive his second wife, Anne, as well as all his children. At his order, Anne's tombstone was incised with the words "O my companion, thou hast left me to finish my journey alone."

The notes John Adams kept at the Second Continental Congress in 1776 mention the Rhode Islander, a man almost thirty years Adams's senior. Adams admired the elderly Hopkins for his long experience in public life and good judgment in chambers, but it was the postprandial Hopkins he enjoyed most. "His custom was to drink nothing all day, nor 'til eight o'clock in the evening, and then his beverage was Jamaica spirits and water," Adams wrote in his diary. "He read Greek, Roman, and British history . . . and the flow of his soul made his reading our own, and seemed to bring to recollection of all we had ever read." As Adams remembered the spirited old man of those evenings, "He kept us alive."

This ground-floor room has been interpreted as Hopkins's office, with a tall secretary desk and a chair that belonged to him. The delft tiles around the firebox portray a variety of Old Testament scenes, including the story of David and Goliath.

Richard Stockton's Morven

Good fortune and enduring fame came to many Founding Fathers after independence. Richard Stockton (1730–1781) belongs in a separate category, as a man who lost his reputation—and his life—during the Revolutionary War. His tale falls well short of the truly heroic.

After signing the Declaration of Independence in Philadelphia, Stockton, a New Jersey attorney, accepted an assignment. The Continental Army in upstate New York was reported to be in disarray, and Congress dispatched Stockton to find out why. Together with the Pennsylvanian George Clymer, a fellow Signer, Stockton traveled to Fort Ticonderoga and Albany. On October 28, 1776, he reported from Saratoga that, even though the soldiers were "marching with cheerfulness . . . the great part of the men [are] barefooted and barelegged." He also volunteered, "There is not a single shoe or stocking to be had in this part of the world, or I would ride a hundred miles through the woods and purchase them with my own money."

The earliest deeds and account books disappeared after the British ransacking of Morven during the winter of 1777, so the construction history of the house is uncertain. The Stocktons probably built their "Mansion House" in the 1760s, and a recent detailed study revealed that portions of one wing of that house still stand (on the right when viewed from the garden behind the house). However, the main block of the house was evidently the work of Annis and Richard's son, Dick. Ensuing generations of Stocktons also altered and enlarged the house in the late nineteenth and early twentieth centuries.

> [Richard] Stockton is not very well in health & much spoken against for his Conduct. He Signed Howe's declaration & also gave his Word of honour that he would not meddle in the least in American affairs during the War.

—*John Witherspoon, Signer, March 17, 1777*

Richard Stockton of New Jersey.

By the time Stockton returned home, in late November, the British forces had the Continental Army in full retreat after having forced General Washington to abandon New York. The Redcoats followed closely, and Stockton's hometown, Princeton, New Jersey, was in their path. On November 29, he and wife, Annis, and their daughters, Julia, Polly, and Sukey, made their getaway. Rather than follow Washington's lead to Pennsylvania, however, Stockton took refuge with friends in New Jersey. He paid dearly for his decision; Tory sympathizers betrayed him, and British soldiers arrested Stockton and took him on a forced march northward. Stockton was locked in a cell in New York's Provost Jail and, contrary to the code of the day, treated as if he were a common criminal. He was put in irons and deprived of food.

When the delegates to the Continental Congress in Philadelphia learned what had befallen one of their own, they were outraged. A congressional order, issued on January 3, 1777, directed General Washington to demand Stockton's release. What they didn't know was that Stockton was already free: the British commander, William Howe, had proffered a pardon, which Stockton had accepted. But in return he had agreed to absent himself from the rebellion.

Stockton's courageous act of signing the Declaration—in the eyes of the Crown it was treason, punishable by hanging—had been followed by another signature. By accepting the terms of his pardon, Stockton sullied his reputation, and his public life abruptly ended. As the story was told in the nineteenth century, the British released a broken man, made ill by his harsh treatment. A close examination of the facts suggests the story was more complicated. His imprisonment did not lead directly to Stockton's death; he died almost five years later, at the Princeton home he called Morven, of a malignant cancer. While not precisely a traitor to the American cause, he had become a bystander, living up to his promise to General Howe.

FACING PAGE: *As revised and remodeled by generations of Stocktons, Morven stands apart from Stockton Street in its parklike setting.*

Slave or Son? "My Poor Marcus"

We condemn slavery today as cruel and inhuman. Yet the symbiotic relationship between slaves and their owners, when seen within the context of the eighteenth century, suggests that human kindness wasn't always absent from the lives of the African-Americans who served the American gentry.

Consider a Stockton slave named Marcus. Born at Morven, he was cared for by the mistress of the house after his mother's death. Annis herself became his wet nurse. She would later recall "the numberless times . . . the poor fellow . . . nursed at my breast" and that she "brought him up almost as my own son." As an adult, he knew how to read and write, leading to the assumption that Annis Stockton taught Marcus, just as she did her own children, the rudiments of written communication.

As a young man, Marcus remained one of several slaves at Morven, working as a farmhand and coachman. Later he moved to Philadelphia to work for Annis's daughter Julia and her husband, Benjamin Rush. Marcus became Rush's assistant, mixing medicines and assisting the doctor on his rounds during the yellow fever epidemics of the early 1790s.

In the will he drafted in 1780, Richard Stockton specified that Annis could at "her discretion . . . grant freedom" to any deserving slave. No evidence survives that Marcus was freed, despite his bond of intimacy and trust with the Stocktons.

MEETING MRS. STOCKTON

A look at Mrs. Stockton's days at Morven during her quarter-century marriage and her two-decade widowhood offers a glimpse into the life of one well-to-do woman in revolutionary America.

In 1756, twenty-year-old Annis Boudinot arrived in Princeton. Though not a memorable beauty, she was attractive, slim, and dark-eyed. Across the street from her father's tavern was another new arrival, the College of New Jersey. The school had recently moved to Princeton from Newark, and many years later (in 1896) it would take the name of the town as its own.

The college would prove an important factor in Annis's life. Her dearest friend of the period was Esther Burr, wife of the school's president, Aaron Burr, Sr. Both Burrs were attracted to the younger woman's manner and conversation. A lifelong passion of Miss Boudinot, the writing of poetry, also impressed Esther, who confided in an acquaintance that her new friend's poems "shew some genious."

Within three years of her arrival, Annis married Richard Stockton, himself a recent graduate of the school and the eldest son of a prominent local landowner. In 1759, Richard and Annis welcomed their first child, a daughter named Julia, one of the six children born to them who would survive early childhood. In 1762, Richard Stockton's sister Hannah married one of Richard's former law clerks, Elias Boudinot, Annis's brother. In the small world of upper-crust colonial culture, prominent families tended to keep one another close.

Richard Stockton owned some three hundred contiguous acres around what he called his Mansion House in Princeton; he owned seven hundred more in outlying farms leased to tenant farmers. When added to the earnings from his law practice, the real estate income allowed the family to live comfortably.

Once bounded by a privet hedge and catalpa trees, the Stockton garden featured ornamental flowers, including tulips, hyacinths, daffodils, roses, lilies, stock, and scarlet creeper. Some acres in Richard and Annis's time were forested, allowing woodland rambles. The landscape was a pleasure the couple had shared; as Annis wrote in one of her annual elegies on the occasion of her husband's death, "Ye stately Elms and lofty Cedars! Mourn! / Slow through your avenues you saw him borne, / The friend who rear'd you, never to return."

OSSIAN'S "LITTERARY WAY"

A published poet, Annis Stockton took pride in knowing something about what she called "the Litterary way." She was moved in particular by *Ossian,* a pair of epic poems her husband had brought back from Dublin. The saga was said by its Scots "translator," James Macpherson, to date from the third century; he claimed to have discovered the blind bard's stories in the original Gaelic, and he published them between 1761 and 1765. Annis was not alone in admiring *Ossian*: Napoleon carried Macpherson's tale of the Scots warrior Fingal into battle, Goethe translated portions into German, and Thomas Jefferson allowed as how "I am not ashamed to own that I think . . . [Ossian] the greatest Poet that has ever existed."

In fact, Ossian never existed: Macpherson perpetrated the literary hoax of the century, melding a few genuine fragments into his own literary invention. To an audience who had mastered Greek and Latin grammar by reading Homer and Virgil, the epic form was familiar; undoubtedly, it was also a happy discovery for northern Europeans, who wished to believe a culture in the cold north had produced poetry on a par with that of the ancient Mediterranean cultures.

Annis and Richard Stockton so admired Macpherson's books that they chose to name their home Morven after the mythical home of King Fingal.

After being inhabited for generations by Stockton descendants, Morven became home to Robert Wood Johnson (during his residence, he transformed his modest family pharmaceutical company into the international powerhouse Johnson & Johnson). Morven then served as New Jersey's Governor's Mansion. Since 1981, the house has been restored and transformed, and it is now a museum devoted to New Jersey's cultural heritage. Although its rooms have become galleries, Morven's architectural quality shows through in these 1964 photographs.

Floating Island, Anyone?

Annis Stockton sent her daughter a recipe book in 1795 or 1796. "I enclose a book of my receipts which I promised you," she wrote. "They are . . . collected from the experience of my mother, my own, and many of my friends."

Annis's servants undoubtedly did much of the cooking under her supervision, but she herself may have prepared certain dishes, in particular sweets and delicacies. One favorite "receipt" transcribed in the book was for floating island, a frothy confection of fruit and syllabub that made

a pretty presentation. (Syllabub was a mix of milk, sugar, wine, and whipped cream served as a punch or a thick, creamy dessert.)

Have a bowl nearly full of syllabub made with white wine and sugar, beat the whites of 6 new laid eggs to strong froth then mix with it raspberry or strawberry marmalade enough to flavour and colour it, lay the froth lightly on the syllabub, first putting in some slices of cake, rise it in little mounds, and garnish with something light.

Stockton traveled to Europe before the Revolutionary War, but his wife chose to remain at home to care for their young children. Stockton met Samuel Johnson in London and was presented to the King; he journeyed to Dublin and Edinburgh. Away from home for months, he missed his family, writing to Annis: "The peaceful retreat which God has blessed me with at Princeton, you and the sweet children you have brought me, are the sources from which I receive my highest earthly joys." But he took some solace in knowing that his wife was in charge, very much a partner in conducting their affairs. During his long absence, he sent her gentle reminders about farming tasks to be attended to, but unusual for the time, he left her to manage their affairs rather than relying upon a trusted male friend or relative.

THE WIDOW STOCKTON

Annis's experience on her own during her husband's European sojourn was an unwanted rehearsal for the painful and abrupt loss of her husband in the winter of 1781. A still-vigorous forty-five, Annis continued to take pleasure in society. She enjoyed the company of others, and they liked and admired her in return. Annis Stockton could count among her "knot of friends" two men who signed the Declaration, the physician Benjamin Rush and the musician Francis Hopkinson. Prominent churchmen, scholars at the college, and politicians dined at her table.

Though a small village, Princeton was a well-trafficked stop on the King's Highway. In November 1781, General George Washington, always known to enjoy the company of women in society, dined at Morven. He found Mrs. Stockton particularly charming and visited again in later years; Martha Washington also honored Annis with a visit on her way to New York for her husband's first inauguration. For her part, Annis wrote a series of poems eulogizing George Washington, and the two exchanged lighthearted letters that verged on the flirtatious. Princeton was the new nation's capital for five months in the summer and fall of 1783, and Mrs. Stockton entertained visitors frequently. On the Fourth of July that year, she invited all the members of Congress to a fete at Morven.

Although the garden bears little resemblance to the landscape Annis Boudinot Stockton knew, she was a passionate gardener. She found poetry in her plantings. In warm weather, she observed, "The flowers rear their lovely heads / The lily bower its fragrance sheds," whereas in cold, "The tulip and hyacinth sleep in their beds / Nor jonquil nor snow drop dare now show their heads."

Annis Stockton (1736–1801) was a woman of parts. She never remarried and wrote poetic elegies to her late husband over many years, several of them on the anniversary of his death. Her poems appeared in New York and Philadelphia newspapers as well as *Columbian Magazine* and *American Museum*. She was a committed gardener and, during her husband's lifetime, created a substantial pleasure garden at Morven.

Annis Stockton was among the privileged few in her era who had leisure time; though she had the burden of managing the household and farm, slaves and servants were at hand to carry out her orders. She entertained guests, read widely, executed decorative embroidery, corresponded with friends, and wrote poetry. Her husband had bought her stylish clothes in England and Philadelphia. Yet she was a survivor, too, living as a widow for many years in the home she had shared with her husband before giving it to her son, Dick, and his wife. In declining health, Annis spent her final years in Philadelphia at the home of her daughter Julia and Julia's husband, Dr. Benjamin Rush.

NAMING NAMES

There does not seem to have been anyone nicknamed Muffy or Biff in the eighteenth century, but that wasn't because informal names were out of favor. Men tended to address one another by their last names, but most women and children had nicknames. Among the most common Christian names and their diminutives were these:

- Abigail: Nabby

- Ann: Anna, Nancy, or Nan

- Catherine: Kitty or Caty

- Eleanor: Nelly

- Elizabeth: Eliza, Betty, Betsy, or Betsey

- Susannah: Sukey

- Martha: Patsy

- Mary: Polly or Molly

To judge by the diaries and correspondence of the time, very young children were rarely referred to by any name. Acutely aware of the high rate of infant mortality, most parents chose to refer to their newborns generically, calling them "babe," "the little Stranger," or even just "it" until they began to display distinct personalities.

Cliveden

The Americans had lost their capital.

At the Battle of Brandywine, the forces under British General William Howe drove the Continental Army from the field. General Washington retreated, and three thousand British troops and German mercenaries made their way almost unopposed into Philadelphia. To the acclamation of the Tories who remained to greet them, Lord Cornwallis and his men rode victoriously down Second Street on September 26, 1777. Dressed in a scarlet coat trimmed with gold lace, Cornwallis led a parade of grenadiers and dragoons with artillery in tow, accompanied by "God Save the King" played by the British military band.

Washington bided his time. Although the battle had been lost, his army had fought well at Brandywine Creek. He had some twelve thousand troops, and he felt confident that, given the right opportunity, they could reverse the tide. But the plan he devised wasn't to take back Philadelphia—no, he would attack the main British force in Germantown, six miles north of the capital. General Howe had divided his army, sending some with Cornwallis into Philadelphia while keeping eight thousand troops under his command along the main northern road in the German enclave. Washington saw an assault there as his best chance.

The many rounds fired at Cliveden no more than dented the house, but the statues were hit hard. As one visitor noted, "I visited and passed a very agreeable day at this celebrated stone house . . . and saw . . . two or three mutilated statues which stood in front of it."

His strategy called for two columns under cover of night to march fourteen miles south; they were then to overwhelm the British outposts and attack the camp head-on. Two other columns would embark on flanking actions, marching as far as twenty miles in order to sweep in upon Howe's forces from the left and right. A fifth and smaller band of soldiers was to create a diversion at the central crossing of the Schuylkill River, keeping potential reinforcements from coming to Howe's aid.

Today the boldness of the plan stands out, but given historical hindsight, equally apparent is the near impossibility of synchronizing the actions of five military divisions over a large area and a period of many hours when communications were limited to cannon shots and messengers. Nowhere were the logistical challenges better demonstrated than at the confrontation at the country seat of Benjamin Chew, the elegant estate known as Cliveden.

A SUMMER RETREAT

The yellow fever epidemic of 1762 had inspired Benjamin Chew (1722–1810) to purchase eleven acres of gardens and orchards in Germantown. Getting there from Philadelphia was a two-hour journey, but the site had a commanding view of the countryside and seemed a world away from the city and its dreaded summer plague.

Chew was a protégé of the prosperous and powerful Penn family. Following in his father's footsteps, he became the Penns' chief counsel in property matters, a responsibility for which his legal training in London and Philadelphia had prepared him. He also served as attorney general of the province of Pennsylvania. Chew's family connections, his inherited properties (which included a plantation in Delaware), and his high position gave him both wealth and status in prerevolutionary society and politics.

Two marriages to the daughters of prominent Philadelphia families further elevated his prospects and produced, by 1763, five daughters (four of them by his deceased first wife) and a son. Chew needed a country house substantial enough to accommodate his wife, children, and perhaps ten household servants (some of them slaves) when they moved for the summer from their fashionable town house on Philadelphia's South Third Street.

Chew settled upon a design that in outline resembled the home of George Wythe (see page 12). Pairs of windows flanked the first-floor entry; the second-story façade had five more generous windows, aligned with the openings below. The two-room-deep floor plan featured a central passage with parlors on the first floor, chambers above, and more rooms in the attic story. Chew's mansion was to be a classic five-bay, double-pile, two-and-a-half-story house in the Georgian style. A pair of square, two-story dependencies were planned for the rear, one a kitchen, the other a washhouse.

Chew collaborated on the design with another of the Penns' attorneys, William Peters. Both men had visited other local houses of the same configuration, and their sketches reflected the mansions they knew and the printed plates they studied in a 1757 English architectural volume, *A Collection of Designs in Architecture* by Abraham Swan. Nine surviving drawings suggests the evolution of the design, which incorporated a stylish entrance with Doric columns.

Whereas many major eighteenth-century houses evolved over long periods (between them, Jefferson's Monticello and Washington's Mount Vernon required nearly a century to finish), Benjamin Chew completed his in three years. He also kept contracts, account books, and other construction-related paperwork. Many of these documents have descended intact to the twenty-first century, offering an unusually detailed glimpse into the manpower, schedule, materials, and manner of building at Cliveden (pronounced *CLIV-den*).

Chew contracted a master mason in October 1763 to work over the winter to assemble the stone (Wissahickon schist, gray in color and found locally). He ordered timbers in February 1764 so they would cure by the time they were required. As the ground thawed in April, the stonemasons set to work excavating the foundations of all three buildings. By mid-May, the cellar walls were well under way. In July, the house was one story tall; in September, according to Chew's accounts, deliveries of lime ended, meaning the masonry walls were completed. Earlier in the summer, the masons had been joined by carpenters because the interior structure of the house was to consist largely of wood. The carpenters completed the first floor superstructure by mid-July, the second a month later. Racing winter weather, they enclosed the house by the end of the year, with wooden shingles sealing its roof.

ABOVE: *As the American Colonel Timothy Pickering observed of Cliveden after the battle, "[The] house of the Chew's [sic] was a strong stone building, having windows on every side, so that you could not approach it without being exposed to a severe fire; which, in fact, was well-directed." Note the projecting pavilion entrance, the Doric columns and entablature, and the stonework. The higher the course of dressed stonework, the thinner the stones. The result is an optical illusion: the building seems even taller than it is.*

TOP RIGHT: *Cliveden, as illustrated in a 1904 guidebook to historic Germantown.*

RIGHT: *This painting, found in England in 1989 and now at Cliveden, was probably done about 1790. The accuracy of the details—both architectural and military—suggests the artist was at the scene on the day of the battle.*

THE POX AND OTHER INFECTIOUS DISEASES

George Washington seemed an exemplar of good health, but his life history suggests the challenges he and his contemporaries faced. Over the course of his sixty-seven years, Washington repeatedly fell prey to malaria, dysentery, and quinsy (tonsilitis). His brother died of tuberculosis, and George seems to have contracted a case himself at age twenty. And he had bouts with smallpox and anthrax.

Medical practitioners of the day understood little about any of these diseases, believing not in germ theory but that the "four humors" (black and yellow bile, blood, and phlegm) determined health; the prescribed treatment for an "imbalance" of the humors was phlebotomy, or bloodletting.

The era could claim one significant victory in the fight against fatal diseases, and Washington played a role in the story. Smallpox was a dreaded killer, but our first president had contracted a light case at age nineteen. Aside from minor pockmarking on his nose, he made a full recovery. His bout with smallpox also produced an immunity to further infection.

Experiments had been conducted in England using a primitive form of inoculation, in which pustulant matter from a smallpox victim with a light case was scratched into the skin of a healthy person. The procedure usually produced a mild case of the disease—*and* future protection. It didn't always work—some patients died within days of receiving the experimental inoculation—but General Washington became a believer and took the unprecedented precaution as commander in chief of the Continental Army of requiring that his troops be inoculated.

After a winter hiatus, the carpenters began a transformation of the interior in the spring of 1765. Wooden partitions were framed and trim installed. Balusters for the stairs and columns for the front passage arrived from the turners. Lath was applied, and by October the plasterers were at work. Chew paid for cordwood to stoke the fires so the artisans could keep working as winter approached. By mid-December, the bulk of the painting had been completed. In the spring of 1766, door and window architraves with triangular headpieces (pediments) were installed, along with mantels and other trim. The columns that formed the colonnade in the entry passage didn't go up until that December, but with a new baby (the couple's daughter Henrietta was born August 15), the ten members of the family (the newly married eldest daughter brought along her husband) were not ready to move in until the summer of 1768. Their servants included a gardener and coachman, plus domestic staff consisting of a cook, a manservant (who probably doubled as a waiter), maids, a nurse to care for the small children, and a laundress.

When they arrived for their first and subsequent summers, the Chews' caravan consisted not merely of people but of all the furniture, kitchen goods, bedding, and other housewares the family would need. Moving in was not a one-time occurrence; each spring and fall the furnishings traveled between Germantown and South Third Street. Linens, glassware, andirons, and goods of all sorts came and went with the season.

The Chews' summer retreat was huge by the standards of the day, standing tall atop Germantown's highest hill. Its shingles were painted to resemble the gray stone walls, while the trim was yellow, the door brown. It was a suitable house for a powerful man and his large family.

HOW RICH WAS HE?

Benjamin Chew's indentured manservant ran away in June 1776. Chew wanted the English lad back—both because the nineteen-year-old owed him service and because of what he had taken with him. In the advertisement Chew placed in the *Pennsylvania Gazette,* he described John Badger this way:

5 feet 3 or 4 inches high, of ruddy complexion, [wearing] . . . a lightish coloured short cloth coat and waist coat, with white metal buttons, buckskin breeches, blue and white worsted stockings, a pair of new shoes, a white shirt and English cocked hat, with small gold twist around the crown, and pinchbeck shoe and knee buckles.

The advertisement also specified Chew's second grievance:

It is probable that he will change his dress, having carried away with him a claret coloured superfine cloth coat and waistcoat, a whitish coloured cloth coat and waistcoat, and a dark coloured ditto, several white shirts, a pair of English boots, almost new, a pair of speckled silk stockings, with linen soales [soles] to the feet, two pair of white thread ditto, a pair of black worsted ditto, a blue and white silk waistcoat, and a red and white linen ditto.

These clothes undoubtedly were his master's. We know Badger was arrested two months later (thanks to Chew's generous three-pound reward?). What isn't known is whether the luxurious clothing ever made it back to Mr. Chew's linen press.

THE BATTLE WITHIN THE BATTLE

The Battle at Germantown, on October 4, 1777, began auspiciously for General Washington's troops. They had marched all night in silence, with pieces of white paper attached to their hats so they would not jostle one another in the darkness. Just as dawn began to lighten the sky, a British soldier spotted the approaching Sixth Pennsylvania Regiment. British musket shots rang out at 5:30, but the pickets quickly fell back from their outpost, calling out as they rejoined the main body of their forces. Six-pounder alarm cannons soon added to the din.

The Americans pursued them, with the second column of American troops joining the first. From behind the British line, General Howe hurried north on Germantown's Great Road. On the way, he met up with his own troops, as British light infantrymen were abandoning their base camp by 6:15. "For shame, light infantry!" one officer called. "I never saw you in retreat before. Form! Form! It's only a scouting party!" Howe saw it differently. Certain that a major American offensive was at hand, he ordered Lieutenant Colonel Thomas Musgrave and his Fortieth Regiment of Foot to cover the infantrymen in retreat. Howe chose to follow the retreating forces after a round of grapeshot shattered a nearby tree.

ABOVE: *The proud—not to say pretentious—tone of the exterior extends inside. The Chews welcomed visitors through tall double doors. The entrance hall reaches sixteen feet into the house; it is twenty-eight feet wide. Yet the most memorable and dramatic architectural element at Cliveden is undoubtedly the screen of columns that separates the entrance hall from the deep stair hall to the rear.*

RIGHT: *This still life summarizes more than a little of Cliveden's history. The chair in the foreground—technically, it is called a back stool—was made by one of Philadelphia's most prestigious cabinetmakers, Thomas Affleck. The long rifles recall the battle fought around the house, as do the paintings by Edward Lamson Henry, circa 1875. The finished canvas on top is called* The Battle Germantown, *while the one beneath, a study for an unexecuted painting, bears the title* Cliveden Entrance Hall During the Battle of Germantown.

The parlor features a fine sofa (attributed to Thomas Affleck) upholstered in yellow flowered silk damask. The looking glass on the right—one of a pair—is thought to have been by another Philadelphia maker, James Reynolds. It is painted yellow pine and plaster.

Musgrave had fought in the New York campaign the previous year. At the Battle of White Plains, he had taken a bullet to the face, which left him with a permanent hole in his left cheek. He and his men had been encamped behind Cliveden, and as the fighting raged, he did his best to follow the order he had been given to hold his position. As the other British troops hightailed it back toward Germantown's center, Musgrave realized his own men would soon be overrun. With his avenue of retreat closing, Musgrave and more than a hundred British soldiers took refuge in the great stone house. Thus, the scene was set for the battle within the battle: at Cliveden, the British and American troops would enact a smaller version of the larger conflict.

Cliveden was a virtual island, entirely cut off by colonial troops from the British army. The Americans discovered that the house remained in enemy hands when a messenger delivering orders from Washington heard bullets whizzing by his head and spied gun flashes in an upstairs window. Washington convened a meeting of his staff to decide how to deal with what was effectively a fortified castle in enemy hands behind American lines. The youthful adjutant Alexander Hamilton favored a plan to leave a regiment of soldiers to contain the Redcoats at Cliveden. Washington seemed about to agree to this strategy when his chief of artillery, Major General Henry Knox, argued that Cliveden posed a danger to the rear guard. Knox proposed a "reduction by cannonade"—bombarding the house with artillery fire. Washington ordered him to proceed.

A bloody ballet ensued. First, Knox dispatched Lieutenant Colonel William Smith, to parley. Smith marched across an open field to offer Musgrave and his men a chance to surrender. But a thick fog had risen from the damp soil and, mixed with the dense white gunpowder smoke, reduced visibility to no more than a few feet. When a British marksman spied the unidentified figure approaching, he shot him in the leg. The drummer accompanying Smith carried him to cover.

Their peace offering rebuffed, the American forces positioned four cannons beyond the range of British rifles. For nearly an hour, they bombarded the façade of the house from across the Germantown Road, 120 yards away. Fusillades of roundshot and grapeshot blew the front doors off their hinges, smashed through

Remnants of the Battle of Cliveden, the front doors to the house were hauled out of storage in 1927 for a celebration of the 150th anniversary of the battle.

SHOT FROM GUNS

Muzzle-loaded guns were the norm during the Revolutionary War. Soldiers carried flintlock muskets that could fire either balls or shot. Black powder was used to power the projectiles along the smoothbore barrels; the guns were notoriously inaccurate, so the prevailing strategy was to fire volleys with a number of soldiers shooting in unison. While one line fired their muskets, another would load theirs. Reloading was cumbersome, as a premade paper cartridge containing powder and ball or shot was dropped into the barrel, then tamped with a rammer.

Three-, four-, and six-pound cannons were usual in the field, although larger cannons could be mounted on ships or fixed fortifications. Again the ammunition was loaded through the muzzle. The projectiles varied from roundshot (solid balls) and grapeshot (linen bags of small iron balls, typically an inch or more in diameter) to smaller shot or musket balls. Less common were shells, hollow iron balls fitted with fuses and filled with powder.

The range of a musket was less than one hundred yards, with little accuracy beyond fifty yards. Grapeshot from a cannon was deadly at up to two hundred yards; cannons shooting roundshot had a range up to eight hundred yards.

windows and shutters, and scarred the stone walls. When the entrance steps were struck, shards of stone flew in all directions. Some of the shrapnel-like chips flew about the front yard, amputating heads and limbs of the lawn sculpture.

Once the Patriots realized the cannon fire was barely denting the stone edifice, they decided to storm the house. Under artillery cover, infantry from the Third New Jersey Regiment rushed forward, but the attack was quickly repulsed when British riflemen, shooting from upper-story windows, cut down many of the approaching men. The few who reached the front door were met by bayonet-wielding British forces. The next strategy was to burn the house using straw from a nearby barn, but that also failed.

Quite by accident, a brigade of Virginia troops, drawn by the sound of cannon and rifle fire, approached the house from the rear.

THE MEN WHO DID THE WORK

Benjamin Chew knew the difference.

To begin with, he would trust local craftsmen and suppliers from Germantown. That meant John Hesser, master mason, and Jacob Knor, master carpenter. Both men lived nearby, as did Christopher Hargasheimer, the blacksmith who supplied iron hinge pintles, hasps, and other common hardware. Anthony Gilbert was the purveyor of the timber for the large framing members and scantling (smaller-dimension lumber). These men and their laborers were responsible for the main structure, the massive stone box that enclosed the wooden matrix of floors and roof.

Chew then looked to proven Philadelphia artisans for the high-style finishes. The ornamental stonework outside was shaped by the Casper Guyer. Inside, the fancy hinges and locks came from William Rush.

Two master woodcarvers, Nicholas Bernard and Martin Jugiez, provided architectural ornamentation for the main parlor. Among the other Philadelphians were the plasterers Samuel Hastings and David Cauthorn and the painter Philip Warner.

If Chew was pleased with the finished house, he wasn't always happy with how much he had to pay his builders—especially the Philadelphians. The total bill was a then-staggering 3,436 pounds for the several buildings (including a stable). Chew didn't hesitate to object when he received what he regarded as an overstated bill: When Casper Guyer submitted his final invoice, Chew paid the amount due against a total of some 92 pounds. But, he noted, "... this account is most extortionate [and] I have paid him [Guyer] already more than is just & he is entitled to."

As the Virginians neared, they were fired upon by not only the British in the house but, unbeknownst to them, Knox's guns on the other side, as occasional cannon shot flew over the structure. The Virginians promptly set up four cannons and returned fire. Meanwhile, other soldiers who had made their way south to engage the British heard the bombardment. Thinking a counterattack might have been launched to their rear, some troops marched back toward the house. In the thick smoke and fog, two bands of American troops formed lines and fired volleys at each another. Not only did an unknown number of casualties fall to "friendly fire" but a large hole emerged in the American battle line.

Precisely how the tide of battle turned is uncertain, but by 8:00 A.M. the Americans were retreating. The British followed cautiously, suspecting a trap, but Musgrave and his men, still barricaded in Cliveden, heard fifes and drums announcing their countrymen's approach. The Fortieth Regiment of Foot emerged and joined in pursuing the Americans. Fewer than five British soldiers lay dead at Cliveden, but one Hessian captain "counted seventy-five dead Americans around the house. . . . Some lay in the front doorway under the pile of table and chairs; others lay under the front windows."

SIX GENERATIONS

That Cliveden still stood after the Battle of Germantown is nothing less than a miracle. When he saw it a year later, Benjamin Chew himself described it as "an absolute wreck." According to one nineteenth-century source, "Chew's house was so battered that it took five carpenters a whole winter to repair and replace the fractures."

Yet Cliveden's survival as a family home is perhaps just as remarkable. The Chew family owned the property for six generations. The last residents were Samuel and Barbara Chew. Before moving in 1959, they consulted Henry Francis du Pont, whose own home, Winterthur, had opened as a museum in the early 1950s. Within a year, *The Magazine Antiques* published images of the renovated Cliveden in its regular feature "Living with Antiques," showcasing the fine Philadelphia-made eighteenth-century furniture. Meanwhile Sam's brother, Benjamin Chew VI, was proving to

In the study, select pieces of Chew furniture are arrayed as if to serve a gentleman conducting his business. The paper press held Chew papers for generations; the comb-back Windsor chair and library table were both made in Philadelphia in the revolutionary era.

be the historian in the family, spending countless hours organizing more than two hundred thousand family documents. Finally, in 1972, the Chews signed a contract transferring ownership to the National Trust for Historic Preservation.

The happy result of the Chews' brand of personal preservation is the presence in the public trust of both the documents and the house itself. Cliveden is a superb specimen of the Georgian style as practiced in America's finest eighteenth-century city. Cannonball scars remain on the exterior walls, and musket balls are lodged in the plaster inside. It is one of history's ironies that the battle fought in 1777 at the house built by Benjamin Chew—who never could bring himself to throw his lot in with the Patriots—would advance the American cause. The bravery of Washington's forces at Germantown, together with the victory two weeks later at Saratoga (see "The Battle of Saratoga," page 164), helped persuade the French to come to the new nation's aid, an important turning point in the war.

BENJAMIN CHEW . . . TORY?

Benjamin Chew had become chief justice of the province of Pennsylvania in 1774. As such he was an official of the proprietary (that is, British) government. Although he had signed the nonimportation agreement in 1768, his commitment to the Patriot cause was regarded with skepticism in certain quarters.

As cannonballs ricocheted off his home in Germantown, Chew was under house arrest, confined at an ironworks in New Jersey with the colonial governor John Penn. Chew had refused to sign a document swearing to remain neutral, claiming that to do so would infringe upon his rights as a free man. He remained in custody for nearly a year.

After his release, Chew sold Cliveden, rented his Philadelphia town house, and moved to his Delaware plantation. When the war concluded, he returned to Philadelphia and resumed his law practice. He did not participate in the Constitutional Convention of 1787 but became a part of the vibrant social life of the city that in 1790 became the new nation's capital. He and his family—including a son and several marriageable daughters (he had a total of twelve)—joined a circle in which the George Washingtons and the John Adamses also traveled. Having reestablished his good reputation, Chew was appointed president of Pennsylvania's High Court of Errors and Appeals.

In 1797 he bought back Cliveden.

No portraits of Benjamin Chew taken during his lifetime survive, but this silhouette was based on one published a year after his death.

Drayton Hall

The revered revolutionary body the
Continental Congress experienced its share of bitter disagreements.
During his seventeen months as a delegate, William Henry Drayton
of South Carolina participated in a number of long-winded, disor-
derly, and acrimonious debates. An orator respected for strong
opinions and his ability to get to the point, Drayton made his voice
heard on important issues such as military pensions, British propos-
als for peace, and the Articles of Confederation.

Drayton also addressed one matter that paled in importance
but has had a recurring significance down to the present day. As the
third anniversary of the Declaration of Independence approached,
Drayton and the Pennsylvania delegate Gouverneur Morris moved
to order the chaplain to prepare sermons "suitable to the occasion."
In the ensuing discussion, another delegate proposed that
Continental Congress President John Jay organize an entertainment and celebration. Drayton, known in his youth for a self-
indulgent lifestyle, liked the idea of a party to celebrate the nation's
founding. When thirteen other congressmen took exception to the
proposal, a furious debate followed.

Perhaps the most vociferous objections were raised by
Drayton's fellow South Carolinian, Henry Laurens. He and Drayton

*A Drayton descendant replaced the mantel in the withdrawing room in 1802
with one in the then-current Federal style; in the 1970s, vandals made off with the
replacement. But the original overmantel remains, with its split pediment,
brackets, rosettes, and other boldly carved details.*

The two faces of Drayton Hall: One looking landward (left), the other toward the river. Today Drayton Hall stands isolated, virtually all of its many dependencies gone. In the eighteenth century, however, what Palladio would have called the casa di villa *was the center of a busy agricultural operation, overlooking barns, stables, slave quarters, and a range of other buildings, including two flankers (also now gone), one thought to have been a kitchen, the other a laundry.*

had been feuding. Laurens, a former president of the congress, felt the younger man paid him insufficient respect. For his part, Drayton, an English-educated child of the landed gentry, saw Laurens as nothing more than the jumped-up son of a saddler, with political opinions that ran counter to his own.

Laurens prided himself on his piety and abstemious habits. He asserted that an "expensive feast" was unseemly when fighting raged back in South Carolina. He advocated a day of "fasting & mourning" rather than indulgence in "joy & mirth." But Drayton's sunnier approach prevailed. On July 5, 1779 (the Fourth that year fell on a Sunday, so "sabbatarianism" forbade celebration), the delegates trooped to the City Tavern for what the *Pennsylvania Packet* described as a "very elegant dinner." Laurens and a handful of others were notably absent.

A "brilliant exhibition" of fireworks followed the banquet. Undoubtedly the echoing booms only irritated Laurens further, but our Independence Day celebrations, with their skyrockets and firecrackers, originated then, compliments of William Henry Drayton.

AN ENGLISH COUNTRY HOUSE

The year that Billy Drayton (1742–1779) was born, his family moved into Drayton Hall. The new home sat on a lush Low Country riverbank, twelve miles south of Charleston, then called Charles Towne after an English king. Enclosing nearly eight thousand square feet on its two main floors, the house was twice the size of any other in the province. Though it was surrounded by the rice fields that underwrote its construction, Drayton Hall's architectural antecedents were foreign. A well-traveled visitor could have been excused for thinking he was in Wiltshire or Devonshire at the country home of an English aristocrat.

In the early eighteenth century, the British Empire emerged as the dominant world power and, simultaneously, adopted Palladianism as its architectural style. The well-to-do wanted houses that made a statement, and they found in the sixteenth-century architect Andrea Palladio's work porticoes, pediments, domes, and other classical elements that conveyed a sense of grandeur. John Drayton, William Henry Drayton's father, was one of many subjects

LEFT AND CENTER: *The view from the portico, upstairs (left) and down (center). The balustrade on the second floor was a turn-of-the-twentieth-century addition.*

RIGHT: *Aside from the mansion, the only architectural survivor from John Drayton's day is this brick privy. Drayton's desire for style and personal comfort extended even to the outhouse, which had seven seats, including two at a convenient height for children and two with armrests.*

Andrea Palladio

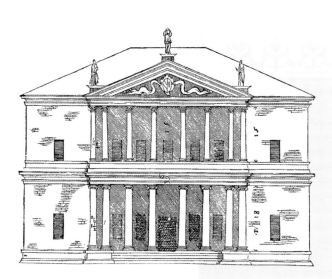

The woodcut from Palladio's Four Books of Architecture *(1570) that may have been the inspiration for Drayton Hall.*

At age thirteen, Andrea della Gondola apprenticed as a stonecutter. When he was in his twenties, a nobleman took him on the first of what would be five trips to Rome. There Palladio studied, measured, and drew ancient Roman temples and other ruins. On his return, he designed buildings *all'antica*—"in the antique manner," demonstrating a deep appreciation for the architecture of antiquity.

Palladio (1508–1580) is remembered best because of *I Quattro Libri dell'Architettura* (1570). Perhaps the most influential architectural text of all time, *The Four Books of Architecture* inspired imitation: John Drayton, for one, seems certain to have examined a freshly printed copy of an English edition at neighboring Middleton Place plantation (see page 210) as he began building his Palladian manse in 1738.

Palladio was the first great architect to devote much of his practice to designing places for people to live. He built churches and municipal commissions, too, but he is best remembered for his *palazzi* for wealthy Venetians and his villas in the Veneto, the terra firma that surrounded the venerable island city in its tidal lagoon. Like Drayton Hall, Palladio's villas were more than bucolic country houses—he designed estates that expressed the personal power of their owners while functioning as nerve centers for agricultural enterprises. In England and its colonies—including Virginia, Ireland, and South Carolina—the same formula fit.

As a young man, he had been known as Andrea della Gondola because his father made deliveries in a gondola. But Andrea Palladio adopted a new name and adapted a classical style that would prove enduring.

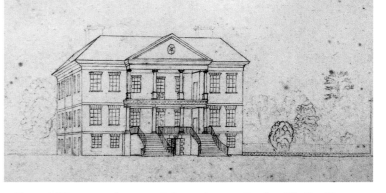

A Doorway To . . . ?

In high-style Georgian architecture, *symmetry* was the watchword. Sometimes the builders were so committed to balance that they would add a false door to a room to give the illusion that everything was symmetrical. And behind the door? Nothing but a brick wall, as in Drayton Hall's first-floor Ionic Room (above).

TOP: *In the cavernous basement at Drayton, dismantled limestone columns rest before an immense fireplace. The four Tuscan columns are thought to have supported the portico's upper level; why they were replaced remains a mystery.*

ABOVE LEFT: *William Henry Drayton, man of property and pamphleteer (in one, signed just "Freeman," he offered an early draft of an American bill of rights). He would die at just thirty-seven.*

ABOVE RIGHT: *A Drayton cousin, Lewis Gibbs, visited in 1846. A professor of mathematics at the University of Charleston, he made this perspective drawing of the mansion's landward elevation.*

of King George II who built a Palladian house symbolic of his power and prominence.

John Drayton's slaves and English craftsmen constructed it of brick and Welsh sandstone on the outside, with fine paneling of local bald cypress lining almost every interior wall. Drayton's nearly cubical house rose two very tall stories atop its raised basement. An examination of some of the interior details indicates that Drayton and his builders pored over not only Palladio's *The Four Books of Architecture* but also William Kent's *Designs of Inigo Jones* (1727), adapting an overall design from the former and many details from the latter.

Drayton Hall was conceived with two faces. One greeted visitors arriving from the Ashley River, the primary route of travel from Charleston, while the other overlooked an array of structures that served the domestic life of the house. Over the years, twenty or more outbuildings—including a kitchen, privy, loom house, poultry house, dovecote, lime kiln, and slave houses—would be constructed on the 660-acre plantation to serve the fields in cultivation as indigo succeeded rice as the main cash crop.

John Drayton had an orangery (greenhouse) along the river in which fresh fruits and berries were grown. He had a fine English garden. Nearby were live oak trees hung with garlands of Spanish moss; a lake; a fenced deer park, where animals were kept for the hunt; and a geometric array of gardens filled with roses, gardenias, lilacs, and other blooms.

The presence of such a sophisticated house in England in 1740 would have been worthy of remark; in South Carolina, it was astonishing, particularly considering it was built for a twenty-three-year-old man who had never crossed the Atlantic. Perhaps that was the point: in the decades before independence, John Drayton's aspiration for his family was to attain full status as members of the English gentry, albeit from an outpost in the American colonies.

The eldest son, William Henry, would never become master of Drayton Hall. His father angrily disinherited him when William remained in Philadelphia, serving in the Continental Congress rather than coming home to defend South Carolina as British troops invaded in 1779. The lost inheritance would prove unimportant; William Henry died in Philadelphia of a "putrid nervous fever"

THE ELEMENTS ARE THE ENEMY

Once the banks of the Ashley River were lined with plantations, but today Drayton Hall is the sole survivor. Drayton itself served as headquarters for the British Generals Clinton, Cornwallis, and Tarleton during the Revolution. The Union Army during the Civil War burned many neighboring mansions but, for reasons that are obscure, left Drayton Hall standing.

Rather than mankind, Mother Nature posed the greatest threat. But the massive house has withstood many natural challenges, too. Among them were these:

✣ THE HURRICANE OF 1752
A major storm destroys five hundred Low Country homes, blows ships ashore, and raises the waters of the Ashley almost to the door of Drayton Hall.

✣ THE HURRICANE OF 1813
Winds and torrential rains blow out most of the windows in the house, leading to the replacement of the original twelve-over-twelve sash with six-over-six windows.

✣ THE EARTHQUAKE OF 1886
Much of Charleston is leveled. At Drayton Hall, the dependency used as a laundry (the northeast flanker) is demolished.

✣ THE GREAT STORM OF 1893
Another hurricane blows through; this time, the kitchen flanker is destroyed.

✣ HURRICANE GRACIE
In 1959, Gracie strikes, and one Drayton descendant notes in his diary that the azaleas were "almost leveled" and the garden looked "like match sticks had been thrown up in the air."

✣ HURRICANE HUGO
Nearly three-quarters of the property's trees and a nineteenth-century barn are lost in 1989 to 135-mile-per-hour winds. But, as the photograph above shows, aside from a few broken windows and damaged chimney caps, the house stood essentially unscathed.

✣ In the years 1804, 1854, 1871, 1873, 1885, 1911, 1940, and 1979, Drayton Hall was visited by other major hurricanes.

Although the main house periodically sustained damage to its roof, chimneys, and windows, it remains largely intact. Many other buildings that once surrounded it—slave quarter, barns, stables, and other structures—fared less well, and Drayton Hall today stands alone at the center of the landscape.

Drayton Hall's Other Family

In 1679, when the first Drayton immigrated to South Carolina from Barbados, slaves accompanied him. Descendants of these enslaved people would remain connected to Drayton Hall for more than *three hundred* years.

The early days survive only as oral history, but by 1851 a slave named Caesar appears in the Drayton family documents. After emancipation, he took the surname Bowens. Both Caesar and his grandson, Richmond Bowens, were born on the property; like his grandfather and so many other ancestors, Richmond spent many years at Drayton Hall, working as gatekeeper for the National Trust until his death, in 1998. A lay preacher, farmer, and chauffeur, Richmond Bowens had memories that proved invaluable in reconstructing the Drayton past.

In an African-American graveyard fewer than fifty yards from Drayton Hall's main drive, Caesar and Raymond are buried in wood caskets alongside other former slaves and their descendants. Although the age of the burial ground is unknown, at least thirty-three graves have been identified, all dug on an east-west axis, so that the departed would face the rising sun.

Though sacred, the cemetery was not isolated. The African-American servant village accepted the spirits of the past as essential to their place, surrounding the cemetery with humble wood-frame houses, kitchen gardens, yards, and the very life of the slave community.

William Henry Drayton regarded slavery as a "peculiar institution," but the history of slave ownership in his family extended at least two hundred years, and the connection between the Bowenses and Draytons survived even the Civil War. Today many Bowens descendants still reside in the Charleston area.

The grandson of slaves, Richmond Bowens was born on the property in 1908 and maintained lifelong ties to Drayton Hall.

(probably typhus), two months after the Independence Day celebration, on September 4, 1779.

Other Draytons assumed ownership—after John's death, six generations of descendants would own Drayton Hall. William Henry's brother Charles came next, purchasing it from his widowed stepmother in 1783. Charles, an Edinburgh-trained physician, was deeply interested in horticulture, and the gardens became his testing grounds. Friends brought him plant materials from their travels (of the 118 olive pits Thomas Jefferson sent for planting, none produced a tree). In later generations, the house was abandoned, its roof penetrated by rain because the lead flashing had been removed to make bullets for the Confederate Army. During Reconstruction, the family could not afford to make repairs, but by the 1880s, the fifth-generation owner founded the self-titled Charles Henry Drayton & Company to mine phosphate on the property. After he restored the family's fortunes, he made the house his country retreat, but it would be one of Charles Henry's daughters who would recognize the larger significance of Drayton Hall. During her time as caretaker, the maiden Miss Charlotta positioned the place for posterity.

PRESERVING THE PRESERVED

Each year between 1915 and 1969, Charlotta Drayton and her dog—she had a series of them, but Nipper was the best remembered—"camped" for several weeks at Drayton Hall. The only creature comforts available there were an icebox and a woodstove. There were no slaves, and the once-busy farm had gone quiet, but the house had remained remarkably unchanged over nearly 250 years.

Upon Charlotta's death, in 1969, the seventh generation of Drayton owners took over. But Miss Charlotta had realized something essential about the Drayton family place, leaving explicit provisions in her will that her nephews, Charles and Frank Drayton, were not to change Drayton Hall. They went her one better, putting the property into the public trust in 1974. They sold the house and 125 acres to the National Trust for Historic Preservation, while the rest of the plantation acreage went to the state of South Carolina.

ABOVE: *Visitors invited to ascend to the second floor encountered the stair hall, with its twenty-seven-foot ceiling and eye-popping mahogany staircase. Though little remains of it today, the original finish on the woodwork was a vermilion stain.*

TOP LEFT: *The center ceiling medallion in the lower great hall was the result of an 1850s renovation.*

CENTER LEFT AND LEFT: *Drayton Hall's survival in its unspoiled state is miraculous; the ongoing challenge is to preserve it. One task for its caretakers is preservation of its painted surfaces, and in recent years paint conservators have worked to stabilize the remaining finishes, including here in the withdrawing room (center) and the great hall (left).*

Charlotta understood that her family had become caretakers of what was undoubtedly the grandest and the best preserved American home of its era. By forgoing modern amenities such as running water, central heat, and electricity, the Draytons avoided the need to perforate the structure with holes for pipes and wires. Drayton Hall's walls bore no channels or chases for heating, cooling, or ventilation. The house had seen virtually no remodelings, so not only were the structure and its skin of plaster and wood paneling largely intact, but original paint abounded (no more than six coats of paint had been applied to any surface).

When the National Trust took over, it had a decision to make: What approach would best serve the house's unique status? The choice was made not to turn the clock back, a departure from what is often done with house museums. The handful of changes made in the Victorian era would not be reversed. Nothing, in fact, would be restored; the house, instead, would be preserved.

Today Drayton Hall stands alone, its outbuildings long ago demolished. Yet the walk across the surrounding open green can hardly prepare the visitor for the experience of the interior. Drayton Hall is empty of furniture. There are no tables, chairs, or looking glasses, no sofas, no carpets, and no portraits. The experience is architectural: in the absence of decorative arts, the impression is of spaces, of generous room volumes, of light pouring in large windows, of a towering staircase. And of exquisite paneling, plasterwork ceilings, and peeling paint.

Drayton Hall remains the house that William Henry Drayton knew and that, for seven generations, his family cared for. It is an untouched and authentic relic rather than a re-creation. Its survival is as remarkable as was its appearance more than 250 years ago.

TOP: *The ornate ceiling in the withdrawing room dates from circa 1742.*

ABOVE: *The capitals on the pilasters in the great hall feature richly carved acanthus leaves and spiraling scrolls.*

ABOVE: *A member of the sixth generation at Drayton Hall, Charlotta Drayton (1884–1969) was the last person in the family to spend extended periods in residence. On her watch little was changed, and in her will she expressly requested that the house as she knew it be preserved. In 1974, two of Charlotta's nephews sold the property to the National Trust for Historic Preservation and the state of South Carolina.*

LEFT: *Paneled walls, carved cornices, and fine mantels (and overmantels) are the rule throughout the rooms at Drayton Hall.*

The Ford Mansion

War tended to be a warm-weather affair.

That helped make General Washington's decision to embark on his famous Christmas crossing of the Delaware in 1776 a complete surprise. In the midst of a snow and ice storm, American troops overwhelmed the unsuspecting Hessian garrison manning the outpost at Trenton, New Jersey (see "Victory at Trenton," page 143). A week later, Washington's army prevailed once more at the Battle of Princeton. But the more usual eighteenth-century routine found the British and American armies establishing encampments in strategic locations in late autumn; then, aside from minor forays and skirmishes, the troops waited for spring to resume hostilities.

Even in the absence of enemy fire, a soldier's life in cold weather had its hardships. The miserable winter of 1777–78 spent at Valley Forge would become the stuff of grade-school history texts, though the Continental Army actually emerged from its Pennsylvania encampment a newly disciplined and confident fighting force. This happened because of the drilling of Baron von Steuben, formerly an aide-de-camp to the King of Prussia. Yet the toughest weather of the war came two years later, during the winter of 1779–80.

As the days grew shorter and the weather colder in autumn 1779, Washington and his officers were staggered by a double dose

The Widow Ford's "Mansion House." The kitchen ell (right) extends from the main block of the substantial brick dwelling.

George and Martha Washington both slept here; given the tight quarters, Martha also used this as her reception room. Both the highboy chest (below) and the Queen Anne mirror (right) were in the Ford Mansion during the Washington occupancy.

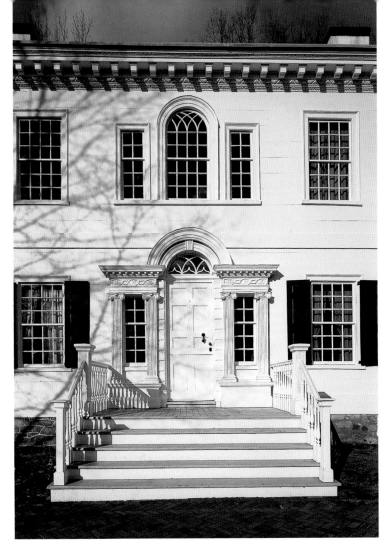

Jacob Ford, Jr., had been a man of means—his wealth came from his father's iron mines—and his desire for a stylish house is perhaps best seen in the fine entrance and window above, both Palladian in style (the central openings have arched tops, the flanking windows are rectangular). The mines, furnaces, and forges in the vicinity were part of what made Morristown a strategic location for a winter encampment.

of bad news. On November 15, tidings reached them of the southern army's defeat in Savannah; making matters worse, the French naval forces supporting the Americans departed for the West Indies, crushing Washington's hopes that the ships would support him in a fall offensive at New York. For the commander in chief, a year of frustration—and of little military progress—neared its end.

Washington moved his army to northern New Jersey, about thirty miles west of New York. His troops chopped down trees to build huts. The area known as Jockey Hollow soon had some twelve hundred log dwellings, each accommodating a dozen soldiers, making the deforested valley temporarily the sixth largest city in the United States. Washington himself settled in the home of Mrs. Jacob Ford in the village of Morristown, four miles from his troops.

Unfortunately for the Continental Army, the weather on the day the general and his staff arrived proved a harbinger of the months to come. The heavy sleet and snow on December 1, 1779, offered a small hint that the most brutal winter of the eighteenth century would soon be upon them.

GEORGE WASHINGTON SLEPT HERE

For the commander in chief and some of his officers, the winter hiatus meant the arrival of their wives. In each of the eight winters of the war, Martha Washington journeyed north from Mount Vernon, bringing a varying collection of family, friends, and slaves. In some years, her appearance was celebrated with grand dinners and balls. But on her arrival in Morristown, in late December 1779, Martha saw an army in dire circumstances.

She had hoped to arrive before Christmas, but heavy weather in Philadelphia delayed her. When she did reach the New Jersey encampment, the troops cheered, but from her carriage she saw soldiers in tattered clothes, many of them lacking shoes, and most with a dangerously lean and hungry look. According to Baron von Steuben, the American troops "exhibited the most shocking picture of misery I have ever seen, scarce a man having wherewithal to cover his nakedness, and a great number very bad with the itch." At night, junior officers lay down together under the stars, their feet to the fire to prevent them from freezing. A late-summer drought had reduced the local harvest of grains, so food was scarce, and General Washington himself complained his soldiers were forced to eat "every kind of horse food but hay."

For Washington, the troubles continued into the winter. He granted many of his officers furloughs, so he himself had to find food and supplies, seek new recruits, and tend to administrative matters rather than develop plans for what he termed the "military parts" of his job. When his starving soldiers began stealing food and livestock from nearby farms, he established a formal requisition system to compensate the local householders and consolidate available food for equitable distribution. Meat and bread repeatedly ran out. Washington lobbied Congress for help, but the government had neither money nor credit. Transporting what supplies there were

Aides to General Washington and visitors were accommodated in upstairs bed chambers. Among the occupants were Don Juan de Mirailles, who died here in April 1780, and the Marquis de Lafayette, who arrived shortly thereafter.

proved difficult through heavy snow and, with the approach of spring, roads mired in mud.

The winter stretched over six months, with twenty-eight snowfalls recorded. The soldiers at times had to make their way around a camp with snow drifts taller than they were. The cold was so extreme that the Hudson River froze, its ice so thick the river became passable by horses pulling cannons. Only once in January did the thermometer rise above freezing. The army that arrived with Washington had numbered some thirteen thousand soldiers; by springtime, a smallpox epidemic, desertion, and the expiration of enlistments had reduced Washington's troops to about eight thousand. Fully a third of those who remained were unfit for duty because of illness. The commander in chief warned that, without more support from Congress and the states, "our cause is lost."

While Washington regarded it as a "fundamental principle" that he "share a common lot and participate [in] the inconveniences" of his men, he and Martha experienced few real privations at Mrs. Ford's. Colonel Jacob Ford had died of pneumonia after the Battle

of Princeton, two years earlier, leaving the fine brick house he completed in 1774 to his widow, Theodosia. The substantial mass of the main structure was joined to a wing containing a kitchen and pantry on the first floor and a sleeping area for the servants above. As large as the house was, it could barely accommodate the Washington entourage.

Mrs. Ford squeezed herself, her four children, and all her household goods into two rooms. The Washingtons inhabited one upstairs chamber, which doubled during daylight hours as Martha's sitting room, where she sewed, read, and received company. Mrs. Ford did the same with the converted dining room, where she and her twelve-year-old daughter slept, and her three sons occupied a converted library. The unheated second-floor central hallway was lined with the cots and trunks of Washington's body servants. Two other chambers accommodated his aides, while the general himself worked in a small office.

On a typical day, Washington's headquarters had the look of a military barracks. The elite corps of his "Life Guard," the men charged with his safety, occupied the first-floor passage and screened visitors. The busiest room in the house was the conference room just off the hall, where aides wrote orders and Washington held conferences. Yet the Ford Mansion also functioned as a home, and Mrs. Washington and Mrs. Ford made it a welcoming place.

Martha saw her role as her husband's helpmate, even at a military encampment. Her philosophy, as she confided in a friend, was simple: "I am still determined to be cheerful and happy, in whatever situation I may be; for I have also learned from experience that the greater part of our happiness or misery depends upon our dispositions, and not upon our circumstances." That meant she adopted the same regime in Morristown that she practiced at Mount Vernon, including a midafternoon dinner. The furniture in the conference room was rearranged for a meal of three courses, often lasting three hours. The talk was as likely to involve light banter as military matters.

Washington always enjoyed company at table, and during the war, his guests included officers and neighbors. Martha invited her friends, too, including Catherine Littlefield Greene, wife of General Nathanael Greene. Immense with child, Kitty Greene would give birth to a son that winter. During their time at the Ford Mansion, the Washingtons were also joined by Benedict Arnold, Baron von Steuben, General Israel Putnam, and on most days, the young Alexander Hamilton.

Hamilton was Washington's principal aide, and many of the field orders issuing from the commander in chief's headquarters were in Hamilton's hand. He was both a gifted stylist in the literary sense and a fine penman, and as he won the general's trust, he quickly rose to the unofficial role of Washington's chief of staff. But that winter, with his military duties slowed by the weather, the handsome and lively Hamilton provided welcome entertainment.

He became a favorite of the ladies, including Mrs. Washington (she slyly named a tomcat she adopted Hamilton). A lively presence at table, he refilled glasses and offered gallant toasts. Despite the hardships suffered by the enlisted men, Hamilton and the other officers attended receptions, sleighing parties, and dancing assemblies. Washington, though his wife had retired from the pastime, remained a demon dancer, who appeared at one dancing party that winter in a striking black velvet suit.

The original of Emanuel Leutze's often reproduced painting George Washington Crossing the Delaware *is enormous (20 × 12 ft.). The 1851 image made a metaphor of the Battle of Trenton, transforming Washington into a virtual figurehead, leading his troops into a new day. When executing his painting, Leutze took many liberties. For instance, the ferrying mission was actually undertaken at night, in a snowstorm, and in a different sort of boat (it should be a flat-bottomed ore boat called a durham, which would have carried perhaps twice the number of soldiers Leutze painted).*

Victory at Trenton

The morning of December 26, 1776, may be remembered best because of the iconic image of Washington posed at the prow of a boat crossing the Delaware. Yet the significance of that day lies in what happened after the Continental Army reached the New Jersey shore.

In the autumn, the American army had retreated across New Jersey after losing New York. Seeking safety from the British force, General Washington crossed the Delaware River to take refuge in Pennsylvania. But as winter approached, he saw an opportunity to reverse his military fortunes by counterattacking when his enemy least expected it. On Christmas night, twenty-four hundred American troops were ferried back to New Jersey. In a raging snowstorm, two columns of Continental troops then marched ten miles to Trenton. At 8:00 A.M., the American forces surprised the Hessian garrison; by 9:30, Washington's men had won a stunning victory.

The victory provided an immense boost to American morale and shocked the overconfident British commanders. Washington, still wary of his enemy's greater strength, led his army quickly back across the Delaware, together with almost a thousand prisoners and a cache of captured supplies. A week later, another American victory would come at Princeton, and in the winter that followed, British troops were repeatedly attacked by militia forces, reducing the invaders' ranks by half.

The night river crossing, the many small skirmishes, the night march on Princeton, and other stratagems presaged the American way of war. It was a mix of "boldness and prudence, flexibility and opportunism, initiative and tempo, speed and concentration, force multipliers, and intelligence," explained the military historian David Hackett Fischer in his book *Washington's Crossing.* "They defined a new way of war that would continue to appear through the Revolution and in many American wars."

RIGHT AND FACING PAGE, BOTTOM: *To welcome the Continental Army into her home, Mrs. Ford consolidated her most cherished possessions into what had been the dining room, which then functioned as her living room and bed chamber as well as her dining room. The upholstered panels (or "wings") of the familiar wing chair helped shield its occupant from drafts in an era when the primary source of heat was the fireplace.*

Morristown National Historic Park

After the Continental Army moved on, in the spring of 1780, the Ford Mansion remained in the family, with title passing from Mrs. Ford to her son Gabriel following the Revolution, then to his son, Henry A. Ford, in 1849. The Fords took pride in the house's historic association with Washington, sharing with historians and other visitors their family's oral history of the general's months of residence. After Henry's death, in 1872, the house was sold at auction, but several historically minded New Jerseyans purchased it and organized the Washington Association of New Jersey. The mansion then was opened to the public as a house museum honoring America's first commander in chief.

In 1933 an act of Congress established the Morristown National Historic Park to commemorate the revolutionary encampments of General Washington at the Ford Mansion and the ragtag band of regulars and militiamen who weathered the brutal winter at Jockey Hollow, where five huts have been reconstructed. The house thus became part of the first national historical park and the first historic house owned by the nation.

Hamilton's roving eye fixed on at least two ladies that January, but early the following month, the company at the Ford Mansion observed a change in the rakish aide. On the second day of February, Elizabeth Schuyler, daughter of General Philip Schuyler, arrived to reside with Washington's personal physician, Dr. John Cochran, just a few hundreds yards from the Ford Mansion. Hamilton's feelings for Betsy Schuyler leapfrogged beyond infatuation almost immediately. Tench Tilghman, a Washington aide who shared quarters with Hamilton, observed, "[He] is a gone man." Before Hamilton left on a mission for Washington in March, the couple had agreed to wed (see "The Schuyler Mansion and Farm," page 156).

As spring approached, and two foreign emissaries, the Marquis de la Luzerne and Don Juan de Mirailles, arrived, an elaborate entertainment seemed called for. Washington made it a grand affair, with a formal review of the troops and a cannon salute, followed by a ball Martha organized. Luzerne stayed nearly a week, during which he and Washington spoke of desperately needed French military assistance for the 1780 military campaign. The Frenchman made no promises but, despite having seen the deplorable condition of the American fighting force, reported back to Paris that he was persuaded "more than ever . . . of the very great advantage which the republic derives from [Washington's] services."

The Spanish envoy unexpectedly became Martha Washington's special responsibility when he fell deathly ill. She nursed de Mirailles as he suffered with an ailment identified as a "biliary complaint" (possibly typhus, also known as "camp fever" because it was rife in the unsanitary conditions characteristic of a miliary camp). De Mirailles died nine days later and was given a funeral with full honors. The death seemed to Washington just one more blow delivered during the hardest months of the war.

A LETTER FROM LAFAYETTE

On May 7, 1780, George Washington finally met up with a cause for rejoicing.

The dinner dishes had been cleared and the candles lit in the early evening when a messenger appeared carrying a letter. Penned "at the entrance of Boston harbour" ten days earlier, the

Washington wrote letters in this room and often conferred here with his officers. At midafternoon each day the soldiers would vacate long enough for the servants to arrange the furniture for dinner, a leisurely meal that was typically taken at about three o'clock. The tall desk against the wall is a Ford family piece, believed to have been in this room during Washington's residence.

opening line read, "Here I am my dear general, and in the midst of the joy I feel in finding myself again one of your loving soldiers." Signed simply "La Fayette," the letter brought tears of joy to Washington's eyes.

The young Frenchman—he was then twenty-three—had become the highest ranking foreign officer in the Continental Army, Washington having named him an honorary major general. They respected each other's military expertise, but each man also discovered that the other filled a void in his private life. Washington had no children of his own; of the two stepchildren Martha had brought to their marriage, Patsy had died of an epileptic fit at seventeen and her brother, Jack, was rapidly proving a ne'er-do-well. Lafayette's father had died in battle before his son turned two. Washington and Lafayette assumed the status of father and son, a relationship Washington acknowledged when Lafayette sustained a wound at the Battle of Brandywine and the older man ordered the battlefield surgeon to "treat him as my son, for I love him the same."

Upon receiving Lafayette's letter from Boston, an elated Washington promptly wrote back, promising "I . . . shall embrace

you with all the warmth of an affectionate friend when you come to headquarters, where a bed is prepared for you."

The news of Lafayette's return boosted his spirits at a time when Washington most needed encouragement. Beyond being the cause of personal rejoicing, Lafayette's letter contained a promise of potential strategic importance: "I have affairs," he had written, "of utmost importance that I should at first communicate to you alone." When he arrived, the two men closeted themselves. Lafayette confided the news of Louis XVI's added commitment to the cause: six powerful warships were bound for America, as were six thousand well-trained troops. Lafayette also brought more personal news that deeply moved both George and Martha Washington. The Marquis's wife had given birth to a boy child, and they had named him George Washington Lafayette.

The season of difficulties was by no means over—Washington would have to suppress a mutiny in the ranks, and news of the fall of Charleston soon came to him—but buttressed by his friend and a winter spent with his wife and military family at the Ford House, he readied to face another year of war.

> Mrs. Washington is excessive fond of the General and he of her. They are very happy in each other.

— General Nathanael Greene, writing to his wife, Kitty

"Lady Washington," A Military Wife's Life on the Road

Her upbringing disposed her to the roles of wife, mother, and mistress of her husband's plantation, but Martha Washington was seized by history. During the winter pauses in the Revolutionary War (1775–1783), she joined General Washington at military encampments. Though they were not her natural milieu ("I shudder every time I hear the sound of a gun," she admitted), Mrs. Washington quickly adapted.

A heroine to her husband's soldiers, she was cheered on her arrival each year. During the rigors at Valley Forge in 1777–78, she organized a sewing circle to make shirts and socks, and to patch clothing for poorly dressed soldiers. She delivered many items herself, basket in hand. Lady Washington, as she was called, offered consolation to cold, hungry, and sick enlisted men.

The women around her were deeply impressed. When they met during the terrible winter at Morristown in 1779–80, Elizabeth Schuyler (soon to be Mrs. Alexander Hamilton) immediately took to Martha Washington. "She received [my aunt and me] so kindly, kissing us both, for the general and papa were very warm friends. She was then nearly fifty years old, but was still handsome. She was quite short: a plump little woman with dark brown eyes, her hair a little frosty, and very plainly dressed for such a grand lady as I considered her. She wore a plain, brown gown of homespun stuff, a large white handkerchief, a neat cap, and her plain gold wedding ring, which she had worn for more than twenty years. She was always my ideal of a true woman."

Later, during her husband's presidency (1789–1797), circumstances once again drew Martha Washington away from the comforts of Mount Vernon. She hated New York and later had to adapt to Philadelphia. But she maintained an equanimity that impressed even Abigail Adams, a woman whose letters reveal her reliable good sense and sharp perceptions. Abigail liked Martha immediately when the wives of the new president and vice president joined forces in New York. "She received me with great ease and politeness. She is plain in her dress, but that plainness is the best of every article. . . . Her manners are modest and unassuming, dignified and feminine, not the tincture of hauteur about her," wrote Abigail Adams.

Martha Washington became the very model for America's First Lady and not only because she did it first. Her contemporaries recognized in her a charisma that blended duty, kindness, gentility, and hope.

Martha Washington, in a lithograph based on Gilbert Stuart's 1796 portrait.

The Heyward-Washington House

In the early years of the war, the British concentrated their military efforts in the North. King George III and his counselors believed the rebellion could be put down with a decisive victory over the colonials' ragtag army, confident the most powerful military force in the world must prevail. Yet the under-manned Continental Army remained very much at large after several years of war, despite having been forced to flee both New York and Philadelphia. General Washington had proved cautious, elusive, and a bit lucky, with an instinct for knowing when to strike the British forces—*and* when to strike camp and disappear into the night.

Sir Henry Clinton changed strategy. He dispatched troops southward from Philadelphia, and by November 1778, the British had moved on Georgia. Savannah fell as the year ended, and the city's Loyalists greeted the conquering army warmly. The Southern strategy seemed sound as Clinton shifted his sights to a bigger prize, Charleston, the largest and most prosperous city in the South.

The Redcoats swept up the coast, planning to lay siege to the exposed city built on a peninsula between the Ashley and Cooper Rivers. By March 1780, the smoke of the invading army's campfires

A portrait of the builder's wife overlooks the dining room; she was Thomas Heyward's stepmother. The table in the foreground is one of a pair; it was common at the time to have a matched set that could be used singly or put together when needed. On the right is a wine cooler, called a cellarette, which was de rigueur for the man of means in the late eighteenth century. Typically lined with lead and some-times loaded with ice, the cellarette would keep the wine cool and near at hand.

The first-floor rooms are simple, but the drawing room on the second floor has floor-to-ceiling paneling on all four walls. That is Thomas Heyward, Jr., age twenty-five, looking down from his perch over the fireplace. Although English-made about 1735, the settee (opposite) has a Charleston connection, having belonged to the Drayton clan (see "Drayton Hall," page 128).

could be seen from the city's steeples, and a fleet of British ships appeared on the horizon. Led by Massachusetts's General Benjamin Lincoln, the colonials dug in. Civilians were evacuated as the British approached. By mid-April, Charleston was entirely surrounded and under almost constant bombardment. The situation seemed more hopeless by the day.

Finally, on May 12, some fifty-five hundred colonial soldiers and officers surrendered, ending a forty-two-day siege. Celebrating what was to be their greatest victory of the war, British troops marched into the city. They would hold it for more than two years, occupying it long after word reached South Carolina of Cornwallis's defeat at Yorktown. The last of the troops were not evacuated until December 1782, when General Nathanael Greene's army repossessed the city.

THE TALE OF THOMAS HEYWARD, JR.

Among the colonials who surrendered in May 1780 was a Patriot named Thomas Heyward, Jr. (1746–1809). The son of a wealthy rice planter, he had, like many of his well-born Southern contemporaries, been educated in England. Upon his return to America in 1771 from the study of law in London and a Grand Tour of the continent, Heyward immediately joined the revolutionary cause. He served in the provincial assembly, joined the South Carolina Committee of Safety, and in 1775 was designated a delegate to the Continental Congress. Five days short of his thirtieth birthday, he signed the Declaration of Independence, along with his fellow South Carolin-ians Henry Middleton (see "Middleton Place," page 210), Thomas Lynch, Jr. ("Hopsewee," page 217), and Edward Rutledge ("The Brothers Rutledge," page 153). After leaving the

The city looks like a beautiful village and consists of about eight hundred houses. It is built at the end of the Neck between the Cooper and Ashley rivers and is approximately a good English mile long and half a mile wide. The streets are broad and intersect one another at right angles. Most of the buildings are of wood and are small, but near the rivers one sees beautiful buildings of brick, behind which there are usually very fine gardens. If one can judge by appearances, these people show better taste and live in greater luxury than those of the northern provinces.

—*Captain Johann Ewald, Hessian officer, 1779*

The master bed chamber is dominated by a four-poster bedstead that belonged to Thomas and Elizabeth Heyward.

Continental Congress, he served as an artillery captain in the South Carolina militia, sustaining a gunshot wound at the Battle of Port Royal.

The sheer number of American soldiers captured after the fall of Charleston made imprisonment of all of them impractical. Some soldiers were confined aboard prison ships in the harbor, others were allowed to slip away and resume their civilian lives. Many officers, among them Captain Heyward, were transported to St. Augustine, Florida, where they were incarcerated in the Castillo de San Marcos.

According to local oral history, Thomas's wife, Elizabeth Matthews Heyward, remained in their Charleston mansion, along with her sister, whose husband had also been exiled to Florida. Before the surrender, Americans had celebrated military advances by illuminating the windows in the city's houses; in the days after, the invaders ordered that the same be done to commemorate the British victory. When the Matthews sisters refused to comply, a Tory mob assaulted the house with stones and mud. Mrs. Heyward's sister is said to have miscarried in the hours that followed and subsequently died.

In the coming months, Elizabeth Heyward would also die. Thomas Heyward regained his freedom in a 1781 prisoner exchange but nearly lost his life in transit, reportedly falling overboard on the sea journey to Philadelphia. He saved himself from drowning only by clinging to the ship's rudder.

A VISITOR TO CHURCH STREET

In the days before the Revolution, Daniel Heyward built a brick town house; by the time of Thomas and Elizabeth's marriage, in 1773, they were able to reside there on visits to town from their plantation in St. Luke's Parish in the Beaufort district.

Nearly cubical in shape, the three-story house has a classic Georgian plan, with a center hall and pairs of front and back rooms on either side. Each of the house's twelve rooms was served by a fireplace. Like those of many other Charleston mansions of the time, the principal rooms in the Heyward House, among them the grand, paneled parlor overlooking Church Street, were on the *piano nobile* (second floor).

The view from the street of the Heyward-Washington House. The doorway is a reconstruction, the original having been lost by the 1920s, when the house was in commercial use as a bakery.

THE BROTHERS RUTLEDGE

John Rutledge (1739–1800) was out of town when George Washington came to visit, but his wife, German-born Eliza Grimké, gave the great man breakfast at their home. Rutledge had had a distinguished career in the law and in public service, leading South Carolina as its governor, representing the state at the Constitutional Convention, and serving as an original member of the Supreme Court. No less a rhetorician than Patrick Henry remembered him as "by far the greatest orator" in the first Continental Congress. Back in 1763, when he and Eliza were newlyweds, they had opened their elegant new downtown home to Charleston society for a Christmas fete, which was remembered as the social event of the season.

John's younger brother, Edward Rutledge (1749–1800), followed his sibling's path, obtaining his legal training in London before returning to South Carolina. As

Edward Rutledge, South Carolina delegate to the Continental Congress and one of the youngest men to sign the Declaration of Independence.

a delegate to the Continental Congress, he signed the Declaration of Independence; as a lieutenant colonel in the Charleston artillery, he was taken prisoner (along with Thomas Heyward) by the British when they seized the city in 1780. Today both the brothers' houses, standing across Broad Street from each other, are operated as inns.

Thomas Heyward, Jr., of South Carolina, Signer and, later, prisoner of war.

The John Rutledge house (left) was constructed about 1763; its ironwork porches were added in 1853. Across Broad Street sits brother Edward Rutledge's home (right).

LEFT: *The Heyward-Washington House contains much fine furniture, including the secretary bookcase at the left and the larger bookcase at center. Before the Revolution and after, Charleston was a furniture-making center, where English-trained artisans established a high-style tradition. Ships arriving from the West Indies brought fine mahogany; local cypress was used for secondary woods (the mahogany was reserved for surfaces on display, while drawer boxes, backs, and the hidden structures of the furniture were shaped of the less expensive cypress).*

RIGHT: *This bookcase was made in Charleston, circa 1795, and it dominates one wall in the first-floor reception room.*

After the war, the widower Heyward remarried, but he chose to reside at his Low Country plantation. He rented out his town house, and in May 1791 George Washington took up temporary residence there on his Southern tour. For 60 pounds, the Charleston city council leased Heyward's house for a week, complete with a housekeeper, several servants, and "a proper stock of liquors, groceries, and provisions." The accommodations pleased Washington. He wrote, "The lodgings provided for me in this place were very good, being the furnished house of a Gentleman at present in the Country."

Washington enjoyed seven formal dinners and three receptions, and was the object of four admiring speeches in seven days—it was a week that one historian has characterized as "the most socially hectic . . . of Washington's career." By the President's own account, he was charmed by Charleston's ladies and impressed by the sumptuous entertainments put on for his amusement, but matters military remained much on the old general's mind.

He devoted one morning to visiting the city's ramparts. The next day he reviewed the island forts that, during the siege of Charleston, had been essential to defending the harbor. "Scarcely a trace" remained of Fort Moultrie, Washington noted, and Fort Johnson was "quite fallen." Still, the President wished to reconstruct the events that had culminated in General Benjamin Lincoln's surrender. Encamped in Morristown, New Jersey, Washington had wondered at the time about the wisdom of digging in for the siege. When he himself had been outmanned at New York and Philadelphia by superior forces, he chose to abandon the towns, saving his army to fight another day. He noted in his diary during his Charleston visit that, having "examined the lines of Attack and defence of the City [I] was satisfied that the defence was noble & honorable alto' the measure was undertaken upon wrong principles and impolitic."

Washington's grandson George Washington Custis reported the great man was "remarkably fond of fish." That being so, he must have enjoyed the cuisine in Charleston.

Although Charleston's cooks drew upon European, Native American, African-American, and West Indian traditions, the raw materials tended to be local. Aside from tea, molasses, coffee, and spices, foodstuffs did not travel very well, so homegrown produce, domesticated animals, indigenous game, and fowl were usual—but with a generous quantity of fish on hand, too.

When in Williamsburg, Washington found different fare: at a typical gentry house in that town (see "What's for Dinner?" page 73), roughly four-fifths of the animal protein consumed seems to have been from domesticated animals. But Charleston's was a coastal culture, with easy access to its surrounding rivers and the sea. From the docks came turtles, catfish, flounder (or flatfish), mullet, and shellfish, including oyster and crab.

Other local ingredients included wild game (in particular venison), wild turkey, geese, and a range of fowl, such as pigeons, herons, and doves. Domesticated animals were sources of beef, pork, and less often, lamb (sheep were poorly adapted to the hot climate). Another local product made its way to the table in a multitude of ways; native rice was used in many recipes, among them pilpy, a rice bread made from flour, cooked rice, water, and egg. Meat and fish stews, soups, and *pilaus* (pilafs) were common in the Low Country, too.

TOP AND ABOVE: *There were no built-ins or countertops in the eighteenth-century kitchen (top)—the cook had to make do with the hearth, a crude worktable, and a range of basic kitchen tools. The laundry facilities (above) were similaly rudimentary.*

RIGHT: *The kitchen quarter, seen at the rear, predates the house, having been constructed about 1740. The hip-roofed, brick structure encloses two stories, with a kitchen on the ground level and the five small rooms of the slave quarter above. Like the main house, this dependency had a period during which it was adapted to other uses (for a time, it was a poolroom). There was a well near the entrance; a dirt cellar beneath was used for storage.*

The Schuyler Mansion and Farm

Some would say the two were well matched. Rachel Faucette Lavien had been jailed for adultery and James Hamilton was a lifelong spendthrift. Although they remained together for fifteen years, they never married; as a result, two sons born to Rachel during those years were regarded by the law as "obscene children." Predictably, perhaps, James deserted his family—he may not have been the father of Alexander, the younger son—and less than two years later Rachel died of a "feverish disease," effectively orphaning the boys.

At age twelve, Alexander Hamilton became a penniless bastard, marooned in the West Indies with no prospects. Yet by the time he was twenty-five, Hamilton's fortunes would come full circle when he married the lovely and affectionate Elizabeth Schuyler, second daughter of Major General Philip Schuyler (pronounced *SKY-ler*).

Under the sponsorship of a friend, Hamilton had arrived in America in 1772 and studied finance at King's College (now Columbia University). He won respect and social status because of his service to General George Washington, whose trust earned Hamilton the role of chief of staff. In a happy accident of timing, that post had provided him the opportunity to woo Betsy when, during the

This tall clock descended in the Schuyler family. Nicknamed "grandfather clocks" in more recent times and called "long case clocks" in England, timepieces like this one were both functional and impressive (it stands almost nine feet tall and its works are brass). The clockmaker was Eliphalet Hull, though the case was probably made by Jeremiah Knowles; both were tradesmen in nearby Schenectady.

1779–80 winter in Morristown, New Jersey, she and an aunt arrived in the neighborhood of Washington's headquarters (see "The Ford Mansion," page 138).

As he prepared to take his vows at noon on December 14, 1780, Hamilton knew the wedding represented a redemption. Not only had he found a woman to love who was devoted to him, but the marriage represented a political and economic liaison with one of the wealthiest and most powerful men in New York. Further, the Schuylers were a warm, cultured, and welcoming family of the sort his childhood had utterly lacked.

According to Dutch custom, Alexander and Betsy took their vows not at a church altar but in the bride's home, standing in the sharp winter light of the southeast parlor of the Schuyler Mansion, one of Albany's most impressive houses. Witnessing the marriage of Hamilton and twenty-two-year-old Betsy were members of her family, including three living sisters, three brothers, and her mother, Catharine, who though age forty-six was seven months into her twelfth pregnancy.

Hamilton would wield vast political influence as the new nation's government evolved in the years after the Revolution. But that day in Albany, even the ambitious Mr. Hamilton must have sensed that he had reached an unexpected pinnacle in a life that so easily might have come to nothing. Instead, he was surrounded by his bride's extended family, a formidable array of uncles and aunts that included powerful descendants of the Livingston, Van Rensselaer, and other first families of the Hudson Valley. However, the groom had no family at hand with whom to share his first great triumph.

TOP: *A copy of the John Trumbull portrait of Schuyler's son-in-law Alexander Hamilton. Done in 1792, Trumbull's original portrays Hamilton as the nation's first secretary of the treasury.*

RIGHT: *The blue parlor at the Schuyler Mansion has grand Georgian details and generous proportions. It's just the sort of place to marry off one's daughter, as Philip Schuyler did on December 14, 1780.*

Participate afresh in the satisfaction I experience from the connection you have made with my beloved Hamilton. . . . I daily experience the pleasure of hearing encomiums on his virtue and abilities from those who are capable of distinguishing between real and pretended merit. He is considered, as he certainly is, the ornament of his country.

—*Philip Schuyler, writing to his daughter Mrs. Alexander Hamilton*

THE PERFECT WOMAN?

Though just twenty-five and given to frequent flirtations with young women he met, Alexander Hamilton chose his spouse carefully; his marriage to Betsy Schuyler was no hormonal accident. The calculating Hamilton established a checklist for what he wanted in a wife, which he confided to another of Washington's most trusted aides, Henry Laurens.

She must be young, handsome (I lay most stress upon a good shape), sensible (a little learning will do), well-bred . . . chaste and tender (I am an enthusiast in my notions of fidelity and fondness), of some good nature, a great deal of generosity (she must neither love money nor scolding, for I dislike equally a termagant and an economist). In politics, I am indifferent what side she may be of; I think I have arguments that will easily convert her to mine. . . .

As to fortune, the larger stock of that the better. You know my temper and circumstances and will therefore pay special attention to this article in this treaty. Though I run no risk of going to purgatory for my avarice, yet as money is an essential ingredient to happiness in this world—as I have not much of my own and as I am very little calculated to get more either by my address or industry—it must be needs that my wife, if I get one, bring at least a sufficiency to administer to her own extravagancies.

Hamilton considered carefully what he wanted—then went about getting it. Elizabeth Schuyler nicely fulfilled his requirements.

Elizabeth Schuyler Hamilton (1757–1854), painted by Ralph Earl in 1787.

LEFT: *The simpler yellow parlor was probably the place the family gathered, as distinct from the more formal blue parlor, where guests would be entertained.*

RIGHT: *On his trip to London in 1761, Philip Schuyler purchased the flock crimson wallpaper for the dining room, along with yellow, green, and blue papers that he used in a total of six other rooms. Flock papers are made by adhering fibers (silk or, as in this case, wool) to the surface to give the paper texture.*

GENERAL AND GENTLEMAN, PHILIP SCHUYLER

When the first Schuyler arrived in the Hudson Valley, in the midseventeenth century, his status was not that of a patroon, the name given to owners of huge tracts of land granted by the Dutch West India Company. Over the generations, the Schuylers gradually earned their membership in the Hudson River gentry, accumulating wealth by trading furs, grains, and timber. By the time Philip was born, in 1733, the Schuylers had become a part of the Dutch aristocracy.

Philip appears to have married Catharine Van Rensselaer for love. At the same time, their 1755 union consolidated the Schuylers' wealth and power, since Catharine brought to the match both her bloodlines (her father was a Van Rensselaer, her mother a Livingston) and an estate of 120,000 acres in a nearby county (Philip himself would eventually inherit tens of thousands of acres). During the early years of their marriage, Schuyler served in four campaigns of the French and Indian War, and if his military service proved unremarkable, it gained him vast experience as a quartermaster provisioning the British army. The young colonel managed the

finances and logistics of feeding and housing thousands of troops, skills he would hone upon his return to private life and, later, in the Continental Army.

An educated and cultured man, Philip Schuyler (1733–1804) spoke Dutch (most everyone in Albany did) as well as French, English, and the Mohawk Indian dialect. His success in business, as well as his powerful family connections, made possible his service in the New York Assembly in the years between the wars. There his increasing hostility to Parliament's interference with colonial affairs led to his appointment as one of New York's delegates to the Second Continental Congress.

In Philadelphia, Schuyler met George Washington. The men found they shared a great deal. They were the same height and nearly the same age (Washington had been born a year earlier), and both were veterans of the French and Indian War, patrician landowners and slave owners, and committed to the cause of independence. After Washington was named commander in chief that June, he chose four men as major generals, and one of them was Philip Schuyler. Schuyler's command of the Northern Department

The sunlit daybed and folding lap desk suggest a moment's peace within the larger setting of the upstairs yellow chamber.

Philip Schuyler in an oil-on-linen portrait painted from a John Trumbull miniature.

ABOVE: *When Philip Schuyler completed his mansion, in 1765, it stood virtually alone, a half mile south of the busy port town of Albany (population 4,000), on an eighty-acre parcel that climbed the hillside to where the mansion stands. With its vista of the Hudson River, the house itself was a showplace, but around it was a highly integrated agricultural property, with gardens for both pleasure (a formal parterre) and function (a kitchen and vegetable garden), along with fields, orchards, and a large Dutch barn.*

RIGHT: *The captured British general "Gentleman Johnny" Burgoyne called the green chamber a home during his stay as guest—and prisoner—at the Schuyler Mansion after the Battle of Saratoga.*

Boys Will Be Boys . . .

According to Schuyler family lore, General John Burgoyne, having surrendered his entire army to the enemy, was treated with great consideration at the Schuyler Mansion. Except, that is, for one small incident.

Nine-year-old Philip Schuyler, Jr., had been warned by his mother that he should say nothing that might offend the captured officers. After a time—and, undoubtedly, feeling ignored in all the commotion—the rather spoiled lad conceived a means of drawing attention to himself. Burgoyne and his officers were closed in a room when Philip burst in, proclaiming, "You're my father's prisoners! You're my father's prisoners!"

Burgoyne's response to the lad's taunt has not come down to us.

LEFT: *The tea set in the foreground is Chinese export porcelain; the cups, as was usual for the day, have no handles.*

RIGHT: *The Schuyler daughters are thought to have slept in this bedroom. Catharine Schuyler birthed fifteen children in twelve pregnancies; the cradle is a family heirloom.*

would last only two years; he was relieved of duty in August 1777, shouldering the blame when the outmanned Continental Army suffered defeats in Canada and on Lake Champlain. (The following year, a court-martial conducted at Schuyler's insistence acquitted him of any wrongdoing.)

Just two months after Schuyler's demotion, a crucial American victory at Saratoga led to the surrender of British General John Burgoyne's entire force of fifty-seven hundred troops. When the British soldiers marched out of their camp, carrying their muskets in accord with "the honors of war," Burgoyne and his staff were met not only by the victorious American general Horatio Gates but also by Major General Philip Schuyler (ret.). The scene is thick with irony: in the days before the battle, Burgoyne's troops had swept through the countryside, burning crops and buildings, including Schuyler's Saratoga farm, with its fine house and many outbuildings. Schuyler came to the ceremony not to seek revenge but to invite Burgoyne to enjoy the hospitality of his Albany home (military tradition called for gentlemanly treatment of defeated officers).

A sometime playwright married to an earl's daughter but notably fond of mistresses, "Gentleman Johnny" Burgoyne knew a social opportunity when he encountered one. He, General William Phillips, the Hessian commander Major General Friedrich von Riesdesel and his wife, Baroness Riesdesel, the Riesdesel children, and other officers were among about sixty people who traveled to Albany. Perhaps twenty of them enjoyed the comforts of Schuyler Mansion for some days, enjoying lavish meals and entertainments. Even the haughty Burgoyne had to acknowledge Schuyler's generosity. "Is it to me, who you have done so much injury that you show so much kindness!" His infallibly polite host is said to have responded, "That is the fate of war, let us say no more about it."

The last Britisher to leave Schuyler's home was Major John Acland, an officer on Burgoyne's staff who remained behind when his commanding officer departed for Boston. More than two months later, Acland and his pregnant wife, Lady Harriet, journeyed to New York in one of Schuyler's sleighs, their host having facilitated an exchange of prisoners that permitted the Aclands to return to England.

America's military fortunes were at low ebb. The British held Philadelphia *and* New York City, and their strategy to separate New England from the other colonies seemed to be working.

General John Burgoyne advanced along the Hudson River, having traveled south from Canada. His plan to capture Albany required two additional columns of troops, with one approaching along the Mohawk River from the west while the other was to move up the Hudson from New York. But the American general Benedict Arnold beat back the western force, and the force from the south never materialized, because Sir William Howe chose to pursue other military targets.

When Burgoyne's forces faced the Americans on September 19, 1777, the Continental Army held its ground until German reinforcements arrived to support the British troops. But a long afternoon's fighting ended with Burgoyne well short of his objective, the American camp a mile to the south. A waiting game ensued. Burgoyne hoped for reinforcements from Howe, but it was the American force that grew larger. By the time Burgoyne engaged the Americans again, on October 7, he was badly outnumbered. When darkness fell, the British withdrew, and surrounded by American forces that outnumbered them three to one, the British had little choice but to surrender.

The outcome at Saratoga represented more than a battle won to the Americans. The decisive victory demonstrated to the British, the French (who would soon join the war on the colonists' side), and even the American troops that they could defeat the much vaunted Royal British Army.

THE FARM AT SARATOGA

After the twin blows in 1777—his dismissal from the army and the destruction of his Saratoga property—Philip Schuyler confided to his friend John Jay that he was relieved to "be as far out of the noise and hustle of the great world as possible." And he went further: "I am confident . . . that I shall enjoy more true felicity in my retreat, than ever was experienced by any man engaged in public life. . . . My hobby-horse has long been a country life; I dismounted once with reluctance, and now saddle him again with a considerable share of satisfaction . . . and hope to canter him on to the end of the journey of life."

Less than two years later, Schuyler returned to public service. He negotiated with the Mohawk tribe on Washington's behalf; in 1779 he also began a second term of service as a New York delegate to the Continental Congress. At Washington's request (the two remained enduring friends) Schuyler helped integrate French reinforcements into the Continental Army in 1780. After the war, when the Articles of Confederation proved a wobbly means of governing, Schuyler worked with his son-in-law Alexander Hamilton to secure ratification in New York of the newly drafted Constitution; then he served twice as a U.S. senator from New York.

When Schuyler wrote to Jay of his "retreat," though, all that was well in the future. In the late autumn months of 1777, his focus was on his Saratoga property. The British army had burned his house, barns, four of five mills, the houses of his tenant farmers, and other structures. The gardens and fences were ruined, leaving nothing at the site of his once fine farm but—in an implied insult—a single necessary (outhouse). Schuyler resolved to start again. Using an upland sawmill that had escaped the torch, and employing American workers as well as some of Burgoyne's imprisoned men, Schuyler set to work. Within six weeks he was able to report that there stood "a comfortable house for reception of my family."

The mills, barns, and other buildings are gone, but once the Schuyler Farm was the center of a village inhabited by hundreds of workers and slaves. It was a huge working farm and more (Schuyler built the first water-powered flax mill in the province). Timber was sawn at the sawmill, the gristmill ground wheat. Herring was salted for winter consumption and sale. Schuyler also had a small navy of boats for shipping goods south to Albany.

This may have been their home away from home, but the Schuylers were accustomed to creature comforts and handsome surroundings. Their penchant for yellow is in evidence here, too. The yellow wallpaper, though a reproduction, is based on a surviving section of the original.

The new house was much plainer than its predecessor. The windows were small, the ceilings unfinished, and the exterior cladding unpainted weatherboards. It was, Schuyler reported, "only a frame house," making it a distinct departure from the mansion where he had entertained Burgoyne just weeks before some thirty miles downstream in Albany.

The house survives today much as Philip Schuyler knew it in his years there. He remained a frequent visitor to the Saratoga property even after 1787, when he renovated the house for his newlywed son, John Bradstreet Schuyler, and John's wife, Elizabeth Van Rensselaer. He wrote then to his eldest child, Angelica Schuyler Church, to tell her of John's marriage. He explained, "They reside at Saratoga, which I have put into good order, the house which I built there in 1777. . . . It is now a neat and very commodious box."

In 1787, the general wasn't quite ready to hand over all responsibilities to a son whose business sense was untested. The deed remained in Philip's name, and the repairs he made to the house that year included the addition of an office off the rear for himself. Management of the house reverted to Philip eight years later, when John Bradstreet Schuyler died at age thirty of a fever. Philip himself died in 1804, and his grandson and namesake, Philip Schuyler II, inherited the house with thirty-two hundred adjoining acres.

General Philip Schuyler played important roles as a politician, military man, and confidant of George Washington. Both his mansion in Albany and his farmhouse in Saratoga survive as valuable records of the styles, decorative arts, and mode of living of the Hudson Valley gentry in the revolutionary era (the appointments at Saratoga were less elaborate, since the finest furniture remained in Albany, but the Schuylers always lived with grace and ease).

Schuyler is remembered for his role in military affairs in the French and Indian War and, later, for impeding Burgoyne's progress to Saratoga, which contributed to the American victory at that battlefield. His friendship with the man who married Betsy Schuyler also adds to his historic luster. The two men became political confidants as Alexander Hamilton emerged as a national figure, a rise aided by an early but crucial boost in prestige and power gained from his association with General Philip Schuyler.

FACING PAGE: *This pleasing still life is in the Schuyler Farm dining room. The drop-leaf table is a family piece, made in New York, with ball-and-claw feet. The chocolate pot is Chinese export porcelain, the teapot of painted tin, and the tray over the table dates from about 1790. The wallpaper, with a wheat-sheaf motif, is a reproduction of a circa 1787 paper.*

TOP: *The upstairs bed chamber known as Mother's Room. The pencil-post bed was made nearby; the sampler on the mantel is English.*

ABOVE: *Even during his son John Bradstreet Schuyler's years at the farm, the general maintained an office here. The wheeled device pictured here is a waywiser, a surveyor's tool used to measure distances.*

The Silas Deane and Joseph Webb Houses

*The two houses sit side by side in Wethers-*field, a town overlooking a bend in the Connecticut River, forty miles north of Long Island Sound. On first glance, the proud buildings remind the viewer of the colonial past, a time much revered for its honest simplicity. Yet, like its most famous cash crop, the red onion, Wethersfield's quiet streetscapes can be deceiving. The innocent setting conveys nothing about the hidden layers, the stories of secret plots and military plans that helped change the course of the Revolution.

John Adams had visited Wethersfield on his way to Philadelphia to join the Continental Congress in 1774. He saw a port town, with a long history of trading with England and the West Indies, from which ships sailed with their holds filled with grains and other local agricultural products; they returned with cherished salt, molasses, rum, and tea, as well as luxury products from England, such as books, fabrics, ceramics, and glass. Both the prosperity of the town and its setting impressed the visitor. After ascending the steeple of Wethersfield's meeting house, Adams proclaimed the view "the most grand and beautiful prospect in the World, at least that I ever saw."

On that August sojourn, Adams reported being "most cordially and genteely entertained with Punch Wine and coffee." But that cozy description of his time at the home of Silas Deane,

If the cliché fits . . . yes, George Washington slept here.

RIGHT: *The doorway of the Deane House is an expression of its builder's skills and its owner's desire to send a message about his means. The inspiration is certainly classical—note the pilasters supporting the entablature—but the execution owes more to the tools and available material (that is, wood) than to ancient Roman monuments built of stone. The moldings, fluted pilasters, and modillion blocks all add detail and shadows, making a statement on an otherwise simple façade.*

MIDDLE ROW: *The Webb House (left) has a gambrel roof (note the double pitch of the roofline; the steep roof encloses a tall attic). The floor plan is Georgian, consisting of a center hall and stairway, with four rooms downstairs and four bed chambers above. Samuel Deane's house (right) presents an interesting contrast, with its unusual plan. The location of the entrance to one side means the floor plan is asymmetrical, with a tall stairway in the front, right quadrant.*

ABOVE: *Deane's parlor, featuring portraits of himself and his second wife, Elizabeth Saltonstall, as well as a carved brownstone mantel.*

a Connecticut delegate to the Continental Congress, also proved somewhat misleading. Deane was destined to become America's first secret agent abroad and the focus of a controversy that destroyed his reputation.

The house next to "Brother Deane's" would have revolutionary connections, too; Samuel B. Webb, son of its builder, fought at the Battles of Bunker Hill and Trenton, and became an aide-de-camp to General Washington. By happenstance, Washington himself would spend some days at the Webb House, in the spring of 1781, meeting French military officers to plan the final phase of the Revolutionary War.

Today the Webb and Deane Houses contain handsome collections of eighteenth-century objects and anchor Connecticut's largest historic district. In interpreting these sites, the caretakers seek to convey a mix of eighteenth-century comfort and a sense that, when we look back in time, not all we see is quite as it seems.

AMERICA'S FIRST SECRET AGENT

The Revolution produced its share of enduring heroes; one need go no further than the nearest cash register to encounter honored images of Washington, Jefferson, Hamilton, and Franklin. But the names of some Founding Fathers come down to us somewhat tarnished. One of those was Silas Deane (1737–1789).

His story has the mathematical symmetry of a bell curve. The son of a farmer in Groton, Connecticut, Deane parlayed an education (at Yale) and his law studies (he was admitted to the bar in 1761) into a more refined station in Wethersfield, where he opened a law office in 1762. Consulted by Mehitabel Webb concerning her late husband's merchant business, Deane soon wedded the well-to-do widow. After Mehitabel's death, he married Elizabeth Saltonstall, the granddaughter of a former governor. At age thirty, Deane could boast of substantial wealth, social status, and a fine house. A few years later, the Connecticut Committee on Correspondence appointed Silas Deane one of their three representatives in Philadelphia.

After serving in the Continental Congress during 1774 and 1775, Deane wasn't reappointed for 1776. The reasons for his dis-

missal remain obscure, but his congressional peers did assign him a new task. In March 1776, he was appointed by Benjamin Franklin and Congress's Committee on Secret Correspondence to travel to France "to transact such Business, commercial and political, as we have committed to his care." In translation: he was to behave as a merchant, purchasing "goods for the Indian trade," but undertake a covert mission to solicit money and military assistance from France ("the supply at present that we want is clothing and arms for twenty five thousand men with a suitable quantity of ammunition, and one hundred field pieces").

By most standards, Deane's mission would appear to have been a success. Aided by the playwright and adventurer Pierre de Beaumarchais and under cover of a shell corporation, Deane arranged for the shipment of eight shiploads of military supplies to America; the matériel arrived in time to be of inestimable value in the Battle of Saratoga. In seeking experienced military men, he met with the Marquis de Lafayette, commissioned him a major general, and enlisted other foreign officers (some of whom would prove more useful than others). Joined in France by Franklin and the Virginian Arthur Lee (see "The Lees' Stratford," page 92), Deane became a signatory to the Treaty of Alliance and the Treaty of Amity, both signed with France in February 1778. These essential documents recognized the independence of the United States.

The precipitous decline in Deane's fortunes soon followed. Recalled to Philadelphia, he learned that Arthur Lee had accused him of misusing funds. Even today the story is difficult to unravel. On the one hand, the unimpeachable John Adams thought Deane somewhat wasteful (as his successor in France, Adams reported that Deane had lived in "such Splendor that I fear there will be Altercation in America about him"). Deane, it appears, had also lined his pockets in an insurance scheme. On the other hand, Arthur Lee had been angered that Deane had taken advantage of some business opportunities that Lee himself had coveted. Much later—in 1842, after intense lobbying by a Deane granddaughter—Congress voted thirty-seven thousand dollars in restitution to his heirs and described Lee's audit of Deane's accounts "a gross injustice." Benjamin Franklin never seems to have doubted Deane's patriotic intentions.

Whatever the truth of the matter, Deane's reputation proved beyond repair, at least in his lifetime. When private correspondence in his hand, in which he advocated reconciliation with England, was published in 1781, his critics branded him a traitor as well as a profiteer. During a decade-long exile in Europe, he attempted to rehabilitate his good name. Finally, in 1789, he booked passage to Boston in order to make his case in person. He died on board the ship after experiencing intense abdominal pains and dizziness. The cause of death—like much else about Deane's final years—remains in dispute, with various theories holding that he was poisoned by an American double agent, that he died of an overdose of laudanum, or that he committed suicide.

Compelled to work in the shadows as a secret agent, Deane remains the subject of speculation among historians, as do his motives. In a way, that makes him all the more interesting: the ambiguities that surround the life and death of the Connecticut Yankee Silas Deane contrast with the usual hagiographic view of the Founding Fathers.

This portrait of Deane was painted at about the time his house was completed. The poised young man seems confident of his imminent rise.

A MILITARY MEETING

General Washington understood, of course, that France's military support could be decisive in the Revolutionary War. But coordinating the ships and ground troops of America's most important ally was proving difficult. True, some six thousand French troops had landed at Rhode Island the previous year, but the promised fleet of French ships still sat in a harbor in the West Indies. When the slightly exasperated Washington received an invitation to meet the French commander, Jean-Baptiste-Donatien de Vimeur (the Comte de Rochambeau), he hoped a breakthrough was at hand.

A meeting at the midpoint meant Wethersfield. Washington and his officers traveled from their headquarters in the Hudson Valley, the French from Newport. On May 20, 1781, Washington and Major General Henry Knox met with a salute of thirteen guns and found accommodations at the Webb House. The French officers, Rochambeau and the Marquis de Chastellux, arrived a day later, taking Stillman's Tavern as their quarters.

Washington had visited Wethersfield on his 1775 trip to Boston to assume command of the Continental Army (see "The Vassall-Craigie-Longfellow House," page 82), but the 1781 visit was no mere stopover; as General Knox observed, they journeyed here "upon matters of great consequence." The American troops in the northern colonies had just suffered through another difficult winter, and Knox reported that powder was so low his troops would be unable to fire their cannons. Recognizing how desperate the situation was, Washington had dispatched Knox a few weeks earlier to call on the governors of his native New England, seeking money and supplies. The army's condition in the South was no better, leaving General Nathanael Greene unable to make a stand against British forces. Instead he harassed the Redcoats' flanks.

Time had also become the Americans' enemy. Washington feared the Continental Army might simply cease to exist without a decisive victory; making matters worse, at that moment, the British held Charleston, Savannah, and New York. Washington determined to take back one of those key cities—and New York was his choice. The enemy had held the city since October 1776, but the British garrison there had been rendered more vulnerable by the departure of many British troops for the Southern theater.

For students of American decorative arts, the bed chamber Washington slept in is even more memorable for the surface of its walls. A rare eighteenth-century survivor, the wallpaper is a red wool flock with a leafy Rococo print. To judge from Webb family account books, the paper was hung to coincide with the general's arrival.

Washington described his plan when the combined staffs met on May 22. The Marquis de Chastellux had to translate for Rochambeau (the latter had arrived in America speaking no English), but language proved no barrier. As Washington confided in his May 22 diary entry, he "[f]ixed with Count de Rochambeau upon a plan of Campaign." The count departed the next day for Newport to prepare his troops for a joint French-American assault on New York, to be supported from the sea by French ships. Washington remained another day in Wethersfield, dispatching several letters pleading for more American troops and supplies in support of the plan. Then he, too, departed.

THE BATTLE OF YORKTOWN

George Washington won his big victory in 1781—only it wasn't in New York, as he had wished.

First Washington learned that Lafayette's small force in Virginia was badly outmanned; then word reached him, on August 14, that the long-awaited French fleet had set sail not for New York but for Chesapeake Bay. For just two months, twenty-nine warships and more than three thousand French troops would be at his disposal in the mid-Atlantic. Immediately the plans were revised: American and French forces would concentrate in Virginia, where British General Cornwallis had assumed a defensive position at Yorktown.

Washington, with some sixty-five hundred French and American troops, marched from New York. Meanwhile, Lafayette positioned his men south of Yorktown to prevent a British retreat. The subsequent arrival of the French fleet off the coast of Virginia ended Cornwallis's hopes for reinforcements by sea.

By the end of September, the British were surrounded, and American bombardments forced the Redcoats to cede territory around the town and gradually withdraw into Yorktown. On October 19, after a three-week siege, his army outnumbered and low on food, Cornwallis surrendered.

With the Battle of Yorktown, major hostilities ended. But no one recognized then the significance of the Virginia victory. It would not be until late 1782 that the British evacuated Charleston and a year later that Washington marched into New York, watching the last of the British troops and Loyalists sail for England. The Treaty of Paris—signed on September 3, 1783—affirmed American independence.

TOP: *A slave or servant might well have lived in the unheated attic, sharing the space with out-of-season equipment—woodstoves, fire screens, and andirons—as well as trunks full of clothes and bed hangings. Looms and spinning wheels often resided in attics, as did the beds and toys the children had outgrown. Strings of herbs were often suspended from the rafters to dry, along with fruit, such as peaches and apples.*

ABOVE: *The servants' room over the kitchen at the Silas Deane House is outfitted as a work and living space where spinning, weaving, and sewing were done.*

The equipment in the Deane kitchen includes a large fireplace and bake oven (left of hearth) and a stone sink (right). Various jugs, jars, and foodstuffs on the table suggest that dinner is in preparation. The white cone on the table is a rock-hard loaf of sugar.

TWO NEW ENGLAND SLAVES

Members of the New England gentry owned slaves. While the day-to-day existence of the lowest caste in any culture is difficult to reconstruct, a glimpse into the life histories of two of Wethersfield's enslaved can be gained at the Deane and Webb Houses.

At the Deane House, the chamber over the kitchen is interpreted today as Hagar Dorus's room. Part Pequot Indian and part African-American, Dorus arrived in town with Deane's second wife, Elizabeth Saltonstall. Her mistress was sickly (she suffered from "the asthma"), and Hagar tended to her personal needs. Hagar survived both Mr. and Mrs. Deane; her name appeared on the inventory of his goods after his death, in 1789.

Born in 1740, Cloe Prut came to Wethersfield as a young woman but gained her freedom when her owner's will was probated, in 1777. Her owner specified Cloe was to be given "the bed that she lyeth on," along with a loom, a "porige pot," a chest, two chairs, a trunk, a table, a few books, and her mistress's "everyday wearing apparel & a red short cloak and two spoons *and the remainder of my estate.*"

Cloe had the means to make a living ("the loom that she weaveth on"). After her friend Hagar Dorus was emancipated (the circumstances are uncertain), the two women purchased a dwelling house in town for twenty-five pounds. Cloe died in 1810, but Hagar lived on at least another twenty years in that house.

As students of the Revolutionary War know, the agreed-upon strategy did not unfold as planned; the military focus shifted south (see "The Battle of Yorktown," page 174). Yet the meetings at Wethersfield provided the foundation for an effective working relationship between Washington and Rochambeau. As the American commander later confided in Lafayette, "It may, I believe, with much truth be said that a greater harmony between two armies never subsisted."

The paneled wall in the Webb House parlor (below) features a fine shell cupboard, intended both to store and to display the china and other goods the merchant family owned. The Connecticut-made mahogany secretary (left) also incorporates a carved shell, a common eighteenth-century motif.

Turkey Day, 1779

Thanksgiving has not always been a national holiday; it was a regional New England tradition until Abraham Lincoln proclaimed it a national holiday in 1863. One richly detailed account survives of Thanksgiving 1779. Written by a Connecticut girl named Juliana Smith, it describes the day for the benefit of her absent cousin, Betsy.

The Venue. "This year it was Uncle Simeon's turn to have the dinner at his house," Juliana reported. The day began with meeting, but the letter writer's father, Parson Smith, kept the service shorter than usual because the day (and the church) was bitterly cold. When the family reached Uncle Simeon's house afterward, the fire in "Uncle's Dining Hall" seemed particularly welcoming. The fireplace was enormous—it could accommodate logs eight feet long—and warmed the large room (some thirty by twenty-two feet). The fire was so hot that those seated in front of the fireplace resorted to fire screens behind their chairs.

The Guests. The crowd numbered more than thirty, not counting the servants, so two tables were set. Both of Juliana's grandmothers attended; she reported that the two balanced each other out (Grandmother Smith, the girl thought, was "a little desponding of spirit," but Grandmother Worthington "always sees the bright side"). The two old widows sat side by side ("handsomer than ever, & happy they were to look around upon so many of their descendants"). Juliana's uncle and aunt presided at one table, at the other Parson and Mrs. Smith. Some twenty members of Juliana's generation were on hand. The Smiths alone accounted for twelve, with Juliana, her four siblings, plus seven orphans the family had taken in. The other guests included "four Old Ladies who have no longer Homes or Children of their own," two cousins, a couple of students, and six members of a new family from next door. The newcomers, the Livingstons, came from New York and "had never seen a Thanksgiving Dinner before."

The Menu. Much of the cooking had been done in advance, with the pies and cakes prepared at Juliana's home. "We had the big oven heated & filled twice each day for three days," she told Betsy. The cooks had to adapt their recipes—this *was,* after all, wartime, and no raisins were to be had—but Uncle Simeon had some spices, so there were mince pies. Simeon's West Indian preserved ginger also made possible a tasty "Suet Pudding," thick with "Plumbs and Cherries." Although no roast beef was on offer ("it all must go to the army"), the meal included venison, pork, turkey, goose, and "two pig Pigeon Pasties" (pigeon pies). Lots of vegetables were served, too, including an unfamiliar one called "Sellery" that Uncle Simeon had cultivated using seed ordered from England.

The Entertainment. Uncle Simeon, an Edinburgh-trained physician, regaled the crowd with "droll stories." Hymns and ballads were sung by the men, and Parson Smith led a prayer for "Absent Friends." After the table was cleared—by then it was dark—the grandmothers told tales of early New England. "My Father says it is a goodly custom to hand down all worthy deeds and traditions from Father to Son," Juliana told Betsy, "because the Word that is spoken is remembered longer than the one that is written."

PART THREE

The Federal Era

1787

On May 25, the Constitutional Convention opens in Philadelphia; on September 17, the convention approves a draft of the Constitution.

October 27, the first issue of *The Federalist* appears. The collaboration among John Jay, James Madison, and Alexander Hamilton helps sway public opinion in favor of ratifying the Constitution.

1788

Between January and August, eleven states ratify the Constitution; North Carolina (1789) and Rhode Island (1790) eventually do the same.

1789

On March 4, the first U.S. Congress convenes.

On April 14, a letter from the Senate president pro tempore, John Langdon of New Hampshire, informs George Washington that he has been unanimously elected president of the United States; on April 30 in New York, Washington is inaugurated as the first president

In 1789, George Wythe becomes professor of law at the College of William and Mary, the first man to hold such a post in America.

1790

James Iredell of North Carolina and John Rutledge of South Carolina are appointed associate justices by President Washington to serve with Chief Justice John Jay on the nation's first Supreme Court.

1791

On April 7, President Washington embarks on a three-month journey to North Carolina, South Carolina, and Georgia, covering a total of 1,887 miles. Among his favorite stops is Charleston, where he stays at the home of Thomas Heyward, Jr.

On December 15, the first ten amendments to the Constitution (the Bill of Rights) are adopted by Congress.

1792

George Mason of Virginia, a powerful intellectual force in the Continental Congress and at the Constitutional Convention, dies on October 7.

1796

The first contested presidential election ends with John Adams and Thomas Jefferson elected president and vice president, respectively.

1799

George Washington, retired general and president, dies at Mount Vernon on December 14 at age sixty-seven.

Led by John Marshall, the Supreme Court asserts in *Marbury v. Madison* the principle of judicial review, enabling the Court to declare a statute unconstitutional.

The United States purchases the Louisiana Territory from France.

Congress bans the importation of slaves to the United States.

James Madison is elected the fourth president of the United States; in 1812, he will be reelected.

Word not having reached the warring armies, the Battle of New Orleans is fought. The Americans prevail on January 8, and the victory establishes Andrew Jackson as a national hero.

John Quincy Adams, son of John Adams, is elected president.

In August the Marquis de Lafayette, along with his son George Washington Lafayette, returns to America for what will be a thirteen-month victory tour to each of the twenty-four states.

1801 1803 1804 1808 1814 1815 1816 1824 1826

Nominated by the outgoing president, John Adams, John Marshall becomes chief justice of the United States.

Thomas Jefferson is inaugurated the nation's third president on March 4.

Aaron Burr kills Alexander Hamilton in a duel at Weehawken, New Jersey.

Thomas Jefferson is reelected president.

On December 24, the Treaty of Ghent is signed, ending the War of 1812.

James Monroe is elected to the first of two terms as president.

On July 4, fifty years to the day after they presented the Declaration of Independence to the Continental Congress, John Adams and Thomas Jefferson die peacefully in their beds.

The Matthias Hammond House

News had belatedly reached American shores that the Treaty of Paris was signed on September 3, 1783. With the war officially over, Thomas Jefferson traveled to Annapolis for a session of the Continental Congress. That winter the new nation's legislative body ratified the peace treaty and, with many toasts and tears, honored General Washington as he resigned his commission. Otherwise the divided body accomplished little, which meant Jefferson, despite his service on virtually every congressional committee, found time to walk the streets of pretty Annapolis town. On one of his walkabouts, Jefferson encountered the Hammond House.

The mansion overlooked North East Street. The neighborhood was the newest and perhaps the town's most fashionable, featuring several imposing colonial mansions, including one that had belonged to Samuel Chase (see "The Chase-Lloyd House," page 185) and another owned by William Paca (see page 36). Both of those men had affixed their signatures to Jefferson's Declaration at the Continental Congress of 1776, but neither of their houses enchanted him as did Matthias Hammond's.

Just two years before, Jefferson had written of American architecture that "the first principles of the art are unknown, and there exists scarcely a model among us sufficiently chaste to give an idea of them." He set himself the task of changing that and, perhaps

Teatime in the large parlor at Matthias Hammond's house.

LEFT: *Seen from the rear, the garden façade of the Hammond House stretches 131 feet. The house contains twenty-one rooms, and researchers believe about a dozen slaves were required to prepare the food, wash the clothes, manage the fires, keep the gardens, and otherwise tend to the needs of the white inhabitants.*

RIGHT: *The renowned street entrance to the house—it has often been termed the most beautiful in America—has a triangular pediment atop a boldly carved entablature; below is a fanlight flanked with spandrels of carved fruits and flowers. Such bold carving was characteristic of William Buckland, the builder-designer.*

more than any other individual, would help establish a new standard for American design over the next several decades. As he asked rhetorically of his friend James Madison, "How is a taste in this beautiful art to be formed in our countrymen, unless we avail ourselves of every occasion when public buildings are to be erected, of presenting to them models for their study and imitation?" Jefferson himself produced such models in giving the Virginia State Capitol the form of a Roman temple and planning the University of Virginia in an idiom that we now call Jeffersonian Classical. Further, as the nation's first secretary of state and third president, he would nurture in the new Federal City of Washington, D.C., the movement that gave American civic architecture the recognizable form that survives to the present day, with its columns, cornices, and domes.

Back in 1783 Annapolis, the forty-year-old Jefferson looked with wonder upon a house the likes of which he had never seen. He recognized immediately that a building of such quality represented an advance in American design. Its size alone was remarkable, with the scale of a grand country estate despite its in-town setting. But Jefferson was struck most by its architectural sophistication.

As he gazed at the Hammond House, he reached for the notebook he always carried and began sketching. Some elements, such as the overall scheme of the Maryland five-part plan which resembled the Paca House around the corner, were familiar. Jefferson conjectured that the builder of this house owned a copy of one of his own favorite architectural volumes, Robert Morris's *Select Architecture,* published in England in 1755.

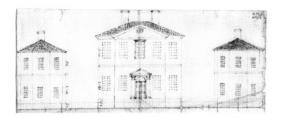

This drawing was the work of Thomas Jefferson, who transformed the freehand sketch he'd made in his pocket notebook into a more formal architectural rendering of the front elevation of Hammond's great in-town mansion.

Overlooking the roof of the kitchen pavilion is a tall window that lights the stairway.

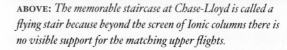

ABOVE: *The memorable staircase at Chase-Lloyd is called a flying stair because beyond the screen of Ionic columns there is no visible support for the matching upper flights.*

RIGHT: *Samuel Chase, Signer: The man who began construction on what we know today as the Chase-Lloyd House (top, right), Samuel was also a cousin of the Judge Chase who later purchased the Matthias Hammond House, across the street.*

THE CHASE-LLOYD HOUSE

The lawyer and Patriot Samuel Chase (1741–1811) began construction of this grand house in 1769, before going on to be one of Maryland's four Signers and later a member of the Supreme Court. When the costs of his architectural dream exceeded the limits of his pocketbook, he was forced to sell the unfinished brick shell to Edward Lloyd IV (1767–1825), who completed it.

A tobacco planter quite unembarrassed about his wealth, Lloyd liked to distinguish himself from his paternal ancestors with the sobriquet Edward the Magnificent (he also liked to travel to his plantation home, Wye House in Talbot County, Maryland, on a barge rowed by slaves in livery). Upon taking title to Chase's half-finished house, Lloyd set about completing it to his own high standards.

Little is known of the undertaker (builder) Chase commissioned, but the man he chose to finish the house was William Buckland, who would later design the Matthias Hammond House. Buckland had worked for Elizabeth Tayloe Lloyd's father, Colonel John Tayloe of Mount Airy in Virginia, and he completed the house for Tayloe's son-in-law in the high style the showy Lloyd desired.

A glance at the main hall alone must have pleased the client: it is forty feet deep, with a divided, cantilevered staircase that soars upward at its far end, and has a grandly carved Palladian window on the landing.

In 1886, when the will of Hester Chase Ridout, a Chase descendant, established it as a home for elderly women, the house became the Chase Home. Although the upper two floors were adapted as residential suites, the exterior and the ground-floor public spaces remain much as they did when Mr. Buckland and his carvers and joiners moved across the street to begin work on Mr. Hammond's home.

The study. The gentleman's desk was made in Annapolis, by the cabinetmaker John Shaw. Notice the folio open on the table—it is the British architect James Gibbs's Book of Architecture *(1728), from which a number of the architectural details in the house were derived.*

Jefferson drew an elevation of the house's façade, locating the chimneys, low-pitched roofs, and large windows. But his focus became the decorative elements at the center of the house, specifically the richly carved front entrance, which would later often be called the most beautiful doorway in America. Although Mr. Jefferson's drawing survives as an important document, he is not at the fulcrum of this chapter. Two other men made the house that impressed him: Matthias Hammond himself and a carver-joiner-architect named William Buckland.

MR. HAMMOND'S HEARTBREAK

In 1773, Matthias Hammond, age twenty-five, was already acquainted with the rich and powerful of his colony. Hammond had substantial wealth from his family's tobacco plantations and, having trained as a lawyer, established a law practice in prosperous Annapolis. It was a city whose literary clubs, theater, balls, and card parties offered ample social opportunity for a worldly and eligible young bachelor such as Hammond. The intoxicating political ferment of the time affected him, too, and he served on both the Maryland Committee of Correspondence and the Committee of Safety, and as quartermaster of his local militia.

Having decided to build himself a permanent home in Annapolis, Hammond acquired a four-acre site in the town. He commissioned the best man available to design and build his house—the story of William Buckland follows—and construction was undertaken the following year. The end result would be the edifice Jefferson admired, although Hammond himself resigned his offices the year it was completed (1776) and left the town, retiring to his plantation in Anne Arundel County.

The facts end there, and the conjecture begins. According to the most likely explanation (or at least the most repeated), Hammond departed because of a failure in his love life. According to an account written almost 150 years later, "The house was designed as a wedding gift . . . from Matthias Hammond to his intended bride. He had even ordered all the furnishings with punctilious care, and the wedding day was set, when the lady declared that he paid more attention to his new house than he did to her."

LEFT: *In an upstairs bed chamber hangs a picture of a girl named Ann Proctor; remarkably, the very doll pictured rests on a nearby chair. The painting is a work of Charles Willson Peale, who completed it in 1789.*

RIGHT: *In this detail from an 1858 engraving, two of the great houses of prerevolutionary Annapolis are identifiable. At the top, right, in the parklike forest at the center of the image, is the Hammond-Harwood House. The William Paca House (see page 36), at left, center, also overlooks the undeveloped acres of what once was a fine landscape garden.*

IMAGINING MOTHER HAMMOND

Matthias Hammond and his fiancée never became man and wife. But let's suppose they had. What would Mrs. Hammond's life have been like?

On the basis of surviving diaries, census data, church records, and countless other documents, a what-if scenario can be composed that lays out what a well-to-do bride such as Hammond's almost-wife might have expected.

Let's call her Polly. On her wedding she is perhaps twenty years old (in the eighteenth century, the typical American woman married between the ages of nineteen and twenty-three). After taking her vows, Polly moves into the just completed mansion her husband has built for her. Within the year she is with child. For much of her pregnancy,

she continues to perform her myriad duties around the house. As delivery approaches, a younger, unmarried sister comes to help Polly ready for the arrival.

The child is born with the assistance of a midwife. A period of lying-in follows, and for a month after the birth, Polly avoids all strenuous activity (her husband's wealth affords her that luxury). She remains at home, welcoming only a few visitors. Even when she emerges from her confinement, she does not resume some of her more laborious duties but turns over chores to servants and slaves (the staff at Hammond House numbers twelve). She and a nurse care for the child.

Polly will nurse this and subsequent babies herself (even among the gentry, mothers in colonial America were expected to nurse, but hiring a

wet nurse was a common practice in England and Europe). Polly nurses each child between ten and eighteen months. In at least one instance, a baby is weaned when another pregnancy intervenes.

Being a bit younger than her husband, Polly will become pregnant nine more times, resulting in a total of seven live births. Bearing a child every two or three years seems entirely normal to the Hammonds; it is the pattern they observe among their friends, family, and neighbors. Five of Matthias and Polly's progeny live to adulthood; of the others, two are stillborn, one dies in infancy, another as an adolescent, and a tenth pregnancy ends in a miscarriage. Even after their christenings, Matthias and Polly Hammond rarely call their children by name. Each remains anonymous until his or her

behaviors and responses reveal an unmistakably individual temperament.

At about the time Matthias and Polly welcome their last child, they become proud grandparents; their firstborn is now a parent, so their younger children and the first grandchildren become playmates.

Polly proves to be a fortunate lady: almost half of her husband's friends have lost their wives, though most have married again and begun producing more children with their second wives. Even when Polly reaches menopause and her childbearing ceases, her parenting skills remain on call, since her younger children and the influx of grandchildren keep her home buzzing.

Responsibilities for her household and her children would have filled our imaginary Polly's life.

Whereas Mother Hammond is imagined, three generations of Thomas Jefferson's family were well documented.

❧ Jefferson himself was one of ten children. He and five siblings lived to adulthood; three others died in infancy and one at age fifteen.

❧ After his marriage to Martha Wayles Skelton Jefferson, she birthed five children. A son and a daughter died in infancy, another girl child died as a toddler, and two daughters lived to adulthood. Before marrying Jefferson, the Widow Skelton had lost a son from her first marriage.

❧ When her turn came to marry, Thomas and Martha Jefferson's daughter Mary Jefferson Eppes had three children. One died an infant and one as a toddler, while the third lived to age eighty. Mary herself died at age twenty-five. Her sister, Martha Jefferson Randolph, proved hardier, delivering twelve children, a remarkable eleven of whom lived to adulthood. She herself survived to age sixty-four.

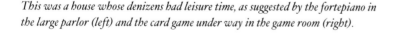

This was a house whose denizens had leisure time, as suggested by the fortepiano in the large parlor (left) and the card game under way in the game room (right).

She left, he left, and the house stood abandoned—a true story? No evidence survives to prove the lost-love tale but for whatever reason, Matthias Hammond (1748–1786) never occupied his fine brick residence in Annapolis.

WILLIAM BUCKLAND, ARCHITECT

Like Matthias Hammond's, the life of William Buckland has its little mysteries. Unlike most artisans of his time, this tradesman turned architect is survived by an unusual array of personal documents, buildings, and even a portrait.

Born in Oxford and trained in London, Buckland came to America as an indentured servant at age twenty-one. Along with many other tradesmen and laborers who wished to come to colonial America, he signed a contract that guaranteed him an annual wage for a fixed period (in his case, 20 pounds per year for four years). In return, his passage to America was paid for, and he received room and board for the duration of his indenture.

Buckland, trained as a joiner and carpenter, traveled to "Virginia beyond the seas" in the autumn of 1755. He brought with him a working knowledge of contemporary London tastes, as well as a substantial library of architectural books. He completed his four-year obligation, filling George Mason's fine new house with extravagant carving (see "George Mason's Gunston Hall," page 218). Upon gaining his freedom, Buckland found work with other members of the Virginia gentry. He took on apprentices and a partner, bought slaves, and established a workshop. His reputation soon reached beyond Virginia, and in September 1771 he was invited to Annapolis to finish and decorate a mansion (see "The Chase-Lloyd House," page 185). Buckland saw Annapolis as an opportunity; houses were rising there, and the town's gentlemen wanted the kind of elaborate and showy dwellings Buckland soon demonstrated he could build better than anyone in America. In the spring of 1772, he relocated his shop and family to the Maryland capital.

Buckland proved to be more than an average craftsman—and he saw himself in grander terms, too. Not content to build houses, he wanted to be able to style himself William Buckland, Architect; he imagined a design in his mind, rendered it as paper plans, then

The large parlor on the second floor is a grand space, suited to entertaining and dancing. But notice the architectural finish: Unlike the grand and bold cornice and fireplace decorations in the dining room the woodwork in this room has the lighter character of the Neoclassical taste that came with the Federal period.

executed it in bricks, mortar, timber, plaster, and boards. Mr. Hammond gave him that chance. Fine hardware was ordered from England, and at least a half dozen craftsmen went to work on the house: a carver, a painter, a carpenter, a stonemason, and two bricklayers.

Buckland would not live to see the Hammond House completed. In November 1774, he was hard at work not only on Hammond's house but on plans for a new courthouse in a nearby county; by December he was dead, at forty. The cause and circumstances of his end are unknown, and completing the Hammond House was left to his onetime apprentice and longtime partner, John Randall.

Today the massive brick villa on what is now called Maryland Avenue is universally known as the Hammond-Harwood House. After Matthias Hammond's departure from Annapolis, the north wing was rented as an office. The property passed through various hands before being purchased in 1811 by Judge Jeremiah Townley Chase. Chase left his house in trust for his descendants, one of whom married a man named William Harwood. In a quirky crisscrossing of fate, Harwood proved to be William Buckland's great-grandson. When Mr. and Mrs. William Harwood took up residence, they brought with them a family heirloom, the Charles Willson Peale portrait of Buckland.

The Harwoods' spinster daughter, Hester Ann, would be the last private resident of the house. After her death, in 1924, the house went into the public domain, and since 1940 it has been the property of the Hammond-Harwood House Association, which operates it as a museum displaying a collection of Annapolis furniture and a number of paintings by the town's own Charles Willson Peale. The house that Buckland built, remarkably intact, signifies the birth of capital-*A* Architecture (as distinct from vernacular building) in America.

One appealing contrivance in the house is the "jib door" that leads from the dining room to the garden behind. On the outside, it appears to be a door, while inside, when closed, it matches the other windows that line the wall and thereby maintains the symmetry of the room.

"Oh, Say Can You See . . . ?"

In 1802, one of Elizabeth and Edward Lloyd's six daughters, Mary Tayloe Lloyd, married Francis Scott Key, an Annapolis lawyer. A dozen years later, he witnessed the twenty-five-hour bombardment of Baltimore and Fort McHenry during the War of 1812. The sight "by the dawn's early light" of the fort's giant flag—it was forty-two feet wide and thirty high—inspired the amateur poet to compose new lyrics for a familiar tune.

Key gave it the rather unimaginative title "The Defence of Fort McHenry." His lines were soon published in the Baltimore *Patriot,* and the song got its more familiar title in 1814 at a public performance in Baltimore. "The Star-Spangled Banner" was adopted as the national anthem in 1931.

The dining room was one of two important entertaining spaces in the house. Today it reflects William Buckland as well as Matthias Hammond: The Annapolis-made sideboard belonged to Buckland descendants, several of whom are portrayed in the Charles Willson Peale portraits on the wall above.

This 1947 copy of Charles Willson Peale's William Buckland, *painted by Mrs. Douglas Gordon, hangs at the Hammond-Harwood House today. Buckland designed the mansion and two generations of his descendants inhabited it in the nineteenth and early twentieth centuries.*

PORTRAIT OF A CRAFTSMAN

Another man of modest origins who made good in Annapolis was Charles Willson Peale, perhaps the most important recorder of the revolutionary generation (see "Peale's Portrait of Paca," page 39). One of the likenesses he painted was of his friend William Buckland.

The portrait remained unfinished at the time of Buckland's unexpected death, with a field of blank canvas surrounding a disembodied head and the architect's hand, the fingers grasping his *porte-crayon,* the pencil of the day. Peale soon packed up his studio and moved to Philadelphia, where thirteen years after beginning the portrait, he put the canvas back on his easel. He added a variety of symbolic elements, including a classical portico, architectural books, and drawing instruments. Most important, he incorporated a large drawing recognizable as an architectural rendering of the Matthias Hammond House.

Having completed the portrait, Peale delivered it on a 1787 journey to Annapolis, where his diary records he sold it for 10 pounds to John Callahan. The buyer's wife, Sally Callahan, née Buckland, was the architect's daughter. The painting—regarded by scholars as among Peale's most penetrating and likable—portrays a man of gentlemanly aspirations who, to judge from his expression of wry detachment, seems pleased indeed with his new station.

The Homes of Governor John Langdon and William Whipple

Settled in 1630 at the mouth of Piscataqua

River, Portsmouth emerged in the eighteenth century as one of the nation's most prosperous cities. Its ships often carried the state's most valuable export, "the Treasure and glory of its woods," in the words of one eighteenth-century historian. Those were tall and straight eastern white pines *(Pinus strobus)* from New Hampshire's virgin forests. In an era when maritime transport was paramount, demand was great for the trunks—often two feet in diameter and as long as forty yards—which made excellent masts and spars for sails. By 1720, some seventy sawmills lined the shores of the Piscataqua; by the early 1760s, two hundred or more ships departed from there annually for the West Indies and Europe.

The son of a local farmer, John Langdon (1741–1819) recognized when he was a lad that the sea represented the quickest route to wealth. After apprenticing in the countinghouse of a local merchant, he became a ship's captain at age twenty-two. Within a decade, he established himself as a merchant in his own right, with business associations in London as well as the colonies. He dispatched ships loaded with lumber and fish for export and welcomed on their return a miscellany of imported goods—rum, sugar, tea, molasses, coffee, salt, and English products—which he sold at wholesale and retail. His knowledge of the sea, his relations with

Portsmouth joiners were noted for their staircases, and this one at the Langdon house is a fine example, with its elaborately carved newel and sets of three finely turned balusters per tread.

LEFT: *Although John Langdon built his dream house between 1783 and 1785, its substantial mass shares certain geometric characteristics with a number of earlier Portsmouth homes. It is nearly cubical, topped with a steep hipped roof, three dormers, and a balustrade. All in all, the design is not far removed from that of the Wentworth-Gardner House, which was constructed almost twenty-five years earlier. Perhaps it is not surprising that Langdon obtained a "draft" for his house from the same man who had supervised construction at the Moffatt house, Michael Whidden III.*

RIGHT: *This spacious dining room—an elongated octagon—was not original to Langdon's mansion but is a 1905–6 addition, designed by the New York firm McKim, Mead & White, working in their Colonial Revival mode. The room did have a Portsmouth precedent, however; Woodbury Langdon, John's brother, had a similar, Federal-style oval room in his house. Woodbury's house, which was demolished in the nineteenth century, had been completed the same year as John's.*

upland loggers, and a good marriage into a successful merchant family made him a man to be reckoned with in Portsmouth.

In the years leading up to the Revolution, Langdon accumulated more than money. He joined the Portsmouth Committee of Correspondence, was a leader of the local militia, and represented New Hampshire at the Second Continental Congress. When the war began, he got himself appointed New Hampshire's Continental agent, charged with constructing and provisioning naval vessels for the nation. A second appointment made him agent for prizes, meaning he distributed the cargoes captured by privateers, the privately owned ships commissioned to interfere with the British navy and shipping.

By the time the long-expected news reached Portsmouth that the Treaty of Paris had been signed, Langdon's unquestioned service to the Patriot cause had made him a hugely wealthy man. And his new house—commensurate with his affluence as well as his political and social ambitions—rose rapidly on Pleasant Street. Upon his arrival on his New England tour a few years later, President Washington took tea with Langdon, by then a member of the U.S. Senate. That night Washington noted in his diary, "Portsmouth, it is said, contains about 5,000 inhabitants. There are some good houses, (among which Col°. Langdon's may be esteemed the first)."

TWO FINE MANSIONS

As early as 1775, John Langdon had acquired land for his dream house. By 1783, he was certain he wanted a traditional design and had hired two local craftsmen, Michael Whidden III and Daniel Hart. Through marriage and training, they represented three generations of building Portsmouth mansions, among them the residence of William Whipple. They prepared a plan for Langdon, and he hired a local housewright to raise the frame. Although its proportions resembled those of a number of earlier houses, it was bigger and more elaborately detailed.

For much of the eighteenth century, the Wentworth clan had dominated Portsmouth as its royal governors and wealthiest mer-

TOP LEFT: *Thomas Wentworth, a wealthy and well-connected merchant (his brother would be the last royal governor of New Hampshire), built this house for his son, Richard. Known today as the Wentworth-Gardner House, it looks out on Portsmouth's harbor, its handsome façade decorated with corner quoins and a bold doorway. Note two of the three dormers have pediments while the third is topped by a segmental arch.*

BOTTOM LEFT: *A New Hampshire native, Tobias Lear became George Washington's secretary, friend, and confidant. Lear's Portsmouth house is adjacent to Richard Wentworth's mansion. It is certainly a humbler dwelling, despite a more-than-passing resemblance to its fancier neighbor.*

RIGHT: *Portsmouth's natural harbor was the key to its economic growth—and the source of its merchants' wealth—in the eighteenth century.*

chants, and their mansions dotted the city's streetscapes. But the Revolution effected a shift in the social and political fabric, enabling men of the middling sort, such as Langdon, to rise. Emerging as New Hampshire's most powerful man, with his financial and political fortunes waxing, Langdon would soon sign the Constitution and serve in the U.S. Senate (for two terms) as well as govern his state in the early years of the nineteenth century. But first he built a statement house to serve his political and social ambitions.

William Whipple, a Founding Father whose shorter life made fewer ripples than John Langdon's, inhabited an elegant house across town. In 1763, a "three-decker" house had been constructed for twenty-five-year-old Samuel Moffatt by his father, John. But the scion would prove less successful in business than his father and, deeply in debt, Samuel fled the country and his creditors in 1768. The elder Moffatt managed to retain title to the mansion and its contents, and he resided there until his death in 1786. Sharing the imposing mansion were his daughter, Katherine, and her husband, William Whipple, who was also John Moffatt's nephew.

Like Langdon and Moffatt, William Whipple (1730–1785) owed his fortune to commerce. Rising from cabin boy to captain before reaching his twenty-first birthday, he retired from the sea to marry his cousin Katherine Moffatt and engage in mercantile pursuits in partnership with his brother, Joseph. In 1775, he sold his share in the business and devoted himself to public service. He served as a member of New Hampshire's Committee of Safety and the state provincial congress, and in 1776 went to Philadelphia as a delegate to the Continental Congress and signed the Declaration of Independence. Later, as a brigadier general in the New Hampshire militia, he commanded a brigade at the crucial Battle of Saratoga, and was one of the chief negotiators of the surrender.

The childless Whipples and Katherine's father had ample room in the great Georgian house on Market Street, which overlooked Portsmouth's busy harbor in general and the Moffatt family wharf in particular.

A WASHINGTON SLAVE FINDS REFUGE

New Englanders would soon share a deep sense of abolitionist outrage, but at the time of the Revolution, slavery remained legal in the region. In towns such as Portsmouth, where the gentry resided in houses of aristocratic pretension, servants were usual and some were enslaved. The two Founding Fathers featured in this chapter were inured to the practice from birth. William Whipple in his days as a ship's captain probably engaged in the slave trade; John Langdon grew up on a farm where slaves owned by his father and grandfather worked the fields.

Repellent as the notion of human bondage has become, today's righteous indignation can blind us to a more nuanced understanding of the historical paradigm in which the Founding Fathers lived. Many of them wrestled with conflicting and evolving thoughts about slavery, and the story of one slave in particular offers a means of considering human ownership from the perspective of the slaver and the enslaved. The narrative of Ona Marie Judge reaches its climax in Portsmouth.

Oney and her sister Delphy (short for Philadelphia) were born at Mount Vernon. Their white father, Andrew Judge, was a carpenter who disappeared to points unknown after completing a seven-year indenture to George Washington. His departure had little impact on his daughters, since according to the prevailing slave laws, the status of a child followed the mother's, and Judge's mate, Mulatto Betty, was a "dower slave." She belong to the Custis estate, entrusted to Martha Dandridge Custis Washington on the death of her first husband and under the administration of her second, Washington. Since they were Mulatto Betty's children, neither Oney nor Delphy had any reasonable prospect of being freed.

Nevertheless, by the standards of the enslaved, Oney was fortunate. Her mother's high status in the slave hierarchy as a skilled house slave meant the girl was always well fed and clothed. Oney received training for household tasks from Martha herself and later became Mrs. Washington's personal maid. The fair-skinned Oney was a deft seamstress and Oney helped Martha dress in the morning and prepare for bed at night. She cared for her mistress's clothing,

One candlepower at bedside . . . and in the parlor.

accompanied her on calls to friends, and by all accounts (including her own) was treated with affection and respect. Upon occasion during Washington's presidency, Oney and two other trusted house slaves were even granted a degree of individual freedom, attending the theater by themselves in Philadelphia.

Although Oney professed affection and reverence for the Washingtons, she desired her freedom. Her years in Philadelphia exposed her to a society that was moving to reject slavery; one means of doing so was a state law decreeing that any slave brought into Pennsylvania became free after six consecutive months in residence. Washington avoided the emancipation of Oney and the other slaves who served him in the executive mansion by regularly shuttling them back to Mount Vernon. But they were not deceived. They learned the particulars of the law from freemen of color living and working in Philadelphia, where in 1775 Quakers had founded the first abolitionist society in America.

Sometime in the spring of 1796, Martha confided in Oney that she planned to bequeath her to a favorite granddaughter. Her mistress regarded this as an act of kindness, but Oney realized that the illusions she had begun to nurture of eventual freedom were fading before her eyes. She was twenty-two years old, promised to a woman younger than she for whom she had little affection, and she had no voice in the matter. "I knew that if I went back to Virginia," she explained many years later, "I never should get my freedom."

Oney resolved to alter her destiny. With everyone in the household packing to return to Mount Vernon for the summer, she smuggled a few clothes and personal belongings out of the house. Then, as her owners ate their dinner, she simply walked away. She found refuge in Philadelphia's underground (a network of Friends and freed blacks probably sheltered her) until the sympathetic captain of the *Nancy* took her aboard. The sloop sailed for Portsmouth, where the escaped slave hoped to begin a new life.

FACING PAGE: *Despite the date—this house was built after the Revolution—the restrained Federal style then coming into vogue seems to have had less appeal for Langdon than the Rococo ornamentation common in his fancy town before the war. The leafy carving on this chimneypiece is so plastic it seems almost to be coming into bloom; it is the work of Ebenezer Deering, another craftsman employed in building the Moffatt House.*

CANDLEPOWER

In our time, candlelight has a distinct charm—in restaurants, at the dinner table, perhaps even accompanying a bath. For the revolutionary generation, however, candlelight was the primary means of lighting interiors after sundown. (In 1784, the French inventor Amie Argand patented the fuel-burning lamp that bears his name, but it was only in the last decade of the eighteenth century that Argand lamps appeared on American tables and mantels.)

For those of us accustomed to Thomas Edison's electric light, life by candlelight is almost impossible to imagine. A candle produces a tiny fraction of the light emitted by even a low-wattage bulb, and none of that light is directed downward. Candles during the era of the Founding Fathers were smoky, and until the introduction of stearin in the nineteenth century and the development of the self-consuming wick, they required almost constant "snuffing." This meant that more than a dozen times an hour each candle needed to have the charred portion of its wick (the snuff) removed to prevent it from falling into the hot, liquid tallow. Left unsnuffed, the candle would gutter, meaning a channel would form and the candle rapidly melt away. An unsnuffed candle also grew dim.

In rural areas, candles were usually homemade. The basic material was animal fat (tallow). Mutton was best because of its whiteness (beef tended to yellow), and wicks were made of spun cotton. Melted over the fire in a pot, the tallow was poured into molds, or the wicks were dipped repeatedly into the molten tallow. The manufacturing had to be done in cold weather (so the candles would harden properly), and it was tiresome, odorous, and backbreaking work. A few day's supply of candles might be stored in the kitchen or pantry, usually in a tightly closed (that is, mouse-proof) box, but the larger supply needed to be kept cool. Candles, along with tubs of tallow, were typically stored in cellars.

In cities, candles could be economically bought in stores, and bayberry and myrtleberry candles, as well as candles made of beeswax and spermaceti (whale oil) were available. They were more expensive, and thus most people reserved them for special occasions. In a given year, many hundreds, even thousands, of candles were required in a typical household.

Oney's story might have ended in anonymity, but that summer she heard a familiar voice call her name on a Portsmouth Street. She had been recognized by nineteen-year-old Elizabeth Langdon, daughter of Senator John Langdon. Elizabeth was a close friend of another of Martha's granddaughters, Nelly Custis. The girl quite naturally looked around for Oney's mistress. Puzzled that Mrs. Washington was nowhere to be seen, she questioned Oney, who confessed the truth. "I wanted to be free missis; wanted to learn to read and write."

Word of Oney's whereabouts inevitably reached the Washingtons, and Martha demanded her return, outraged at the young woman's disloyalty. But George recognized the delicacy of the situation. The Fugitive Slave Act of 1793, which he had signed into law, entitled slave owners to reclaim escaped slaves; however, it also required an owner to present evidence of ownership to a magistrate before transporting the slave across state lines. Washington understood that the public perception of slavery was rapidly changing, and he knew an airing in court of the dispute—the President himself remanding a slave girl from New Hampshire—would inevitably produce a public outcry and harm his reputation. Out of the desire to keep the matter private, he also refused to advertise a reward, a common means of recapturing slaves, for Oney's return.

Yet Washington still felt bound to do his wife's bidding and asked the nation's secretary of the treasury to pursue the matter quietly on his behalf. He suggested the government's collector in Portsmouth might "seize, and put her on board a Vessel bound immediately to this place." The secretary agreed to handle the delicate affair.

The New Hampshire man charged with acting upon the President's request was Joseph Whipple, Portsmouth's collector and the brother and former business partner of the Signer William Whipple. At first, the task seemed simple. Whipple found Oney without difficulty and reserved a place for her on a ship readying to sail south. But upon talking to her, he had second thoughts. Although he had been told that a "French seducer" had lured her away, Whipple reported, "[I]t appeared to me that she had not been decoyed . . . but . . . a wish for complete freedom had been her only motive for absconding." Rather than bundling her aboard a ship, he chose to

TOP: *John Langdon, the first president pro tempore of the U.S. Senate, as painted about 1790. The artist was probably the self-trained, Massachusetts-born portraitist Edward Savage.*

ABOVE: *This portrait of William Whipple, painted by the New Hampshire artist U. D. Tenney in the nineteenth century, descended in the Whipple family.*

Although slavery persisted in New Hampshire well into the next century, an increasing number of free men and women of color made independent lives for themselves there after the Revolution.

Siras Bruce was probably born a slave, but by 1783 he was able to contract as a freeman to work as a "domestic servant . . . for a term of twelve months in exchange for wages." His pay was six dollars a month, payable half in cash and half in goods. His employer was Colonel Langdon, who rendered his new servant's name Cyrus de-Bruce. Siras signed the document with an X.

At first Bruce worked at the converted tavern that Langdon inhabited, but in 1785 he moved with the Langdons to their new mansion. Bruce was known about town for his attire. According to one later account, when he was dressed in his livery, "there could scarcely be found in Portsmouth one who dressed more elegantly or exhibited a more gentlemanly appearance." Surviving bills confirm that the clothing featured fine buttons, silk thread, and other materials beyond the means of most working people.

Bruce remained in Langdon's employ for many years and married another former slave, Flora. His compensation included the use of a small house rent-free. His role in the escape of Oney Judge is uncertain, but Siras Bruce probably alerted the young mother that she and her child were in danger of being abducted.

TOP LEFT: *Samuel Moffatt's fine house was completed just three years after the Wentworth-Gardner House and incorporated three full stories beneath its roofline (it was the first in town to do so). The façade is framed by the zigzag of corner quoins and capped by a balustrade. Remarkably, the Moffatt-Ladd House remained in the hands of Moffatt's descendants (a Ladd married a Moffatt granddaughter) until 1911, when the property became a museum home. The builder, Michael Whidden III, was one of New Hampshire's best craftsmen. The details add up nicely: the lines of the fence are set off by the urns on its posts, the fine line of narrow-show clapboards contrasts with the deeper shadows cast by the wooden details of the portico, and the various shapes over the window and door architraves imply the hierarchy of the levels of this three-decker house.*

TOP RIGHT: *According to family records, the "green chamber" in the Moffatt-Ladd House was William and Katharine Whipple's bed chamber. It is furnished consistent with inventories prepared in 1785 and 1786.*

ABOVE: *The great hall, as it is known, dates from the construction of the house, although the scenic wallpaper was installed by the Ladds about 1820. The large room dominates the first level, while the stair offers an implied invitation to ascend to the second floor.*

write on Oney's behalf (she was unlettered), conveying her willingness to return if the Washingtons would promise to free her upon their deaths.

To George and Martha, this proposition smacked of blackmail—and from a *slave*—so they would not make such a promise. Oney remained in Portsmouth, soon marrying a "Black Jack," as African-American sailors were called. She bore Jack Staines's child and once more seemed destined for obscurity. Then, in 1799, her past resurfaced once more.

One afternoon a nephew of Martha's, Burwell Bassett, Jr., mentioned while dining at Mount Vernon that he was soon to depart for Portsmouth. A few days later, George Washington wrote to him: "I do not however wish you to undertake anything . . . unpleasant or troublesome . . . [but] it would be a pleasing circumstance to your aunt" if Oney could be returned to Mount Vernon. Whether the Virginians knew Oney had a child is unclear, but the infant would have been an added inducement to resume pursuit of the young woman, since by law the baby also belonged to the Custis estate.

The details of the next stage are murky. Bassett, apparently on his own initiative, decided that he, if necessary, would bring Oney and her child by force. While dining with Senator Langdon in his grand Portsmouth house, he confided in his host. Whether out of moral courage or political instinct (that is, as the state's most powerful man and future governor, Langdon would certainly have wanted to avoid involvment in a potentially volatile situation), the senator apparently instructed his manservant, a black man named Cyrus deBruce, to warn Oney of the danger. Learning of Bassett's plan, Oney fled Portsmouth and found refuge with a free black family in the town of Greenland. She would live out her life there, but before her death, half a century later, she confided her story to the Reverend T. H. Adams, who published it in the *Granite Freeman* in 1845.

Ironically, Oney's life was undoubtedly harder as a freewoman living a hardscrabble existence on a rural New Hampshire farm than it would have been as a high-caste house slave in the wealthy and genteel home of a descendant basking in the afterglow of Martha and George Washington—but she would not have had her freedom. And quite likely, given the fate of other dower slaves, she would have been sold far from her family and even her own child after George and Martha Washington's deaths (Washington himself had made it a rule not to separate families, but Oney probably knew of at least one instance in which a Custis descendant had auctioned slaves without regard to family ties).

FACING PAGE: *William Whipple's office, a "retirer's room" to which he and his gentlemen friends would move after dining with the ladies. According to an inventory prepared after Whipple's death, he furnished the room with, among other items, twelve chairs.*

ABOVE: *The kitchen at Moffatt-Ladd retains its early dresser, the multiple shelves lined with ceramics and pewter.*

A formal garden extends some three hundred feet from the rear of the Moffatt-Ladd House. The last full-time resident, Alexander Hamilton Ladd, designed the gardens with many of the plants his mother and grandmother had used. At least one of the roses (an English damask) is believed to have been planted in 1768 by Mrs. Samuel Moffatt.

John Langdon and Joseph Whipple, it appears, conducted themselves honorably, even by the higher standards of our time, and did so despite pressures exerted from the nation's highest office. And Washington himself, within weeks of halfheartedly asking Bassett to pursue Oney on his wife's behalf, wrote something else on another sheet. It would be his final will, which, after providing for "my dearly beloved wife Martha Washington," ordered that "[U]pon the decease of my wife, it is my Will & desire that all the Slaves which I hold in my *own right,* shall receive their freedom." A controversial decision at the time, it comes down to us as one of his most admirable.

Like Oney herself—a fair and freckled young woman of mixed racial ancestry—slavery in the eighteenth century offered few choices that were purely black or white.

AN APPRAISING EYE

To the careful observer today, houses such as those of Governor Langdon and William Whipple can be read like evidence at a crime scene. Their setting, together with the surprising number of eighteenth-century dwellings that survive on Portsmouth streetscapes, reveals much about the town's economic history. The harbor offers the largest clue, of course, with its implication of a maritime past, but the proud houses of the merchants, most of which date from the decades just before and after the Revolution, mark the period when Portsmouth reached its zenith.

A visitor with the experience of the Marquis de Chastellux, the French aristocrat and officer who came to Portsmouth in 1782, had no difficulty interpreting what he saw. He made the rounds that November, twice taking tea with Colonel Langdon ("He is a large handsome man, and of a very noble bearing . . . one of the leading men of his region"). He visited the Moffatt House, too, where he found Mrs. Whipple "neither young nor pretty but [she] appeared to me to have wit and gaiety." Her house, he reported, like "all those I saw at Portsmouth [was] very handsome and well finished." The bottom line? "This country has a very flourishing appearance."

AN AFRICAN PRINCE

Over the generations, more than a little mythology has added detail to the tissue of true stories about the revolutionary era. The painted image of Washington's Delaware River crossing is a visual case in point (see "Victory at Trenton," page 143), but the tale of a New Hampshire slave owned by William Whipple has its own unique mix of the real and the imagined.

The grand version of Prince's story begins in Africa. Supposedly the son of a prince, he was sold into slavery at age ten, when William Whipple became his master. Later Prince reportedly served at the Battle of Trenton (and, indeed, a black soldier is depicted as an oarsmen in the well-remembered painting *Washington Crossing the Delaware*). Legend has it, as well, that when General Whipple readied to depart for military action, Prince failed to conceal his reluctance. Whipple ordered his slave to explain himself. Prince is said to have replied, "Master, you are going to fight for your liberty, but I have none to fight for." In response, Whipple is said to have promised Prince that, if you "behave like a man and do your duty . . . from this hour you shall be free."

Historians today suspect little or none of the above is true. Prince was unlikely to have had high status in Africa; the timing of the New Hampshire militia's involvement in the war was such that he could not have served at Trenton; and existing documents indicate that Prince was not manumitted until February 1784.

Prince was, however, one of twenty Portsmouth slaves who signed a petition in 1779 asking for their freedom. The New Hampshire House of Representatives briefly considered the petition before deciding "that at this time the house is not ripe for a determination in this matter." Yet Prince Whipple—like other slaves and black freemen in the Continental Army—won the respect and trust of their fellow soldiers. William Whipple died soon after freeing Prince, but his widow, Katherine Whipple, gave Prince the use of land at the rear of her property. He resided there with his wife and children as a freeman prior to his death in 1796, at forty.

Amstel House

The event proved to be a high point in New Castle history. On Thursday, April 29, 1784, Nicholas Van Dyke's daughter, Miss Ann, was married; at noon the next day, a four-horse carriage arrived at the Van Dykes' door. General George Washington emerged to join the marriage feast.

Van Dyke was Delaware's president (the state's chief executive office), but Washington himself had retired to private life. The previous December he had surrendered his commission, returning to his plantation, Mount Vernon, after eight and a half years as commander in chief of the Continental Army. Once again a gentleman planter, he felt free to attend the social events of his friends.

Yet Washington's hero status refused to fade away. Nine years earlier, he had traveled to Philadelphia as just another member of the Virginia delegation, albeit one distinguished by his outfit. When the Second Continental Congress convened, Washington wore his old uniform, made to order by a London tailor. It dated from the French and Indian War, when he'd served in the Twenty-second Virginia Regiment. Although dressed in what was effectively a British uniform, Washington impressed his congressional peers, and soon they expressed their confidence in the tall, reserved, and slightly stiff Virginian. According to the minutes of June 15, 1775, "The Congress . . . proceeded to the choice of a general by ballot, when George Washington, Esq., was unanimously elected."

General Washington's presence is commemorated at Amstel with a 1929 copy of a Gilbert Stuart portrait.

The main parlor suggests the early date of the house, with floor-to-ceiling paneling and a fireplace with a large firebox. Although the exterior door (top left) was not original (it was added in a 1904–5 Colonial Revival renovation), it offers easy access and a pretty view of the garden to the rear. In 1929, Van Dyke descendants helped the newly established house museum commemorate the Van Dykes' time there. Two of the shield-back chairs here in the parlor are Van Dyke pieces; the sofa and portraits are precise copies of others. The man and woman portrayed are Ann Van Dyke Johns and her husband, Kensey.

In New Castle, dressed in mufti, Washington might have imagined his fellow guests regarded him as just another civilian happy to take part in a wedding feast. But records of the event describe the general, standing with his back to the fireplace, receiving compliments and congratulations. Officially, the day belonged to the newly married Mr. and Mrs. Kensey Johns. But in late-eighteenth-century America, with George Washington on hand, the focus inevitably shifted to the general.

NEW CASTLE REMEMBERED

The memory of George Washington at any colonial home has, for more than two centuries, been one reason to visit. But both Amstel House, as the home of Nicholas Van Dyke (1738–1789) is known today, and pretty New Castle have charms that outweigh the lure of a brief visit by the man who would be president.

Although Native Americans long inhabited the region, the town's recorded history begins with the arrival of Peter Stuyvesant, who was the governor of all the Dutch colonies in North America, including portions of modern-day Delaware, New Jersey, and New York. Stuyvesant landed here in 1651 and named the landing at the bend in the river Sand-Hoek (Sand Hook). He fortified the place as Fort Casimir and laid out an orderly street plan that even today defines the neighborhood which extends from the waterfront to the village green. The town itself was known as New Amstel until 1665. Since then this onetime port town on the banks of the Delaware has been called New Castle.

When Pennsylvania's three lower counties separated to become Delaware, New Castle served as the colony's capital and the site of its general assembly and courts. By the time of Washington's visit, the population hovered around a thousand and New Castle had become an important trading center. William Penn had established it as a market town, to which farmers came to sell their produce, and brickmaking and brewing were early local industries.

Ships often stopped there when journeying to the fast-growing metropolis of Philadelphia forty miles upstream; New Castle's situation also made it the last port of call for traders bound for the

THE TWELVE-MILE CIRCLE

When the lower three counties of Pennsylvania split off as Delaware, the boundary between the territories was defined as the "twelve-mile circle." The agreed-upon center of the circle was the cupola of the courthouse in New Castle; an arc was then drawn beginning at the Maryland border to the west and extending to the Delaware River and New Jersey. That neat curve became the north–south, Pennsylvania–Delaware boundary. It wasn't new when it was adopted—a William Penn deed from 1682 mentions it—but it remains the only territorial boundary in the United States that is a true arc.

Many buildings that George Washington saw on his visit, including the courthouse, remain in New Castle. The courthouse's main section dates from about 1732 and the building was Delaware's capitol until 1777. During the early days of revolutionary fervor, the royal portraits that had hung in the courthouse were tossed on a bonfire on the town's green.

Far East. Travelers moving by land stopped, too, using the stagecoach route that linked Philadelphia, Annapolis, Baltimore, and influential eighteenth-century tidewater towns such as Chestertown, Maryland, and Williamsburg, Virginia.

George Washington's visit, quite by accident, heralded New Castle's finest days. In the decades that followed, the town prospered and its streetscape saw the rise of many fine Federal era houses, including an academy (1798), an arsenal (1809), a town hall and market (1823), and homes for Senator Nicholas Van Dyke (Nicholas's son, 1799) and Kensey Johns (Van Dyke's son-in-law, 1789). Yet the town's prospects were circumscribed by its geography. Wedged between the river and lowland swamps, it had little room to develop; when the coastal railroad lines were laid in the mid-nineteenth century, New Castle was bypassed. The result is an out-of-the-way, unspoiled relic. Once wealthy and important, New Castle's streets remain lined with fine houses.

The George Read II House

Over time Governor Van Dyke's dwelling came to be known by various names—the Corner, the Van Dyke House, even the Washington House—but it is now known as Amstel House, after the early name for New Castle itself.

Maryland-born George Read arrived in New Castle in 1754. Trained as a lawyer, he would be a Signer of the Declaration of Independence (though he voted against it on the first roll call, on July 2, 1776). His own home on the Strand in New Castle burned in 1824, but the home of his son, George Read II, survives as a museum.

The scion did not live up to his father's expectations—his political career fizzled early—but George Read II did get to spend his life in a fine home. The house stands very tall, with a raised basement and high ceilings. Decorated with a wrought-iron balcony on the front and a balustrade on the roof that resembles candles on a cake, the house draws attention to itself even as it seems to gaze solemnly at the wide river spread before it.

Built between 1796 and 1803, the George Read II House is high-style Philadelphia Federal, having been constructed by craftsmen from that city who worked with materials that were off-loaded at Read's own wharf. Although his son was no Founding Father, the Signer George Read had a hand in designing the grand house for George II before his death, in 1798.

George Read, Signer of the Declaration, was the codesigner of his son's home in New Castle.

AMSTEL HOUSE

At the time of his daughter's marriage, Nicholas Van Dyke lived in a house known as the Corner, a name derived from its location at the crossing of today's Fourth and Delaware Streets. The design took advantage of the location, with the broad front gable (forty-three feet across) making a bold statement overlooking Fourth Street. A service wing extending to the rear, along Delaware Street, disguised the fact the main structure was only twenty-two feet deep. The L-shaped footprint of the house enclosed a garden, also to the rear.

The dwelling was built about 1738 for a physician educated in Edinburgh; Van Dyke was one of a long series of renters. The frame of the house is oak, the bricks that make up its walls were manufactured at Brickmaker's Point, south of town. Ironically, the occupant that has proved most enduring is the New Castle Historical Society, which purchased the house in 1929. A house museum known as Amstel House, the building features portraits and an array of fine Delaware furniture, some of which belonged to the Van Dykes. It was renovated in the early twentieth century in a way that reflected the romanticized tastes of the Colonial Revival, giving the house a warm and familiar early-twentieth-century character.

As for George Washington's visit for the Van Dyke–Johns nuptials? According to one local historian, Washington "enjoyed himself so much on that occasion that he not only kissed the bride, but all the other pretty girls at the wedding as well."

The south bedroom contains a range of eighteenth-century furniture, including a four-poster bed, a cradle, and a highboy (note the bandboxes on top, used to store hats), as well as a circa 1760 looking glass by John Elliott of Philadelphia (his label survives on the back). The dressing table descended in the Van Dyke family.

Middleton Place

At age forty-four, Arthur Middleton had survived a year of house arrest in St. Augustine, Florida (which was under British rule from 1763 to 1783). A voice for radical change in the days leading up to the Revolutionary War, he served in the Continental Congress, signed the Declaration of Independence, helped write a new constitution for South Carolina, and fought in its militia. After his retirement from public service, Middleton planned to repair the damage done by British troops to his properties, which included one of the largest dwellings in the land.

His anticipated retirement ended abruptly: As his wife recorded in her Bible, "On the 1st of January '87, [he] departed this Life in the Forty fifth Year of his Age, the most respected, and best of men—whose memory will ever be *held sacred* by a disconsolate wife and eight Children."

With an imprecision typical of eighteenth-century medicine, the cause of Middleton's death was reported as a fever. He was known to have been periodically unwell in the preceding years, so malaria may have ended Arthur Middleton's life, a conclusion supported by the fact he was taking "Bark," a preparation made from the cinchona tree that contained quinine, a drug still used to treat malaria. However, according to one nineteenth-century account, his fever came over him "in the preceding month of November,

A wood nymph surveys the Azalea Pool; once there were more sculptures in the garden, but many were destroyed during the Civil War.

ABOVE LEFT: *Arthur Middleton and his wife, Mary Izard Middleton, visited relatives in England before the Revolution. They commissioned Benjamin West, the American-born painter who became a confidant of King George III, to paint a family portrait. The infant pictured with Arthur and Mary is their firstborn son, Henry.*

ABOVE RIGHT: *Middleton Place after the fire started by Union soldiers (the buildings burned to masonry hulks) but before the earthquake of 1886 (which caused the collapse of the main house and one of the flankers).*

LEFT: *Paolina Bentivoglio Middleton, Arthur Middleton's granddaughter-in-law, was a capable artist. Her 1841 sketch of the main house with its two flankers is the best surviving image of it. Two of the original three large buildings are gone; the third, though restored, today looks little as it did in Paolina's time.*

BURYING YOUR DEAD

Death was never a surprise in the eighteenth century. After the end came, a watcher stayed with the deceased until burial. The dead person was dressed in a shroud or in "grave clothes" (Martha Washington specified which white dress was to be her funeral garb), and laid out in the parlor.

Mourners came to view the deceased. When the coffin was ready, the body would be placed inside with the top left open. The ankles of the deceased were tied together, the arms bound to the waist.

Held the day following the death, the funeral ceremony tended to be a simple affair, with mourners dressed in black with veils and ribbons. The minister offered a prayer, the family members bid the deceased farewell, and the coffin was sealed. A black funeral pall sheeted the coffin, though sometimes honored pall-bearers held the pall as a canopy. At the funerals of some Founding Fathers, a flag as well as the pall enshrouded the coffin, and a horse followed with the deceased's boots reversed in the stirrups. Depending upon the prominence of the deceased, the funeral cortege might consist of many carriages or a few.

After the burial, the mourners often returned to the home of the deceased. In some areas (Albany, New York, for example, where the traditions were Dutch), revelry and feasting would follow, with wine, tobacco, and funeral cakes. In contrast, New England funerals were followed by simpler fare.

The bosquet is the burial place of Arthur Middleton, with his mother and many descendants. The crypt was built when Arthur's son Henry died in 1846.

The sundial garden is one of the many formal garden spaces, which include a rose garden, an octagonal sunken garden, secret gardens, and other garden "rooms." These spaces were regarded as an extension of the house for walking and talking.

by an injudicious exposure to the unsettled weather of the autumnal season." Perhaps pneumonia or another ailment led to his early demise.

Whatever the cause, Arthur Middleton (1742–1787) died at his birthplace, a plantation twenty miles upstream from Charleston. His survivors interred his remains in the family graveyard, secreted within the bosquet. A woodland wilderness of shrubs and trees penetrated by paths, the bosquet lay at the center of what was probably America's first and certainly its finest landscape garden.

THE ART OF LANDSCAPE

Arthur's father, Henry Middleton (1717–1784), married Mary Williams in 1741. Although the groom owned other major properties (his plantation holdings would reach fifty thousand acres), the newlyweds chose to live at Middleton Place, which came to Mary as part of her dowry. Their home, built circa 1705, towered three and a half stories, but of particular appeal to Middleton was the situation of the house. The land rose from the Ashley River to a plateau well above the tides, offering both protection from the river's waters and a majestic view of the Low Country.

Cultured people in the eighteenth century regarded the shaping of a landscape as a fine art, and for Henry Middleton, the grounds surrounding his tall brick dwelling provided a chance to exercise his imagination. According to oral tradition, he set about transforming the topography of his riverbank by deploying perhaps a hundred slaves, who worked for a decade to create his pleasure ground. The plan, inspired by the classical symmetries of André Le Nôtre's Versailles, included parterres, gardens in formal geometric patterns of circles and squares. Lines of trees (allées), walkways, and dense plantings of shrubs, flower beds, and other vegetation were used to create roomlike outdoor spaces. The composition was formal, as an Enlightenment man's attempt to impose a rigid vision upon the landscape at a time when random forces—such as disease, death, and extremes of weather—were regular reminders that nature would not be tamed.

In the eighteenth century, most visitors to Middleton Place arrived by boat. From the Ashley River their vessels entered a narrow inlet, flanked by a rice field to the north and a dense woodland to the south, both representative of sources of Middleton income ("Carolina gold" and timber, respectively). Upon disembarking, guests strode along a narrow green, flanked by mirror-image, man-made ponds (the Butterfly Lakes). Next a series of gentle curved terraces rose to a wide green, which was bisected by an avenue and flanked by flower beds and decorative shrubs. At its opposite end, narrow terraces stepped up to the site of the house.

Viewed across one of the Butterfly Lakes (the outlines of the mirror-image ponds resemble the wings of a butterfly) are the terraces that rise toward the site of the house.

That was merely the approach—the bulk of the formal gardens were on the opposite side of the house, extending north from the main axis. There was a sunken garden in the shape of an octagon and secret gardens, screened by shrubs and arbors. The landscape's designers sought to surprise and entertain visitors. The colors and textures changed along with the plant materials; the open and sunlit gave way to cool, shaded spaces. The scale shifted from intimate to grand as vignettes opened to broad vistas. The mannered and manicured acres contrasted with the larger waterscape of the powerful river lined by fields and forests. Mute swans, peafowl, fine marble sculpture, topiary, water features, and bursts of colorful blooms coexisted with a mammoth seven-hundred-year-old live oak that once marked a Cherokee trail. The bosquet, with its hallowed tomb, offered a touch of managed wilderness.

Under the aegis of his heirs, the gardens that Henry Middleton planted underwent changes. On Arthur Middleton's watch, the showy Asiatic camellias were introduced, compliments of a Middleton friend, the French botanist André Michaux. After Arthur's death, his son Henry expanded the landscape to sixty-five manicured acres. In turn Henry's son Williams experimented with azaleas (*Azalea indicum*), crepe myrtle, tea olives, and magnolias. But the Civil War brought a temporary end to the luxurious life of the gardens at Middleton Place. A half century of neglect ensued, and only in the 1920s did Middleton descendants return to restore the landscape and open the gardens to the public. As it has for more than two and a half centuries, the landscape garden at Middleton Place today embodies the will of a man—and his descendants—to carve a man-made Eden out of a wilderness on civilization's frontier.

A FAMILY AFFAIR

His father's great wealth had made it possible for Arthur Middleton to obtain the education of an English gentleman. Traveling to England at age twelve, he spent his adolescence at Hackney and Westminster Schools, then earned a degree at Cambridge before studying law at London's Middle Temple. Such a fine education would not have been complete without a Grand Tour of the continent, so Arthur traveled at length, visiting France and Italy before returning home to marry another wealthy Carolinian, Mary Izard. Despite his many years abroad—he would travel again to England with his new wife, and his first son, Henry, was born there—Arthur seems not to have been tempted to become a Tory. Instead he chose the role of radical in the new nation's founding days and expressed nothing but contempt for those Carolinians who remained Loyalists.

His lifelong American home was Middleton Place. Upon his mother's death, in 1761, Middleton's father gave him the property.

In the 1930s, a new generation of Middleton descendants renovated and enlarged the surviving flanker, adding a service wing (left). Today the building contains a collection of Middleton furniture, paintings, china, silver, family papers, and other goods.

TOP: *A view of Rice Mill Pond with the rice mill itself at the vanishing point and the springhouse (left). Opposite the springhouse is the azalea hillside; in springtime, the thousands of blooms there are reflected in the pond's still waters.*

ABOVE: *This immense live oak* (Quercus virginiana) *has been described as the largest living organism east of the Mississippi. Nearly ninety feet tall, with a circumference approaching forty feet, the oak is estimated to be a thousand years old. When the Middletons arrived, it marked an Indian trail.*

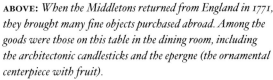

ABOVE: *When the Middletons returned from England in 1771, they brought many fine objects purchased abroad. Among the goods were those on this table in the dining room, including the architectonic candlesticks and the epergne (the ornamental centerpiece with fruit).*

ABOVE RIGHT: *The bedrooms in the south flanker are dressed as a summer bedroom (top) and a winter bedroom (bottom). The camphorwood trunk at the foot of the bed was used to conserve clothing (some of Henry and Arthur Middleton's finest clothes were found in it early in the twentieth century); everyday clothes were more likely to be stowed in the standing clothes press (at left). The sheer fabric on the summer bedstead is mosquito netting.*

THOSE WHO GREW CAROLINA GOLD

Plantations in the Low Country cultivated a golden-colored variety of rice. The crop lent itself to South Carolina's climate, soil conditions, and labor force—the colony's slave population before the Revolution outnumbered whites by about two to one.

Planting, hoeing, and harvesting had to be done by hand (mules and oxen sank into the boggy earth suited to rice growing). Rice fields were repeatedly flooded during the growing cycle to allow the seeds to germinate, to kill weeds and insect pests, and to keep the top-heavy stalks upright before harvest. The rice was harvested using a small sickle called a rice hook, dried in the sun, then separated from the stalks by threshing. Slaves performed each of these labor-intensive operations.

Ironically, rice cultivation offered the slaves at some plantations, including Middleton Place, a modicum of independence. Unlike cotton growing, which involved the "gang system," rice cultivation used the "task system," in which a slave was assigned a daily job, such as hoeing a half acre or threshing a set quantity of rice. When he completed the task, the slave was free to tend to work of his own. Although the sense of independence was largely illusory, the slaves nevertheless maintained some remnant of the social patterns they had known in Africa and even their language, which evolved into the Gullah dialect.

By then, the main house was only one of three grand structures; during Arthur's years in England, his father had constructed matching, detached wings on either side of the original house. One of these two-story flankers was used as guest quarters, the other as a music conservatory and library for what would become a ten-thousand-volume library. Arthur seems to have made few changes to the house during his ownership.

The terrible climax in the history of the house occurred well after Arthur Middleton's death. As the Civil War neared its end, a detachment of the fifty-sixth New York Regiment arrived at Middleton Place, and on February 22, 1865, the main block and the two flankers were ransacked and burned. The flames reached high into the sky, and the ground at the base of the buildings was strewn with books, paintings, and family objects. The fire left only roofless brick walls.

In 1868, Middleton descendants returned to inhabit the property. They stabilized and reroofed the least damaged of the three structures, the gentleman's guest quarters, and it became the main dwelling. Though little more than massive masonry remnants, portions of the main house and north flanker remained standing until the earthquake that struck the Charleston area in 1886. Reduced to no more than mounds of fallen debris, they survive today like some ancient ruin.

The sixty-five-acre garden, the serving house, and the attendant stable yard are today owned by the Middleton Place Foundation. The south flanker has become a museum devoted to surviving Middleton collections. Displayed are paintings, furniture, silver, and other objects from the times of Henry, Arthur, and later generations of Middletons.

HOPSEWEE

Hopsewee was home to both Thomas Lynches.

Thomas Lynch, Sr. (1727–1776), was an indigo and rice planter with enormous holdings near Georgetown, South Carolina. He attended the Stamp Act Congress in New York in 1765 and served in the Continental Congress before the Revolution. During Lynch's time in Philadelphia, his fellow delegate Silas Deane described him in a letter to his wife: "He wears the manufacture of this country, is plain, sensible, above ceremony, and carries with him more force in his very appearance than most powdered folks in their conversation. He wears his hair straight, his clothes in the plainest order, and is highly esteemed."

During the 1776 session of Congress, Lynch suffered what appears to have been a stroke. When word of his illness reached Charleston, the General Assembly of South Carolina elected his son, Thomas Lynch, Jr., to take his father's place. By the time the younger Lynch traveled to Philadelphia, his father showed signs of recovering, and the two decided to attempt the journey home. But the elder Lynch died en route and was buried in Annapolis. Thomas Lynch, Jr. (1749–1779), returned to Philadelphia in time to become a Signer of the Declaration of Independence. The Lynches were the only father and son to serve in the Continental Congress.

TOP: *The younger Lynch contracted a "bilious fever" while serving in the militia. The illness persisted and he and his wife sailed in 1779 for the West Indies, hoping the journey would prove restorative. The ship apparently foundered, ending Lynch's life at age thirty.*

ABOVE: *Hopsewee, one of three Lynch plantation houses in Georgetown County, still stands, overlooking the Santee River. Thomas Lynch, Jr., was born and spent much of his boyhood in the house; the exterior is largely original.*

George Mason's Gunston Hall

If you drive the bear from his lair, don't expect him to be happy.

No longer young, George Mason found himself in Richmond, engaged in a pitched parliamentary battle of the sort he despised. Before the Revolution, he had withdrawn from elective politics, nervous about his health and impatient with other men's inflated oratory. Yet like so many of his generation, George Mason (1725–1792) had come back into public life to fight for his ideals and interests.

In the autumn of 1788, he was taking part in one final debate about the shape of the new American government. The Virginia Assembly had convened to ratify the Constitution, which Mason had helped draft the previous year in Philadelphia. But the irascible old militia colonel was there to oppose it, and his harsh arguments disappointed his colleagues. Unwilling to compromise, Mason found himself witnessing the ratification of the Constitution, which lacked what he thought were essential changes regarding individual rights and the balance of powers.

The embittered Mason retreated to his plantation on Dogue's Neck. Eventually, his personal promontory would be renamed Mason's Neck in honor of the old Patriot. But in his lifetime, his determined opposition to the Constitution cost Mason dearly.

Among historians, the debate continues about how much credit to assign George Mason for the Declaration of Independence (more than he typically gets) and for the Bill of Rights (probably less than some of his admirers claimed). But the laboriously restored Gunston Hall is certainly a monument to an enigmatic man.

Today Gunston Hall sits amid 556 acres, a property roughly a tenth the size of George Mason's plantation on Dogue's Neck.

From his formal garden, Mason's vista reached to the Potomac, a quarter mile away. He could watch ships departing from his own wharf, carrying his cash crop, tobacco, off to market. He himself had often embarked there on the short journey upstream to dine with George Washington at Mount Vernon. The men had a friendship of long standing. Though Mason had not been trained as a lawyer, Washington had called upon his renowned legal expertise in untangling property disputes, as well as for the revolutionary thinking that would prove to be Mason's most important legacy. The two men served as members of the Truro Parish Vestry, overseeing construction of the Pohick church, where their families worshipped together. In a 1776 letter to the Marquis de Lafayette, Washington summed up their relationship, calling Mason "a particular friend of mine."

Yet what Washington had termed their "unreserved friendship" came to an abrupt end after the events of 1788. The two had had other differences over the years, but the thin-skinned Washington broke off the friendship when Mason opposed ratification. After becoming president a few months later, Washington delegated one of his secretaries to respond to Mason's letters. More pointedly, he referred to Mason in a note to Alexander Hamilton in imperfect Latin as his "quandam [former] friend."

In the eighteenth century, when a surprisingly small circle of men founded a nation, it was evident that all politics were personal.

A LANDED GENTLEMAN

George Mason's youth had ended prematurely when his father drowned, his boat capsized in a sudden squall in the Potomac. The ten-year-old remained years away from his majority, but the responsibilities of a large landowner suddenly loomed in the boy's future.

Both temperament and circumstances contributed to Mason's character—he was remote and opinionated—but another important influence was John Mercer, the uncle who emerged as a paternal presence. Most probably it was Mercer's library that introduced the young man to the world of ideas. With some fifteen hundred volumes, Mercer's collection was one of the best in the colonies, and he owned virtually every major legal treatise of the time. His nephew read voraciously, in history as well as the law. He encountered the ideas of John Locke, whose notions of the natural rights of an individual became the basis for much revolutionary thinking. His early immersion in ideas established a pattern for the solitary Mason. It would be the life of the mind, rather than the company of equals or the adulation of the public, that provided him with his greatest satisfactions.

At twenty-one, Mason came into his inheritance of some twenty thousand acres in Virginia and Maryland. A cautious and careful manager who delegated little but monitored everything, he devoted most of his time to his own affairs and would greatly

RIGHT: *If the young Mason was trying to impress his friends and neighbors, the portico overlooking the garden would certainly have done it. This drawing appeared in* Appleton's Magazine *in 1874.*

FAR RIGHT: *The Gothicized arches of the portico, with their ogee curves, and the polygonal footprint distinguished it from every other American porch of its time.*

LEFT: *The ashlar quoins on the corners of the house were quarried in nearby Aquia Creek. A few decades later, the same biscuit-colored stone would be used at the President's House in the new Federal City—later to be known as the White House.*

ABOVE: *There were thirty outbuildings at Gunston Hall, according to the 1785 census, some of which, including the dairy, wellhead, and laundry, have been reconstructed.*

Views of the lower and upper floors from the stair landing suggest the generous scale of the house, despite its modest-seeming exterior.

increase his wealth and landholdings. His eyes and hair were dark, matching what, even at an early age, was quite evidently a serious manner. Mason assumed a prominent place in the community, becoming a county justice. He married well, taking the Marylander Ann Eilbeck as his wife in 1750. The marriage would be a happy one, producing twelve children.

Life in George and Ann's home was typical of well-to-do Virginia gentry. While their home was four miles from the major public thoroughfare along the coast, the road was little more than a rutted dirt track. As a result, many visitors arrived by the river. Since travel was slow—on horseback, a rider might hope to cover thirty miles in a day but in a carriage only twenty—visitors from a distance often stayed several days or even weeks. During the war, military officers were frequent guests at Mason's table and were given quarters for the night.

Ann managed the household's affairs with the same strict control her husband exercised over the plantations. She stowed her and the children's clothes in a tall chest, some of them in locked drawers. Her chamber also had two large closets, one on each side of the fireplace. The first was a locked pantry for valuable foodstuffs (spices, for example, were expensive and doled out with great care). Another held household items, including a horse whip with a silver head. Ann used it when she went riding, although, when the occasion warranted, it also had a disciplinary purpose. The children gave it the respectful nickname "the green Doctor."

"A SUBSTANTIAL BRICK MANSION"

Once Mason inherited his property and married, he lacked only a house that suited his station. All things stylish at the time were thought to come from England, so Mason wrote to a younger brother, Thomson, who was completing his law studies in London. He requested that he engage a capable builder to construct him a fine house.

Thomson Mason made an inspired choice, hiring William Buckland, the gifted undertaker who went on to build grand houses in Annapolis (see "The Matthias Hammond House," page 182). But before Buckland could reach America, the ever impatient Mason began building. Brick walls rose one and a half stories from

ABOVE: *Visitors enter a broad central passage, lined with carved pilasters and fine English reproduction wallpaper. The central passage functioned not only as a corridor but also as a social filter: visitors, depending upon social caste, might or might not be admitted to the private rooms on the left or the public entertaining spaces to the right.*

BELOW: *Recent scholarship has found that the builder William Buckland had a worthy collaborator, a trained London carver, William Bernard Sears, who had been transported to America for the crime of stealing clothes. Indentured to Mason, Sears is thought to have executed much of the extravagant carving in the house under Buckland's guidance. Many surfaces in the house suggest the quality of the woodworkers who labored here, including the turned black walnut balusters and scrolled brackets that decorate the returns of the stair treads.*

WHO WILL MAKE THE TODDY TODAY?

In the Federal era, the cocktail as we know it hadn't been invented, though wines were often drunk at table (they tended to be sweet), and Madeira, wine fortified with brandy, was another popular alcoholic beverage. Potent alcohol-based punches were common, too.

As in most gentry homes of the time, dinner was served at mid-afternoon at Gunston Hall. In George Mason's time, the meal was preceded by the ritual of the toddy. A weak alcoholic drink, it consisted of rum, sugar, and water, with nutmeg grated on top. As Mason's sons matured, they mixed the toddy.

Once prepared, the communal bowl was presented to their father, who would say, "I pledge you, Sir." That was the cue for the boy who had mixed it to take the first sip before handing it back to his father, who would then put it to his lips. The rest of the company would take their turns thereafter.

The ceremonial toddy was, in the words of one contemporary, "then & thus a matter of civility in Society." It was followed by the patriarch or, as they matured, one of his sons, giving the standard blessing, "God bless us, and what we are going to receive." Only then was dinner served.

The Palladian room, as it came to be known in the twentieth century, features much fine carving using classical orders (columns, cornices, and pediments), as well as a portrait of the man of the house, taken in 1750.

a forty-by-sixty-foot print. There would be four rooms downstairs, two on either side of a generous passage, with seven chambers on the upper floor beneath the gabled and dormered roof. At that early stage, the house would have appeared handsome but unremarkable to Mason's Virginia peers. But that was before Mr. Buckland made it a showplace, with his extraordinary carving skill, knowledge of current London styles, and free rein to exercise his imagination.

MASON THE MAN

George Mason might have played a much larger role in the early years of the republic than he did. Peyton Randolph, a fellow Virginian and the first president of the Continental Congress (see "The Peyton Randolph House," page 66), begged Mason—reportedly with tears in his eyes—to accept an appointment to Congress. Mason later refused service in the Virginia House of Delegates, waxing indignant at the very suggestion ("I shou'd look upon some Attempt, in no other Light than as an oppressive & unjust Invasion of my personal Liberty").

Was this just the railing of a wealthy man who could afford to do as he pleased? Was Mason terminally shy? Or a misanthrope?

Mason's health certainly helped explain his taciturn demeanor. He suffered from gout, a recurring and painful joint complaint that made standing upright sheer agony. He was known to use his various ailments—some of them, perhaps, hypochondriacal—to excuse his refusal to travel from his home.

And Mason was not a man who needed to be liked. "I would not forfeit the approbation of my own mind for the approbation of any man, or all the men upon earth," he once wrote. He professed not to care a whit about "the Smiles & Frowns of the Great." He disliked the pomp and even the perquisites of public life ("I begin to grow heartily tired of the etiquette and nonsense so fashionable in this city," he wrote from his unhappy 1787 junket to Philadelphia, the longest journey he ever took).

Even at home, Mason was a private person, often closeting himself with his books and papers. One of his children recalled that "he absented as it were from the Family some times for a week together." He took long, solitary strolls in the garden, "wrapped in meditation [before] return[ing] to his Desk, without Seeing or

[I] would sooner cut off [my] right hand than put it to the Constitution as it now stands.

—*George Mason*

LEFT: *The elaborate scalloped Chinoiserie cresting and other carving in the window headpieces were based on pagodas. They were fabricated on site entirely by hand, using fine carver's chisels.*

RIGHT: *The Chinese Room, set for tea. It features the earliest known Chippendale-style carving in America and was probably inspired by a plate in Thomas Chippendale's* Gentleman & Cabinet-Makers' Director, *published in 1754.*

speaking to any of the Family—and in these walks we all well knew, that he was not to be disturbed."

Yet, his contemporaries report, George Mason was cheerful in company and, particularly at his own table, a gregarious conversationalist. Despite his reputation for "biting cynicism," Mason was regularly consulted for his thoughts about public policy and law. Jefferson once called him "the wisest man of his generation," and his accomplishments included drafting the Virginia Declaration of Rights. Jefferson's own Declaration, which appeared only a month later, owed a conspicuous debt to Mason's. (Jefferson paraphrased portions of Mason's Declaration; the following words, from Mason's pen, sound remarkably familiar to anyone acquainted with Jefferson's legendary document: "That all men are by nature equally free and independent, and have certain inherent rights, . . . namely, the enjoyment of life and liberty, with the means of . . . pursueing and obtaining happiness and safety.")

Mason's philosophical musings helped shape the Declaration of Independence, the Constitution, and the Bill of Rights, even though he tended to grow churlish when his cherished notions were ignored or amended. Mason was a man who, on his own terms, in his own time, and at his own pace, thought long and hard about personal liberty.

TWO OLD ALLIES

Thomas Jefferson had given his notice. Unhappy to have become the object of virulent political attacks, a few of which even questioned his patriotism, he informed President Washington he was resigning as the nation's first secretary of state. He had had enough, he confided in family and friends, and contemplated his retirement the following March ("I look to that period with the longing of a wave worn mariner," he told a friend).

Perhaps, then, his Sunday afternoon visit in September 1792 to another exile from government, his old friend Colonel Mason,

was to be expected. Unlike Washington, Jefferson had worked to remain friends with the aging Mason. He had assured him the previous year, "Whenever I pass your road I shall do myself the honor of turning into it." And he made good on the promise when, on the last day of the month, he arrived, with his handsome fourteen-year-old daughter, Patsy.

Mason made his guests welcome, despite the fact that he was not well. He had been complaining for some time of "fevers" that left him "very weak and low," and Jefferson found him hobbling on a crutch. The younger man, his hair receding but still a vibrant red, brought the news of the day, and the excited talk of politics was just the tonic Mason needed. The elder man may have looked old and exhausted—once he had shaved his head to accommodate a powdered wig, but he had more recently allowed what was left of his hair to grow out—but his thinking was clear, his opinions as sharp as ever.

Jefferson regaled Mason with stories of the happenings in Philadelphia, and particularly of their common enemy, Alexander Hamilton. Mason declared that the New Yorker had "done us more injury than Great Britain and all her fleets and Armies." The men regarded as treacherous the way Hamilton had consolidated political power in the hands of moneyed rather than landed interests; Hamilton and the Federalists favored urban bankers and merchants to the exclusion of the country aristocrats, such as Jefferson and Mason. They also talked of slavery, which Mason had taken to calling, with prophetic vision, "slow poison."

The visit between the two anti-Federalist allies was brief. After an overnight stay—and, no doubt, a meal in the large dining room with its fine carving—Jefferson and Patsy departed early to breakfast with Washington at Mount Vernon. Jefferson did, however, in his usual meticulous fashion, make notes of their conversation in his journal. These would prove to be the last recorded words of Mason's. He died the following Sunday afternoon, October 7, 1792, in the sixty-seventh year of his life.

BELOW: *The family referred to this as the Little Parlor; it was an informal room where Mason conducted business, read, and mused on the matters of the day.*

BOTTOM: *There were eight rooms on the second floor, including these chambers.*

Ann Eilbeck was the love of George Mason's life. She was sixteen when they married (he was twenty-five), but she died at thirty-nine, having birthed a dozen babies, nine of whom would survive to adulthood. One of them, John Mason, was a lad of seven when his mother died in 1773, but almost sixty years later, he recalled the events clearly:

> My mother was attended during her illness by Dr Craig . . . who was afterwards the Surgeon General of the revolutionary army—the intimate personal Friend of General Washington—as he was of my Father—Among the prescriptions for her was weak milk punch to be taken in Bed in the morning—little urchin as I was, it is yet fresh on my mind that I was called sometimes by this beloved Mother to her bed side, to Stand to drink a little of this beverage. . . .

> I believe it was a few days before her death [she] told me she was going to leave us all [and] gave me her blessing—and charged me in terms no doubt suitable to my age and understanding, to be a good Boy, to love & obey my Father and to love and never quarrel with my Brothers & Sisters, to be kind to the Servants and if God spared me when I grew up, to [be] an honest and useful Man.

Martha Washington attended Ann Mason's funeral, and a few days later, George Washington made a special journey to Gunston Hall to deliver his condolences. The Mason household went into deep mourning, and Mason himself "paced the rooms, or from the house to Grave . . . for many Days alone—with his hands crossed behind him." He eventually remarried, but the second marriage appears to have been one more of convenience than of love. When Mason died, he was buried beside Ann in the family plot at Gunston Hall.

William Livingston's Liberty Hall

*Every antique house poses its own ques-*tions, but one issue common to all restorations is, When? That is, given the need to respect the history of a place, which time in its past should be targeted as *the* moment to which it ought to be restored? The caretakers at Monticello designated 1809, the time of Jefferson's retirement from the presidency; at Mount Vernon, the look has become that of 1799, the last year of Washington's life.

At Liberty Hall, no single historic moment has been chosen. Instead, the visitor's experience traces the seven generations of habitation by the builder's family. Like the old Hollywood device in which the pages of a calendar flip past, Liberty Hall offers the opportunity to shift from one era to another in its busy history. One room, for example, commemorates a particular visitor, Martha Washington.

At noontime on April 14, 1789, her husband learned he had a new title: a letter from the president pro tempore of the Senate arrived, informing George Washington of his unanimous election as president of the United States. Eager to take charge of the nation, the president-elect headed north from Mount Vernon to the nation's capital, at New York. His trip became the occasion for an unprecedented outpouring of affection, with parades in every city, delegations of local dignitaries in each town, and toasts and speeches everywhere.

The room where Martha Washington is believed to have stayed.

An image of her husband—one taken some years after her visit to Liberty Hall— hangs on the wall of Martha Washington's bed chamber.

After his inauguration, on April 30, Washington sent for Martha, who took a more leisurely journey north. She rode in her carriage, accompanied by her two wards, the youngest children of her son, Jacky, who had died of "camp fever" (probably typhus) after the Battle of Yorktown. Wash was eight, his sister Nelly two years older. As her husband had, Martha met with one grand welcome after another. "Dear Little Washington," she wrote of her grandson, "seemed to be lost in a maze at the great parade that was made for us all the way we come." In some towns they were serenaded by musicians, at others fireworks lit the sky. But one stop they made before crossing the Hudson to Manhattan was the elegant country home of Governor William Livingston, in Elizabethtown, New Jersey.

Beyond the fact that the visit took place, not a great deal is known. Oral tradition in the Livingston family claims that a new bedroom was added for Mrs. Washington. More likely, she was the first to stay in quarters the Livingstons had just added to the house. But the gathering was of old and familiar friends. Molly Morris, wife of the financier and Washington confidant Robert Morris, had joined Martha's entourage at Philadelphia. During the Revolution, Mrs. Morris had welcomed the Livingstons' daughter Kitty into the safety of her home, and Martha, too, had stayed there on numerous occasions. After years of war and political uncertainty, the old friends could relish the prospects of a new experiment in government masterminded in part by the Virginia general, the Philadelphia banker, and the New Jersey governor, each of whom had played essential roles in shaping and ratifying the Constitution.

To the caretakers charged with conserving Liberty Hall's history, commemorating the reunion of the old friends seemed only proper, so a bed chamber is designated the Martha Washington Room. In the eccentric way of such experiments in historical memory, more objects commemorate George than Martha. But the room, with its carved four-poster bed and several images of the general, strongly conveys an early American character.

Once the Livingston dining room, this space is today a pastiche of family history. In addition to much Victorian furniture, there are earlier pieces, including a shaving mirror and an Empire-style butler's desk (its front swings up and slides into the case, so when closed, it is indistinguishable from a dresser).

LIGHTING THE DARKNESS

Darkness was different then. Aside from bonfires and torches, the Founding Fathers had no artificial light outdoors, so the stars and the moon appeared brighter than they do today. When the moon was full, people were known to sit inside without burning one of their precious candles, calling it a blind man's holiday.

Electric lighting was a century in the future, so sunset meant interiors went to shadow. Typically one lit taper on a candlestand at the center of the parlor was the focus of evening activity, with several people seated around it sewing or reading. The periphery of the room remained shadowy and dark. Unused furniture was typically left "at rest," squared up and flush to the walls, to reduce the tripping hazards in an ill-lit room or hallway.

What light there was seemed in constant motion. Flames wavered in every draft. Craftsmen tried to employ this kinetic quality to good advantage, making corkscrew finials, boldly grained surfaces, and spiraling andirons that seemed to be in motion in flickering lighting conditions.

Some techniques to make the most of the available light were subtle—wallpaper manufacturers sprinkled the paper's surface with mica chips to add sparkle. Gilded picture frames were popular because they reflected light onto the pictures. "Looking glasses," the sheets of glass with backs coated with an amalgam of quicksilver, were signs of wealth, in part because they made rooms seem larger and brighter. Despite such cleverness, however, the rooms remained dim.

ALEXANDER HAMILTON, ALMOST-SON-IN-LAW

In 1780, Alexander Hamilton married into a powerful New York family, but a few years earlier, most observers thought his bride's maiden name would be Livingston, not Schuyler.

William Livingston's five daughters were much admired in New York society ("My principal secretary of state, who is one of my daughters," he once observed, "is gone to New York to shake her heels at the balls and assemblies"). His daughter Sarah married the brilliant lawyer John Jay, who would soon play essential roles as a legislator, diplo-

mat, and jurist (see The "John Jay Homestead," page 274). That same winter, Sally's sister Catherine also had a gentleman caller.

They were immediately drawn to each other. "I challenge you to meet me in whatever path you dare," Hamilton wrote provocatively to the pretty and notably flirtatious Kitty in 1774. "If you have no objection, for variety and amusement, we will even make excursions in the flowery walks and roseate bowers of cupid." He was smitten and perhaps looking to conquer.

The rapidly rising Hamilton soon moved on to King's College in New York, and his wooing of Kitty temporarily ended. But three years later, as an officer in Washington's command, he would suggest in a letter that the war's end might "remove these obstacles which now lie in the way of that most delectable thing called matrimony." Kitty refused his proposal, and Hamilton later married her good friend Elizabeth Schuyler (see "The Perfect Woman?" page 159). But Kitty and Hamilton remained friends for the rest of Hamilton's abbreviated life.

The Alexander Hamilton Room, named for the man who was once a regular guest at Liberty Hall, with its tall clock, cradle with ogee canopy, and rocking horse.

The morning room. The Architect's Tea Service on the table dates from twentieth-century residents while the gilt over mantel mirror (above) is a nineteenth-century addition.

LIVINGSTON'S WORLD

That powerful men tend to congregate is an immutable law of politics, and William Livingston (1723–1790) was living proof. A scion of the wealthy and influential Livingston clan of New York's Hudson Valley, he chose the law over commerce, passing the bar in 1748. For a decade he exercised a strong influence in his native colony's affairs through his writings and as a legislator. When his party's moderate views lost popularity—he preferred parliamentary to royal power and favored civil liberties—he retired from politics in New York in 1769.

Married to Susannah French, the daughter of a wealthy New Jersey landowner, Livingston purchased 120 acres in his wife's colony. There he devoted himself to agricultural experimentation. He wrote poems, penned the occasional polemical essay, and built in 1772–73 the fine house he named Liberty Hall.

His quiet interlude as a gentleman farmer ended when Livingston plunged back into politics in the years just before the Revolution. He began by joining the local Committee for Correspondence but soon traveled to Philadelphia as a New Jersey delegate to the First Continental Congress. Appointed a brigadier general, he took command of the colony's militia and was with his troops

rather than in Philadelphia when the Declaration of Independence was signed. He resigned his commission upon being elected the first governor of the state later that year, succeeding William Franklin, the colony's last royal governor (and the illegitimate son of Benjamin). Livingston would hold the post for fourteen years.

His sphere of influence was broad. His brother, Philip, was a Signer; their cousin Robert Livingston was chancellor of New York and the man who administered the oath of office at George Washington's inauguration. A regular visitor to Liberty Hall before the Revolution was Alexander Hamilton, who was then studying at an academy nearby and became a protégé of Livingston's. One of Livingston's daughters, Sarah, would marry John Jay, a longtime political ally. Their wedding took place in the Great Hall at Liberty Hall (see "The John Jay Homestead," page 274).

Jay and Hamilton would, along with James Madison, write the series of articles published as *The Federalist,* which proved essential to the public relations campaign launched to gain support for passage of the Constitution. William Livingston played a role, too, both as a delegate to the Constitutional Convention and as governor of New Jersey, where he helped assure the Constitution was ratified. He would die in office in 1790.

An early-nineteenth-century engraving of Liberty Hall, much as it appeared when Martha Washington was welcomed there in the spring of 1789.

THE BRITISH ARE COMING

In the winter of 1779, General Washington nurtured hopes of recapturing New York, but he bided his time, waiting out the winter from his inland New Jersey encampment.

In the no-man's-land between the British and American armies, Liberty Hall sat unprotected. When a Loyalist tipster alerted the Redcoats on February 25 that William Livingston would be at home that night, a band of British troops led by Lieutenant Colonel Thomas Sterling pounded on the door, looking to take the rebel governor hostage. But the intelligence was wrong, and only Livingston's wife and his unmarried daughters, Kitty and Susan, were at home.

Miss Susan boldly met the soldiers at the door. Told their quarry was not at home, the British searched the house. When Livingston's absence had been confirmed, Colonel Sterling demanded the governor's papers. Susan appealed that her personal letters ought to be exempted from the search; the colonel agreed, and the British troops left with quantities of irrelevant documents— while the governor's papers remained safely in the box Miss Susan had designated as her own.

John Fell, a New Jersey delegate to the Continental Congress, wrote to Livingston the following month, "I was exceeding happy to hear you was from home, when the Enemy came to pay you a Visit." What he didn't say was that, fortuitously, Miss Susan was—and that she took advantage of the genteel mores of the day to outwit the chivalrous soldier.

Governor Livingston's guests would have entered the great hall. Today the room typifies the history-of-history quality of Liberty Hall, with its 1920s Colonial Revival view of the Founding Fathers' time.

[B]y all Accounts [the Enemy] have penetrated the Country as far as Springfield, & I am told have burnt & destroyed all before them. My Anxiety for you and the Children has been inexpressible & I have had a most miserable Night of it, upon your Account.

—William Livingston, to his wife, Susannah French Livingston, June 9, 1780

The immense chestnut tree shadowing the front of Liberty Hall was planted by William Livingston's daughter Susan. The tall and sprawling Liberty Hall as it looks today, with its extensive Victorian additions.

DINNER BY CANDLELIGHT

The eighteenth-century dining room was a showplace, with the sideboard or buffet at its focus (some houses even had a custom-made recess or archway to display the sideboard). Essentially a movable closet, the typical sideboard held cupboards and drawers for wine as well as cutlery, but its top surface was for display. Above it often hung a mirror (see above); while it may be hard to think of an ornate girandole as a utilitarian object, the round, convex mirror amplified the light from the candles on its branches. Ranks of crystal glassware and silver platters on the buffet top would also refract and reflect the light.

On the nearby dining table were more candles (the rule of thumb was one candle for every two people). The candlesticks were left empty until the time came to light the candles, which were positioned high enough (eighteen inches or more) to be above conversational sight lines. Candles elsewhere in the room—on the mantel, and in wall sconces, ideally with mirrored backdrops—added to the illumination and the ambience. A bright white tablecloth was usual for the first course, but when the cloth was removed for the fruit and wine (always sweet wines), the surface beneath was likely to be mahogany. New to Europeans, this handsome and workable wood from the Indies took a mirrorlike polish that also reflected light.

LIBERTY HALL EVOLVES

The house that William Livingston built still stands, though it has been much changed.

Livingston built a wood-frame house of three connected parts. The center section was two stories tall with a gambrel roof; extending from both ends were two one-story wings with hipped roofs. The main floor consisted of a large room called the Great Hall, with a smaller one to either side for use as a bed chamber and a dining room. Upstairs there were five bed chambers. Before Martha Washington arrived in 1789, a second story, containing a guest room, was added to the west wing.

Much later—about 1860—the entire structure had its roof raised to a uniform height of three stories. Another addition to the rear incorporated a tower and more rooms. While the original floor plan of the house remains largely intact, it is encased by later spaces, the result being a fifty-room Victorian mansion.

The grounds at Liberty Hall today consist of twenty-three acres, although the original setting has been transformed. Once it resembled the Hudson Valley mansions Livingston knew from childhood, with a manicured landscape that rolled gently down to the banks of the Elizabeth River. Today the property is an oasis, the house nearly hidden from dense urban surroundings by some of the oldest trees in New Jersey. More than a few of them were planted by William Livingston himself.

LEFT: *A circa 1938 photograph of the stair hall, looking from back to front, in the era of the Kean family's occupation.* **BELOW:** *The young bride to be Mary Alice Barney Kean, who would be Liberty Hall's principal benefactor.*

THE WIDOW KEAN (1902–1995)

One place to begin the Liberty Hall story is with a beautiful bride who married a man twelve years her senior. The time is just after the war—World War I, that is—and Mary Alice Barney is radiant and beautiful; a veteran of the Great War, her husband has the shrapnel in his shoulder to show for it.

Captain John Kean and his bride became owners of Liberty Hall in 1932 (the surname Livingston, through marriage, had given way to Kean in the early nineteenth century). Sixty-three years later, the widowed Mary Alice died at age ninety-three, but during a thirty-six-year widowhood, she cherished her husband's memory and his house, along with the memory of earlier occupants. In the bicentennial year of 1976, she and her son John established a foundation to maintain Liberty Hall.

Having made it her cause to restore the place, Mary Alice shaped a march through time. Previous generations of her husband's family had left a wealth of furniture and family objects to employ in telling the story of the house's inhabitants. In addition to the Martha Washington Room and the Great Hall, where Governor Livingston welcomed prominent members of the revolutionary generation, other spaces reflect the long history of one of New Jersey's great dynasties, whose members included numerous military men, two U.S. senators, a ten-term congressman, and coming full circle, a twentieth-century governor, Thomas H. Kean. After Mary Alice Barney Kean's death, in 1995, Liberty Hall was given by her son John to the Liberty Hall Foundation, which maintains it as a historic house museum.

The Deshler-Morris House

President Washington wanted to get back

to work. After a few weeks at his plantation, Mount Vernon, he felt compelled to return to the nation's capital. But the scourge that had driven him from Philadelphia still exacted a fearsome daily toll. On October 11, 1793, 120 people had died; on October 22, another 82. The total approached 5,000.

In September, the call "Bring out your dead!" first rang out in the streets, but the disease had arrived quietly at least a month earlier. During the first week of August, a French sailor living in a rooming house down by the docks spiked an intense fever. Unexplained illnesses—often called summer fevers—were common, but this man soon experienced violent seizures and vomited blood and bile. His skin and eyeballs yellowed, and he died in a matter of days.

The loss of the anonymous sailor went little remarked, but the passage of another week saw seven more symptomatic deaths on the same street. Soon after, Dr. Benjamin Rush, perhaps the nation's most esteemed medical practitioner, was consulted by two other physicians about a case of what they termed "bilious fever." Having witnessed an epidemic some thirty years earlier, as a sixteen-year-old, Rush recognized the symptoms. On August 19, he dared name the cause. It was yellow fever.

Washington enjoyed the main meal of the day wherever he was. In Germantown he would have taken his midafternoon repast in this room. The stone in the fireplace came from a quarry in Valley Forge.

On the second level was George and Martha's bedroom (above); across the hall, their ward (and Martha's granddaughter), Nelly Custis, slept (opposite).

General Washington, Neighbor

Although he had become their president, Washington remained known to most Americans by his military title (even Martha referred to him often in her correspondence as "the General"). According to one Germantown resident looking back at Washington's time in the village, "Many remember his very civil and courteous demeanor to all classes in the town, as he occasionally had intercourse with them. He had been seen several times at Henry Fraley's carpenters shop, and at Bringhurst's blacksmith shop, talking freely and cordially with both. They had both been in some of his campaigns. His lady endeared herself to many by her uniform gentleness and kindness."

No cure existed, so the wisest course seemed to be to escape the overheated city (as Rush confided in his wife, Julia Stockton Rush, "There is but one preventative that is certain, that is 'to fly from it.'") Washington himself had little inclination to depart, though he wanted his wife and the children to seek safety (the Washingtons were raising two of Martha's grandchildren, Eleanor Parke Custis and George Washington Parke Custis). The fever of Alexander Hamilton, the secretary of the treasury, who fell ill just two days after dining with the Washingtons, decided the matter. The President wrote, "As Mrs. Washington was unwilling to leave me . . . I could not think of hazarding her and the children . . . by *my* continuing in the City." On September 10, the presidential carriage had begun the journey south.

Washington's plan had been to be gone little more than a fortnight. He left Secretary of War Henry Knox in charge, requesting that Knox dispatch him "a line by every Monday's Post informing me concisely of the then state of matters." The secretary remained in Philadelphia long enough to mail one report. "The streets are lonely to a melancholy degree," he wrote, "hundreds are dying and the merchants have fled." But Knox soon departed, hoping to reach Boston and join his wife, Lucy, and their children. Instead, he found himself quarantined in New Jersey.

As if the killer contagion was not enough, the exiled Washington faced a constitutional crisis: no one was piloting the nation *in* its capital, and his cabinet was divided over whether Congress could meet *outside* the designated capital. What if the "malignant fever" (as Washington called it) was still rife in Philadelphia on December 1, when Congress was scheduled to reconvene? The Constitution seemingly forbade relocation of the government. And all the nation's papers and records were locked away in a city abandoned by half of its forty-two thousand inhabitants and virtually all its government employees.

As October drew to a close, the reports from Philadelphia began to suggest that new cases of yellow fever were growing fewer (indeed, a thick frost had killed the mosquitoes that carried the disease, but neither Washington and Rush nor any of their contemporaries understood the significance of the cold snap). The President decided to journey back and, for a time, to govern from the relative

We are all well at present, but the city is very sickly
and numbers [are] dying daily.

—*George Washington, August 25, 1793*

safety of the village of Germantown, six miles north of the capital. At Baltimore, Thomas Jefferson joined Washington and his secretary in a hired coach, since regularly scheduled stages had not yet resumed running. On November 1, they arrived in Germantown in a pelting rain to establish a temporary seat for the executive branch.

THE GERMANTOWN WHITE HOUSE

At the time of Washington's return to Pennsylvania in November 1793, the epidemic had abated in Philadelphia, though refugees from the city still crowded Germantown. That meant that Secretary of State Jefferson had to satisfy himself for a few nights with a bed in the corner of a public room at an inn called the King of Prussia. The President found other accommodations, eventually settling into the house on Germantown Avenue that had been British General William Howe's headquarters during the Battle of Germantown (see "The Battle Within the Battle," page 122).

The house Washington rented had been constructed in two phases. In 1752, the countrified air of Germantown had attracted David Deshler, a Quaker merchant who built a four-room summer cottage. Twenty years later, he transformed his home into the grander house that Washington adopted. The newer and more impressive portion faced Germantown's Market Square; the original structure was now an ell off the rear. The façade of the nine-room, Georgian-style addition stood two and a half stories tall, topped with ornate dormers that illuminated the generous attic space.

After Deshler's death, in 1792, a former colonel in the Continental Army named Isaac Franks purchased the property. Washington leased the large and comfortable house from Franks and found it served his purposes nicely, providing quarters for his secretary and slaves, and a meeting place for his cabinet. Among

FACING PAGE: *The red camelback sofa with "hairy paw" feet is thought have been used by George and Martha Washington during his presidency; however, it may or may not have come to Germantown on one of the two wagons that brought furniture from the Washingtons' downtown house, on Philadelphia's High Street. What is known for certain is that President Washington's cabinet met in this parlor, and the notables included Thomas Jefferson (secretary of state), Henry Knox (war), Alexander Hamilton (treasury), and Attorney General Edmund Randolph.*

A CITY UNDER SIEGE

Today "yellow jack" is regarded as a tropical disease peculiar to the Southern Hemisphere, but it was a recurrent threat in the young United States. Brought by ships from the West Indies, where yellow fever was endemic, the disease struck not only Philadelphia but Baltimore, Boston, New York, and other coastal cities. More than a century later, the mode of transmission—the bite of the *Aedes aegypti* mosquito— would be determined, but in the 1790s, America's finest physician, Benjamin Rush, believed the cause to be putrefying vegetable matter. In the absence of effective treatment, yellow fever produces high temperatures, jaundice, liver damage, and in many cases, death.

During the plague of 1793, the citizens of Philadelphia who had not departed (and who were well enough to venture out) walked in the middle of the street to avoid infected homes. Some held bags of camphor to their noses, thinking these would protect them, while yellow fever victims were wrapped in blankets dipped in vinegar. Another theory held that gunpowder and tobacco were "salutory preparations," and as a result gunshots regularly echoed in the city and people smoked cigars.

African-Americans were thought to be resistant to yellow fever. For a time, the bulk of the nursing duties thus fell to free blacks and the city's last remaining slaves, but soon the black citizens fell ill, too. A few blacks who had contracted it earlier in their lives in Africa or the West Indies had some antibodies, but yellow jack recognized no racial immunity.

those who visited him there were Jefferson; the recuperating secretary of the treasury, Alexander Hamilton; Henry Knox, who returned from New Jersey; and Attorney General Edmund Randolph. Together they worked on speeches, discussed policies, and dined. Hamilton, his heath still variable, absented himself from at least one cabinet meeting late in November, but his empty chair may have eased the tone—Hamilton and Jefferson were by then avowed enemies and almost invariably took opposing positions.

Washington had moved back to Philadelphia by December 1, but tenant and landlord had a subsequent haggle over the bill. The President, a meticulous record keeper, expressed his unhappiness when Colonel Franks charged him $131.56, a sum that included fees for the loss of a flatiron (one shilling), one fork, and four plates, as well as three ducks, four fowl, a bushel of potatoes, and a hundred bushels of hay. Franks even sought reimbursement for his travel costs to and from Bethlehem, Pennsylvania, where he resided during the President's tenancy in his Germantown house. Washington swallowed his displeasure and paid the bill.

The following summer he returned once more to Franks's house. This time he brought Martha and the grandchildren Nelly and Wash with him. Wash attended the Germantown Union School, a short walk away, and Nelly was tutored at home. Despite the recurrence of yellow fever in Philadelphia that season, an air of normality seemed to prevail in Germantown. On Sundays the family worshipped at the German Reformed Church, just across Market Square. Martha tended to her flower garden. For the period July 30 to September 20, Washington's cashbook records the rental payment: "Isaac Franks in Full for House rent &c. at Germantown pr rect, $201.60."

Mr. Stuart's Washington

On April 12, 1796, President Washington returned to Germantown, ferrying across the Schuylkill to assume a seat in what he called "the Painters Chair."

Washington found no joy in having his picture painted. He never did, though he sat repeatedly for Charles Willson Peale, John Trumbull, and a number of other American, French, and English artists. He disliked sitting still, and on this day he was self-conscious about his new false teeth. Having promised wealthy friends he would pose for a standing portrait, the President arrived at Gilbert Stuart's studio in a converted barn.

A Rhode Island–born, English-trained artist, Stuart had become the ex officio portraitist of Federalist Philadelphia; his three Washington portraits would be the most famous of his works. All of them were executed in the mid-1790s; more accurately, the *originals* were. Stuart spent much of the next three decades producing knockoffs of his work to keep himself in snuff and liquor ("hundred dollar bills," he called his copies). The seated portrait had come first, the standing one last, but the best known would be the second, the one called the Athenaeum portrait because it was purchased after Stuart's death by the Boston Athenaeum. This portrait consists only of the General's head and neck, but it would eventually become the most reproduced portrait in history, engraved on every one-dollar bill since 1918.

Though commissioned by Martha to paint it, Gilbert Stuart refused to relinquish the original canvas of this Washington portrait. Instead, he kept it in his studio in order to make copies for clients eager to own an image of the great man.

The tearoom, just to the rear of the parlor, was probably used by Martha Washington as her reception room. The mahogany tea table belonged to James Smith, a Pennsylvania Signer.

A large hearth with some of the tools essential to the eighteenth-century cook.

FIREPLACE COOKERY

Cooking in the time of the Founding Mothers was done by processes we recognize—boiling, baking, roasting, and frying—but their tools and techniques are utterly unfamiliar.

Gas and electricity were not yet harnessed as fuels, so cooks relied upon wood. The kitchen fireplace, with its fire—well stoked in both summer and winter—was the equivalent of today's kitchen range (iron cookstoves did not become commonplace until after 1825).

Coals from the main fire were raked into a pile on the hearth;

a trivet positioned on top became the cook's burner. Reflector ovens called tin kitchens roasted turkey, beef, or mutton. An iron arm called a crane fastened to one of the fireplace jambs swung in and out of the firebox; suspended from the crane were pots and kettles, often including a water pot fitted with a spigot.

Pies, breads, and cakes were baked in a dome-shaped masonry bake oven built into the same masonry mass as the fireplace. A wood fire was built in the oven itself; once the fuel burned down, the coals and ash were raked out

and the door closed. The bricks inside held the heat for hours. Typically, the oven was fired up once a week, when large quantities of foods were prepared for later consumption.

Aside from damp, cool root cellars and, in major households, hay-covered ice stored in icehouses (little more than excavated holes in the yard with roofs), nothing in the age resembled refrigeration as we know it. That meant leftovers from the main, midafternoon meal were usually eaten at supper and breakfast, before the food spoiled.

On display at the Deshler-Morris House are a range of period bottles (above) and a traveling clock, document box, and tavern table (right), all objects familiar to late-eighteenth-century Philadelphians.

Today the home where Washington spent portions of the summers of 1793 and 1794 is known as the Deshler-Morris House (David Deshler was its first owner; Samuel B. Morris and his descendants owned it for many years before donating it to the National Park Service in 1948). The nickname by which the site is often known, the Germantown White House, is an anachronism. It came to be applied well after Washington's time, since today's White House was little more than a muddy hole in the ground in 1793, and even after President John Adams moved in, in 1799, the house would remain known for many years as the President's House. The Deshler-Morris House is the earliest surviving presidential residence.

LEFT: *From the ell to the rear of the dwelling, a doorway led to a pleasant garden.*

ABOVE: *Note the twelve-over-twelve windows and the sturdy doorway of the Deshler-Morris House, as illustrated in a plate from a 1904 guidebook to historic Germantown.*

BENJAMIN FRANKLIN'S HOUSE?

There is a poetic appropriateness to the skeletal frame that limns the outlines of Benjamin Franklin's house in Philadelphia: even when his substantial brick dwelling stood on the site, the man himself was almost never there.

In 1763, Benjamin Franklin (1706–1790) hired the builder Robert Smith to construct his High Street house, but before the three-story structure could be completed, Franklin departed for England. During his absence, the home was finished and his common-law wife, Deborah Read Rogers Franklin, resided there with their daughter, Sarah, and her husband, Richard Bache. By the time Franklin returned, in 1775,

Deborah was dead, and Franklin remained in America only sixteen months before going back to Europe on the new nation's business. After spending another nine years abroad, he returned to America for good in 1785 and promptly planned an addition to the house. He then enjoyed the new drawing room and library until his death.

Only archaeological remnants survived of Franklin's house (it was demolished in 1812), so as part of the bicentennial celebration, the National Park Service commissioned the architect Robert Venturi to design a remembrance of the man and his Philadelphia dwelling. The result is the so-called Ghost House, the steel frame that outlines the approximate mass of Franklin's long-lost home.

General Knox's Montpelier

His friends called him Harry—and Henry

Knox, in his two decades of government service, managed to make friends with just about everyone he met. The Marquis de Chastellux described him as "gay and amiable." Other contemporaries wrote of his "cheerful smile," "affable speech," and "[j]ubilant character."

But Henry Knox (1750–1806) was more than likable. People also respected him for his abilities and long service as a major general under Commander in Chief George Washington and as secretary of war during the Confederation years and in President Washington's cabinet. Only after serving his country for almost twenty years did Knox return to private life. He saw the financial chaos General Nathanael Greene's wife inherited after the death of his old friend (see "Three Yankees Who Went Down to Georgia," page 313), and in December 1794, Secretary Knox resigned, explaining "The natural and powerful claims of a numerous family will no longer permit me to neglect their essential interest."

Henry and his wife, Lucy Flucker Knox, embarked on a new adventure with their six children. The Knoxes had moved house fourteen times in the preceding nineteen years, but now they were ready to settle in the Maine district. Henry had consolidated the

Henry Knox specified in a letter to housewright Ebenezer Dunton, in August of 1793, that his mansion was to have "an oval room . . . [and] staircases in the rear of the oval room to be lighted from the top of the house by a sky light or rather by two skylights, or one pretty large." Many architects in the Federal era incorporated curved rooms, moving beyond the traditional boxy forms of colonial architecture.

LEFT: *Montpelier is reminiscent of the White House. Built in the same decade, the main façades of both mansions swell boldly in elliptical curves. The President's House and Knox's home shared another similarity: both were built atop small hills overlooking rugged, undeveloped tracts of land. By employing the Renaissance notion of the* piano nobile, *in which the primary living floor is elevated to the second level, the designers enhanced both grand entrances to Montpelier.*

RIGHT: *At the Knox mansion, the clerestory windows immediately below the roof railing illuminate the central stair hall inside.*

'Tis high time that I should quit public life and attend
to the solid interest of my family, so that they may
not be left dependent upon the cold hand of charity.

—*Henry Knox, writing to his daughter Lucy, 1792*

General Knox in uniform—jowly, sanguine, yet with a military bearing. As one of his Maine neighbors said of him, "His features were regular, his Grecian nose prominent, his face full and open . . . his eyes gray, sharp and penetrating, seldom failing to recognize a countenance they had rested upon. His mental perception was equally penetrating, and he needed little time to form an opinion of a person's character." This portrait, a later copy of the circa 1805 Gilbert Stuart original, hangs at Montpelier in the oval salon.

Flucker family inheritance of some 576,000 acres along the rocky coast between the Kennebec and Penobscot Rivers. For the previous two years he had managed from afar the building of a grand mansion in the village of Thomas Town (later Thomaston).

Knox anticipated the pleasure of life after government service. One of his old colleagues wrote to cheer him on from his own retirement. "Have you become a farmer?" inquired former Secretary of State Thomas Jefferson from Monticello. "Is it not pleasanter than to be shut up with four walls and delving eternally with the pen? I am becoming the most ardent farmer in the state."

The Knoxes left Philadelphia in June 1795, bound for New York, where they boarded a packet for Boston. After a celebratory retirement dinner in Boston, Knox's hometown, the family embarked once more. On June 22, they reached their destination, traveling the last ten miles up the St. Georges River, their immense white house a beacon on the shore ahead of them.

Some townspeople greeted them that day, but the sociable Knox devised another way of getting acquainted with his new neighbors. He invited all the inhabitants of the county for an Independence Day party at the house his wife called Montpelier. More than five hundred people came.

"At early dawn in the morning, the company began to assemble in crowds," remembered their nineteen-year-old daughter, Lucy. "Men, women and children poured in until the house completely filled and babies without number were placed on the different beds—which caused no small confusion among the mothers, who found it difficult to remember where they had placed them. . . . The house was so much larger than anything they had seen before, that everything was a subject of wonder. Every object around had all the attraction of novelty."

The jolly General Knox, determined though he was to fade away to private life, could never resist a party.

THE CHIEF OF ARTILLERY

His father having abandoned the family, Henry Knox was forced to leave school. To help support the family, he apprenticed as a bookbinder in a bookstore. There one of the proprietors kept a watchful eye on the lad, who proved clever, ambitious, and a voracious reader. Knox taught himself French, read Plutarch, and studied military strategy and engineering. His spelling proved to be more intuitive than disciplined, but by age twenty-one he had opened his own

Boston shop, the London Book-Store. According to one advertisement, the wares on offer, "just imported in the last ships from London, [include] a large and very elegant assortment of the most modern Books in all branches of Literature, Arts and Sciences."

The young man welcomed a genteel clientele to his shop. Despite his limited formal education, the gracious, companionable, and well-read Mr. Knox impressed his customers and offered them a congenial place to meet and talk. He paid close attention, too, adopting their manners and dapper dress. One young Loyalist lady, Miss Lucy Flucker, proved especially susceptible to the bookseller's charm, and they soon married.

Knox caught revolutionary fever early when, at twenty, he witnessed the Boston Massacre, in which eight beleaguered Redcoats fired upon a crowd of unarmed Bostonians, killing five people. A hearty, barrel-chested man with a booming voice to match, Knox soon became a lieutenant in the Grenadier Corps, a Boston militia, and welcomed to his bookstore not only English-educated patrons, many of them Tories, but also Patriots, among them Paul Revere and the Rhode Islander Nathanael Greene.

After the Battle of Lexington and Concord, everything changed. With his militia sword sewn inside the lining of Lucy's cloak (or, perhaps, her petticoat; the anecdote varies with the teller), Knox and his wife left town under cover of night, abandoning his bookstore to begin his military life. Barely two months later, he met the new commander in chief when George Washington toured the artillery installation Knox had overseen near Boston. Knox had two obvious physical disadvantages for a soldier. He was overweight, standing slightly over six feet tall and already well on his way to his eventual bulk of three hundred pounds; and he had lost two fingers in a hunting accident in 1773. But the young man's book-learned knowledge of gunnery impressed Washington, who made him his chief of artillery.

Soon General and Mrs. Washington found they also had two new friends; for much of the next two decades, Harry and Lucy Knox remained social intimates and political allies of George and Martha. Knox's loyalty, administrative skills, resourcefulness, and sheer desire to please his friend made him indispensable. During the Revolution, Knox and his artillery played important roles at the siege of Boston as well as the Battles of Trenton, Princeton, Brandywine, Germantown, Monmouth, and Yorktown. Later, in Washington's cabinet, Knox negotiated Indian treaties, planned coastal fortifications, and helped found the U.S. Navy, commissioning the construction of six frigates, among them the USS *Constitution*.

LUCY AND HARRY

Harry and Lucy Knox made a formidable partnership; in the way that George Washington cannot be understood without reference to Martha, Washington's most enduring military confidant must be remembered as Lucy's husband.

Her father was Massachusetts's last provincial secretary and a staunch Loyalist. When the willful Lucy became enamored of a mere bookseller, both her parents opposed the marriage. Harry had been a pauper child, and his politics seemed to them horrifically revolutionary, but Lucy, even at age seventeen, knew precisely what she wanted. Her parents were not present when Harry and Lucy married, in 1774. After the couple fled Boston, in April 1775, Henry's brilliant stratagem of moving the guns from Fort Ticonderoga to Dorchester Heights overlooking the city forced the British to evacuate (see "Tory Row," page 84). Lucy watched in March 1776 as her parents sailed for England, gone forever from her life.

Even in youth, both husband and wife were big-boned, tending to overweight. Equally, though, both were happy people, valued by their friends for their good humor and generous natures. Insistent that she remain with her husband, Lucy spent much of the war as a core member of Martha Washington's sewing circle. At times she left her children in the care of others, but more often she took them with her: as the Marquis de Chastellux observed during the winter encampment of 1781, Lucy and "a child of six months and a little girl of three years old formed a real *family* for the general."

Lucy had her domestic side, but she was nothing if not spirited and independent, and she learned to play the role of great lady from the best of them (she presided at Mount Vernon for a time during the siege of Yorktown, in 1781). She wrote to her husband during one of their separations, musing on life after the war. "I hope you will not consider yourself as commander in chief of our own

TOP: *This elegant travel case contained all the essentials—a tea set for two, silverware, bottles of liquor and perfume, a sewing kit, and toiletries. Known as un nécessaire, the Parisian-made box is believed to have been given to General Knox by his old colleague in arms the Marquis de Lafayette.*

ABOVE: *The core of Montpelier is dominated by its staircase, a dramatic and decorative construct that soars up to the chamber (bedroom) floor. When the original mansion was demolished, in 1871, many of the spiral-turned spindles from the grand stairway were salvaged, and local townspeople kept them as souvenirs, referring to them as "Thomaston Walking Sticks."*

ABOVE: *In the absence of other evidence of the central stair, the twentieth-century architects charged with creating a new Montpelier built a fancy-based-on-fact flying staircase. A good deal was known of a staircase in the Barrell House in Charlestown, Massachusetts, which the architects believed had inspired the one at Montpelier. After studying photos, drawings, and documentation of the Barrell staircase—designed by the Boston architect Charles Bulfinch—they designed the theatrical space pictured here.*

house, but be convinced that there is such a thing as equal command." While their marriage appears to have been a partnership of equals, it was also a love match. "[Harry] is the best and tenderest of friends," Lucy once wrote to her sister, "[but] never were two persons more happily united than we."

Lucy's life was tinged with sadness: she birthed thirteen children, and of the three who lived to adulthood, her son Henry Jackson Knox proved to have a weakness for drink and to be a poor manager of money. During their first April in Maine, Lucy lost two children (Augusta Henrietta, nine, and William Bingham, eleven) to diphtheria; the next year her thirteenth child was stillborn; and a year later, her daughter Julia died of consumption at age thirteen. Local oral history has it that the Knoxes' Maine neighbors began referring to their first-floor room where the deceased children were laid out as the "dead room."

Lucy had been raised in elite Boston society, and her manners and conversation put other members of the gentry at ease. But she was a complex figure: a demon card player (whist and loo were her favorites), indomitable at chess (Dolley Madison called it Madame Knox's "mania . . . she is certainly the best I ever encountered"), and obese in middle age ("Her size is enormous," John and Abigail Adams's daughter Nabby told her mother. "I verily believe her waist is as large as three of yours"). Her friends in Philadelphia found her charming, but Lucy's Maine neighbors thought her aloof and haughty.

A NEW LIFE IN THOMASTON

Henry Knox left public life for Maine in 1795, prepared to embark on new ventures of his own.

FACING PAGE AND ABOVE: *The grandest room in the house, the large oval parlor was heated with two fireplaces and illuminated by a pair of floor-to-ceiling windows that opened on the piazza.*

In this circa 1870 daguerreotype, Montpelier's deterioration is evident, from the overgrown plantings to the absence of the grand front porch that originally ran the length of the house. The first Montpelier would be demolished the following year.

THE SOCIETY OF THE CINCINNATI

At the close of the war, Continental Army officers formed the Society of the Cincinnati. The organization took its name from a Roman farmer, Lucius Quinctius Cincinnatus. In the fifth century B.C., Cincinnatus left his plow upon hearing his nation's call (like so many Revolutionary War officers did), led his troops to victory, and then returned to his fields.

Henry Knox wrote the society's constitution, and George Washington was elected its first president. Membership was limited to officers who had fought in the Revolution, along with their eldest male descendants. Members were required to pledge one month's pay; it was to be a benevolent society, supporting needy officers, widows, and orphans.

The organization had its detractors from the beginning; to critics, a hereditary military organization seemed unegalitarian and inconsistent with the republican ideology. Although the society survives, it proved to be largely unpolitical.

This Society of the Cincinnati medal was Knox's own. Designed by Pierce L'Enfant (who later planned the new "Federal City," Washington, D.C.), the gold medal was suspended from a deep blue ribbon, edged with white, to signify the union of France and the United States.

One contemporary described 1790s Thomaston as "still a woody region, interspersed with straggling clearings, dotted here and there with small, low unpainted houses." Squatters had cleared acreage to make their claims, and a small town was emerging, though it still lacked a church. As Harry and Lucy's immense Federal mansion rose atop a low hill near the harbor, it must have stood out like Gulliver among the Lilliputians. Planning his new domicile from afar, Knox advised his Boston housewright, Ebenezer Dunton, that he wanted the "basement, parlor, [and] chamber . . . stories" to be nine, thirteen, and eleven feet high. The result, a house of some twenty rooms, was both massive and tall.

The true grandeur of the Knox mansion was a function of both size *and* style. Aware of the emerging Neoclassical trend in architecture and its vogue for dramatic interiors, Knox described to Dunton his wish for "an oval room with wing rooms . . . [and]

BELOW: *Known as the General's Bedroom, this chamber contains a fine four-poster bed (note the painted cornice) purchased by Knox in 1796 from the Charlestown, Massachusetts, maker Benjamin Frothingham. The receipt for its purchase survives (the price was 12 pounds, 10); the bureau (bottom) with pigeonhole organizer and drop-front desk surface in its top drawer came from the same maker. The architectural wallpaper, printed in imitation of cut ashlar stonework, was a popular choice circa 1800.*

ABOVE: *On either side of the oval room on the first floor were two square rooms, the drawing room (top) and the dining room (above). Although local legend asserts that the mirrored bookcase in the drawing room once belonged to Marie Antoinette, its materials and manufacture suggest that Knox brought it to Maine from its maker's shop in Philadelphia. Several of the wallpapers, including that in the dining room, were reproduced from surviving scraps salvaged from the original house.*

staircases in the rear of the oval room to be lighted from the top of the house by a sky light or rather by two skylights, or one pretty large." His Maine mansion would feature elliptical rooms and a soaring staircase. (See "The Federal Style," page 290.)

The Boston builders set to work in their shop in the autumn of 1793, making window frames, sashes, shutters, doors, balustrades, cornices, and the smooth sheathing for the front of the house. In the spring Dunton and his partner, Tileston Cushing, signed a contract with Knox agreeing "to build for . . . Henry Knox resident at Philadelphia . . . A dwelling house at Thomas Town agreeable to the plan furnished." Ten carpenters and eight masons traveled to Maine to begin construction on site, while Dunton fabricated architectural elements at his Back Street workshop in Boston.

The sheer size of the place worried Knox's great friend and Boston lawyer Henry Jackson. Charged with managing construction while Knox fulfilled his duties as secretary of war in Philadelphia, Jackson warned his friend, "I believe you do not calculate the expense of this immence Fabrick—twenty-four fire places and all your rooms pretty large." Knox's finances were perilous at best; he had gone into considerable debt to reassemble the Flucker holdings in Maine. His house, its price estimated by Jackson at $8,000 to $10,000, probably cost closer to $15,000 to complete.

Knox arrived in Maine with big plans for his properties. Among the businesses he wished to develop were lumbering, lime burning, shipping, cattle breeding, and brick making. He never did things in a small way—he purchased forty-six mattresses, sixty-six pounds of wallpaper, a billiard table, a fortepiano (his daughter Lucy played), 364 books in French, and even four cannons. There were at least eight outbuildings on the property; he kept twenty horses in his stable. The Knoxes soon found themselves living in straitened circumstances, and the house they had built as a summer home (they expected to winter in Boston) became their year-round home to save money.

Despite financial pressures, Knox confided in an old military friend in 1799, "I am more happy than at any other period of my adult age." He spent just eleven years at Montpelier before his premature death, in 1806, at age fifty-six. Dining at a friend's home, he swallowed a chicken bone that perforated his intestine. The resulting peritonitis killed him three days later.

MONTPELIER II

With Harry dead, Lucy remained at Montpelier, gradually selling off most of their real estate holdings to support herself and clear her husband's debts. When she died, in 1824, the house was already in disrepair; by the time Nathaniel Hawthorne visited, in 1837, he beheld "a large, rusty-looking edifice of wood." In 1871 the mansion was demolished to make way for the Knox and Lincoln Railroad.

The Montpelier on view today is a reconstruction. Early in the twentieth century, a member of the General Knox Chapter of the Daughters of the American Revolution observed that "in nearly every home [in Thomaston] there was something that came from the original Mansion—a chair, table, dishes, plaster, door, or wallpaper." When a descendant agreed to donate his Knox family pieces to the DAR with the proviso that a fireproof home be provided for them, the notion of rebuilding Montpelier began to take shape. A Boston architectural firm, Putnam and Cox, was commissioned to draft plans for a replica, and after more than fifteen years of fundraising, a gift from Cyrus Curtis, publisher of *The Saturday Evening Post* and a native of Maine, enabled construction to get under way in 1929.

The Knox Memorial Association opened the house to the public in 1931. It sits on a hill some distance from the original site. Its appearance is based on extrapolations from minute examinations of antique photographs, a drawing of the interior of uncertain date, a few dimensions specified in correspondence, and frequent reference to houses by the Boston architect Charles Bulfinch, whose works were surely known to Knox and his builders. The interior is based on educated guesses and key pieces of physical evidence that provided some details from the original, among them wooden shutters, staircase and roof balusters, and wallpaper scraps.

Montpelier today cannot be said to be the home of Harry and Lucy Knox. Nor is it fair to say it is a facsimile, given how little its creators knew of the original. Yet to many people the place embodies a significance as real and important as if it were a restored survivor, like the other houses in this volume.

Washington's Mount Vernon

The brave George Washington must have known fear on the battlefield. Yet none of his men reported him exhibiting any reluctance to lead them into battle, even when confronted by flashing bayonets, booming cannons, and musket balls. But the threat of his mother moving to Mount Vernon? George seems to have found that a frightening prospect.

He wrote to her in February 1787. The elderly and long-widowed Mary Washington was in decline, and her son sensibly advised she should "break up housekeeping." Living with one of her children seemed the right thing, he thought, but he was quick to explain that his house would hardly suit her. He put it this way:

> My house is at your service, & [I] would press you most
> sincerely & most devoutly to accept it, but . . . candour
> requires me to say it will never answer your purposes . . .
> in truth it may be compared to a well resorted tavern, as
> scarcely any strangers who are going from north to south,
> or from south to north do not spend a day or two at it.

For once, the notoriously demanding Mary Ball Washington took the hint and chose to remain in Fredericksburg (she would die at home two years later of breast cancer). But her son did not exaggerate when he talked about the plethora of visitors at Mount Vernon. In one year alone, the records document 667 guests. Many

Mount Vernon's porch has breathtaking views of the Potomac River.

ABOVE: *Whether arriving by water or by land, most visitors would enter the passage or central hall, which extends from the front to the back of the house. Near the end of his life, Washington ordered the woodwork in the passage grain-painted, and a faux finish was applied to simulate the grain and color of mahogany.*

ABOVE RIGHT: *The large dining room was called the New Room, because it was the last principal room to be finished. Completed in the mid-1780s, it incorporated the latest in decorative notions, with classical motifs applied to its orna-mented ceiling and Palladian window. Note the crumb cloth beneath the table; used to protect floor and carpets, the fabric would be removed and shaken by the servants after the meal.*

RIGHT: *The marble chimneypiece was a gift from an English merchant and admirer, Samuel Vaughan. Washington was at first reluctant to install it, worrying that it was "too elegant and costly by far . . . for my own room and republican style of living."*

During Washington's time, more than a dozen buildings stood on his Mansion House farm. Pictured above, on either side of the main house are the gardener's house and servants' hall (at left) and the kitchen (at right). The mansion itself was linked to its two flankers (left) by curving colonnades, which functioned as covered walkways.

strangers stayed only a few hours, but more than a few friends and family members remained for weeks at a time.

Custom called for members of Virginia's landed gentry to open their homes to visitors. George Washington (1732–1799) honored that tradition and more; even in his absence he was concerned that charity be extended to the poor as well as the comfortably well-to-do. He instructed from his military quarters in Cambridge in 1775, "Let the hospitality of the House . . . be kept up. Let no one go hungry away." Hospitality was, quite simply, a given for anyone knocking at the door of America's greatest man.

AN ARCHITECTURAL ASSAY

One visitor who appeared unbidden was a brilliant young Englishman named Benjamin Henry Latrobe. He arrived with better auspices than many others, armed with a letter from the President's nephew Bushrod Washington. They had become friends in Richmond, where Bushrod practiced law and Latrobe, a London-trained

architect and engineer, considered establishing a professional practice in America.

Over the next quarter century, Latrobe would have a great impact on the nation's architecture, canals, sanitation, and its capital city, but during the summer of 1796 he was still getting his bearings. He had arrived in Virginia four months earlier, a man of some means but still shocked by the sudden death of his wife and a precipitous downturn in his London practice caused by the French war. He arrived in search of new prospects for work in both engineering and architecture. He was quite literally learning the lay of the land that summer, and during one of his occasional journeys around the commonwealth, he proceeded on horseback to Mount Vernon.

After a visit nearby with Bushrod's father-in-law, Latrobe rode down a wooded road until he reached a large stone gristmill straddling a creek. That landmark stood at the entrance to Washington's eight-thousand-acre plantation. After traveling another two and a half miles on the entrance road, Latrobe reached the mansion house.

AMERICA'S FIRST PROFESSIONAL ARCHITECT

Charles Willson Peale's portrait of Benjamin Henry Latrobe. His spectacles are just visible amid his curly hair; he needed them badly, once remarking, "I am only half alive without their assistance."

Benjamin Henry Latrobe (1764–1820) appraised Mount Vernon differently than other visitors.

As a young man, he traveled Europe, visiting Rome, Paris, and other capitals. In London he apprenticed as an engineer and architect. By the time the thirty-two-year-old Latrobe arrived in America, he could execute precise architectural renderings, devise civil engineering projects, and critique the style of a building as no one else on the continent could.

Thomas Jefferson was among the first Americans to recognize Latrobe's talents, and he created the office of surveyor of public buildings for the young man in 1802. For almost twenty years, Latrobe supervised construction at the Capitol and the President's House, and designed a range of domestic, commercial, civic, and ecclesiastical projects, including banks, canals, a cathedral in Baltimore, municipal water systems in Philadelphia and New Orleans, a prison in Richmond, and various mansions.

When Latrobe arrived, American architecture was in the hands of amateurs; he made it his duty to establish professional standards and set an example for the next generation of architects. Buildings were to be imagined on paper first, Latrobe demonstrated, independent of the builders. He thought of buildings in spatial terms. He imagined volumes from within, then sculpted them—in his mind and on paper—into one composition.

Although the landward approach to Mount Vernon owed a debt to other designers, the elevation that overlooked the Potomac was of Washington's own imagining. The memorable piazza (facing page) was destined to become one of the most imitated American architectural innovations of the revolutionary era. It runs the full ninety-six-foot length and two-story height of the house, and the view from it extends up the Potomac toward the city that bears Washington's name.

Within certain limits, he liked what he saw. He recounted, "The center is an old house to which a good dining room has been added at the north end, and a study &c. &c., at the south. The House is connected with the Kitchen offices by arcades." Still, as a man who had built two substantial stone mansions outside London earlier in the decade, he wasn't overly impressed, concluding, "The whole of . . . the building is in a very indifferent taste."

THE MANSION HOUSE

The plantation once belonged to George's father, Augustine Washington, who deeded it to George's half brother Lawrence. After the premature deaths of Augustine and Lawrence, George acquired title to what was then a 2,126-acre plantation, dubbed Mount Vernon in honor of a British admiral under whom Lawrence had served.

At the age of twenty-two, George Washington became the man of the house, taking over management of the plantation, which had been in his family since 1674. During the next forty-five years, the plantation would be the source of his livelihood. He was a farmer who managed the land carefully, quadrupling the holdings he inher-

ited. He eventually acquired four surrounding farms, where he grew a range of grains, in particular wheat and corn, with a total of some 3,000 acres in tillage. Washington never tired of farming talk—in fact, he and Latrobe conversed on the design of plows, crop rotation, and the nutritive value of corn.

His service in the Virginia militia during the French and Indian War meant Washington spent little time at Mount Vernon until his return to private life in 1758. As he anticipated his marriage—to the wealthy widow Martha Dandridge Custis in 1759—his house suddenly seemed too small. In the year they wed, he embarked on a major remodeling, raising the roof to double the size of the house. But that was not the structure over which Latrobe cast his appraising gaze.

Washington reinvented the place yet again after 1773 as he was about to emerge as a national figure. He added rooms at each end, transforming the modest house of his boyhood—it had four rooms and a passage on the main floor with four smaller rooms above—into a house as grand as the great man himself. It enclosed twenty-odd rooms in an era when most Americans lived in homes of two first-floor rooms with unfinished sleeping quarters in the attic.

Washington's vision of the place led him to add a cupola, a borrowing from the Governor's Palace in Williamsburg; a Palladian window in the "New Room," perhaps the first room in America decorated in the style of the English architect Robert Adam, which had become the rage in England; and two flanking dependencies, along with connecting colonnades, that put a Washingtonian stamp on the then-popular Palladian five-part house (see "The William Paca House" and "The Matthias Hammond House," pages 36 and 182). The house had truly become a mansion, and at his death, Washington was a wealthy man with more than three hundred slaves working his plantation.

Ironically, Washington himself would be little more than a visitor for long periods during his service as commander in chief of the army (1775–1783) and later as president (1789–1797). But his house was (and remains today) the most visible symbol of Washington, his manner of living, and his aspirations. Its story parallels the life history of the man.

CONVERSING WITH THE GENERAL

Following the protocol of the time, Latrobe left his horse at the stable upon arriving at Mount Vernon, and a servant carried his letter of introduction to his master. Meanwhile the visitor ambled onto the porch to the rear.

The river front he liked rather more than what he had seen on the entrance façade, remarking that the "portico supported by 8 square pillars [has] good proportions and effect." The two-story-tall, fourteen-foot-wide porch was enormous. But it was a space where, Latrobe would soon find, the Washingtons and their guests tended to linger, talking, reading, and socializing. While he waited, Latrobe took in the sweeping vista of the Potomac and the Maryland hills beyond.

President Washington came to him in ten minutes, and in his journal that night, Latrobe recorded their meeting: "He was dressed in a plain blue coat, his hair dressed and powdered. There was a reserve but no hauteur in his manner. He shook me by the hand, said he was glad to see a friend of his Nephew, drew a chair and desired me to sit down."

Asymmetry was certainly not a guiding principle of eighteenth-century architecture, but as the old General said to Latrobe, "Sir, you see I take my own way." At Mount Vernon, Washington was remodeling an existing house, and he chose not to reinvent entirely the original structure that remained at the center of his Mansion House, betraying a certain bilateral imbalance.

They talked, moving quickly from pleasantries to the rivers of Virginia and a canal project Washington favored. The President believed firmly that expansion of the frontier was key to the future of the new nation; he also believed that an inland waterway might be engineered to facilitate the flow of goods and people. "I was very much flattered by his attention to my observations," Latrobe noted. The men conversed intently for more than two hours.

Washington invited Latrobe to stay for dinner, which was served at three o'clock. Latrobe was seated at Mrs. Washington's left hand. He found her very agreeable, observing that "she retains strong remains of considerable beauty, seems to enjoy very good health and to have a good humor. She has no affectation of superiority in the slightest degree, but acts compleatly in the character of the Mistress of the house of a respectable and opulent country gentleman."

Washington reinvented a vernacular Virginia planter's dwelling, making it his chief architectural statement. Mount Vernon was the world as he would have it.

While Washington had no children of his own, at sixty-four he had spent a great many years in loco parentis to a number of other people's youngsters. Martha had arrived in 1759 with her son, John Parke Custis, known as Jacky, and daughter, Martha (Patsy) Parke Custis. When Jack died suddenly at just twenty-six, Martha and George took in his two youngest children, Eleanor Parke Custis and George Washington Parke Custis, and brought them up as their own (Jacky's two older daughters remained with their mother, who subsequently remarried).

Now seventeen, Eleanor—Nelly, as she was affectionately known—enraptured Latrobe. "Miss Eleanor Custis . . . has more perfection of form of expression, of color, of softness, and of firmness of mind than I have ever seen before, or conceived consistent with mortality. . . . [T]he soul beaming through her countenance, and glowing in her smile, is as superior to her face, as mind is to matter."

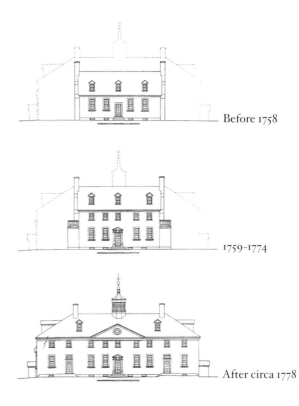

Before 1758

1759-1774

After circa 1778

A second youth of the same age was also at hand. George Washington Motier Lafayette, the son of the Marquis de Lafayette, was in residence at Mount Vernon, since his father was incarcerated in the wake of the French Revolution. (Latrobe: "He talked much, especially with Miss Custis and seemed to possess wit, and fluency.")

Latrobe was privileged to glimpse the domestic Washington; in turn, he left us the priceless record of his visit, in both words and pictures, as he employed his sketchbook while at Mount Vernon and later painted watercolors of the house and those who lived there.

MARTHA WASHINGTON, FOUNDING MOTHER

When George Washington took the oath of office on April 30, 1789, the newly ratified Constitution specified much about his role as the nation's chief executive. But his devoted wife, Martha, was cast in a part for which no lines had been written. Martha Dandridge Custis Washington (1731–1802), barely five feet tall, proved very much up to the task.

As the daughter of a moderately successful planter, she had been trained to tend to the needs of large numbers of people—family, friends, and strangers alike. As the widow of the wealthy Daniel Parke Custis and the wife of George Washington of Mount Vernon, she spent her early adult life endeavoring to make a constant stream of guests comfortable. Likewise, she welcomed a rotating series of officers and wives to her table during the war, along the way winning the admiration of French aristocrats, dying soldiers, wealthy Philadelphia merchants, officers young and old, and virtually every woman who crossed her path.

Martha Washington had a series of surrogate daughters. Nelly, Nelly's older sisters, her daughter-in-law, Martha's own younger sisters, and a variety of nieces all got the benefit of her ministrations. She taught them manners and good posture, arranged for music and dancing lessons, and nursed them when they were ill. Her home was a happy place; the girls in her life returned her love and devotion.

Martha wrote countless letters. Although many seem to have been written for her by various secretaries, her personal style is unmistakable. Unlike George's literary voice, which tended to be mannered, courtly, and wordy, Martha's was economical and to the point. Her grammar, spelling, and punctuation were idiosyncratic, but she said what she had to say, sent her love, and signed off. The dynamic of George and Martha's marriage can be understood only at second hand, since virtually no correspondence between them survives.

The Widow Custis had been a wealthy woman when she married Squire George Washington; in fact, his rise in Virginia society might not have come to pass without the money and social connections she brought to the union. She devoted her life to her husband, just as he devoted his to his nation. "I have been so long accustomed to conform to events which are governed by the public voice," she wrote to a friend as George's first term as president neared an end, "I can hardly dare indulge any personal wishes which cannot yield to that." Perhaps it is only appropriate that Martha Washington—in her own right and as the general's wife—became the most notable American woman of her century.

THE DEATH OF WASHINGTON

Even when he was sixty-seven, a five-hour horseback ride was usual for George Washington. No one was surprised when, on Thursday, December 12, 1799, he returned from inspecting his farms a bit later than usual. It was after three o'clock, but Martha had waited dinner for him. He soon sat down to eat, his hair still damp from the mix of rain, hail, and snow he had encountered.

More snow fell overnight, so Washington took no ride on Friday. He reported having a cold and an accompanying sore throat in the morning but felt well enough by afternoon to mark some trees in the "hanging wood," the facing groves on the hillside that framed the majestic view of the Potomac from the portico. In the evening, he complained of hoarseness, but when his secretary, Tobias Lear, asked if he might take something to treat his cold, Washington rejected the idea: "You know I never take any thing for a cold. Let it go as it came."

Washington awakened in the early hours of the morning, complaining to Martha of an ague (fever and chills). He could barely speak, and his breathing was labored. Presented with a mixture of molasses, vinegar, and butter to soothe his throat, he could not swal-

Washington added a private study at the south end of the mansion, and he filled it with objects essential to his private and public life. At right are the desk and chair he occupied while writing countless letters. Against the far wall is his dressing table, where he readied himself for the day. He surrounded himself with his books, his globe, and even a portrait of his brother Lawrence, who preceded him as master of Mount Vernon.

low it. His doctor was summoned and made an incision to bleed the former president; a prevailing medical theory held that the balance of the "four humors" (black and yellow bile, blood, and phlegm) determined health and that the letting of blood could correct imbalances.

Other treatments were also tried in the course of the day. Washington's neck was bathed with "salvolatila" (an ammonia salt also known as hartshorn; see "Medicaments," page 273); his feet were bathed in warm water. Since he showed no sign of improvement, another doctor was called. A "blister of Cantharides" (also known as Spanish fly, an inflammatory agent) was put on his throat, and more blood was let. He choked and nearly suffocated when given a gargle of vinegar and sage tea. A third doctor was consulted, and he was bled again. Despite Martha's entreaties "that not much be taken from him," more than five pints of blood were let.

Washington knew his condition was dire, and late Saturday afternoon, he asked Martha to bring him two wills from his office. In her absence he confided in his private secretary, "I feel I am going, my breath cannot last long." Between ten and eleven o'clock that night, he expired.

Modern doctors have generally agreed that, based on the symptoms Washington exhibited, the cause of his death was acute epiglottis, in which swelling at the back of throat blocks the airway. Despite the bizarre treatments he was given—the letting of roughly a third of his blood volume certainly did not help matters—his physicians can hardly be faulted; bloodletting was the treatment of choice for many complaints at the time. Certainly all three doctors wanted nothing more than to save the life of the man who was almost universally acclaimed for his military and political leadership.

The Palladian Window

Often misidentified, the Palladian window is not simply a window with a round top; more correctly, the name identifies a grouping of three windows. The one at the center is arch-topped, the shorter ones on either side rectangular. Traditionally the three openings are decorated with flattened columns (pilasters) and other elaborately molded trim.

The man after whom the window was named, Andrea Palladio, was known to use this architectural element—but so was another Italian designer, Sebastiano Serlio (thus another name for the same notion, the Serlian motif). Most likely, the great Renaissance artist Raphael had the idea first, but the notion was transmitted to posterity by Palladio's *Four Books of Architecture,* in which other writers and, eventually, Washington and countless other British and American builders found it (see also "Andrea Palladio," page 131).

The Palladian motif has proved very flexible. Palladio himself used it for ground-floor entrances and upstairs windows. It invites in volumes of light, which is one reason eighteenth-century builders set Palladian windows in central halls and staircases (or, as in Washington's case, in his new, show-off dining room). The triple openings became principal sources of illumination for large spaces, which were often difficult to light in an unelectrified age. And just as a Palladian window lets light *in,* it frames the view *out* in grand style.

PRESERVATION'S FIRST PLACE

The visitors who streamed into Mount Vernon threatened to overwhelm George Washington in life, but after his death they would prove to have been but the trickle that anticipated the deluge. A thousand visitors a year would have been almost unthinkable to him, whereas today's caretakers must plan in terms of a thousand thousands.

After her husband died, in 1799, Martha Washington closed the second-floor bed chamber they had shared. Sealing it off constituted a tribute to her husband, then a common practice. However, rather than leave it for a respectful interval, she moved permanently to a third-floor bedroom, where she died in 1802. Mount Vernon then became the property of Bushrod Washington, the nephew who had written to his uncle on Benjamin Latrobe's behalf (and who had recently been named by President John Adams an associate justice of the Supreme Court). At Bushrod's death, in 1829, his nephew John Augustine Washington inherited, but it would be John Augustine Washington, Jr., from whom the Mount Vernon Ladies' Association would purchase the dilapidated property.

Led by a determined South Carolinian named Ann Pamela Cunningham, the Mount Vernon Ladies' Association of the Union was founded in 1853. By 1858, the Ladies had managed to persuade John A. Washington to sell, had raised the money for a down payment, and had signed a contract to buy the estate over the next several years. Their restoration of the place as a shrine to Washington initiated a historic reverence for America's past as the first successful national effort at preservation. An unbreakable thread connects the Ladies' sense of mission with the subsequent conservation of countless American historic sites, the nation's patriotic view of its past, and even books such as this one.

To visit Mount Vernon today is to revisit 1799, the target year of the restoration. The restoration has evolved over the generations, as recent archaeology studies are making possible the reconstruction of lost outbuildings and a fine-tuning of the landscape in a manner Washington would recognize. The issue of slavery, once virtually ignored, is now confronted and discussed. And the house, with its astonishingly complete collection of Washington artifacts, tells the story of a quiet gentleman who would have wanted you to feel welcome in his home.

LEFT: *The front or west parlor dates from Washington's first renovation of the house, circa 1759 (note the Georgian-style floor-to-ceiling paneling). This room was much used by the family, and it features portraits of Martha (left); her two children, Martha Parke and John Parke Custis; and Washington himself. The last canvas, a nineteenth-century copy of the original painted by Charles Willson Peale, portrays the general in his French and Indian War uniform in 1772.*

RIGHT: *Like the west parlor, the small dining room was used when larger rooms were not required to accommodate guests. Its finish consists of several layers of a glaze pigmented with verdigris (copper acetate) atop a base layer of green paint. The image over the mantel is an engraving of a family portrait by Edward Savage.*

A Ring on Her Finger

Martha Washington's daughter, Martha Parke (Patsy) Custis, began to have seizures at age twelve. Her stepfather and mother did all that they could to boost her spirits (fine London clothes, a dancing master, a pet parrot) and consulted various doctors, who prescribed a variety of medications, even an iron "cramp ring." Such rings, together with their supposedly magical inscriptions, were leftovers from medieval medicine.

Patsy's ring proved less than efficacious. As Washington wrote to his brother-in-law in June 1773, Patsy "rose from dinner about four o'clock in better health and spirits than she had appeared to have been in for some time; soon after which she was seized with one of her usual fits and expired in it in less than two minutes without uttering a word, a groan, or scarce a sigh. This sudden and unexpected blow . . . has almost reduced my poor wife to the lowest ebb of misery."

As the old saying goes, the cure can be worse than the disease. Certainly that was true with bloodletting (phlebotomy), a standard medical procedure in the eighteenth century in which a volume of the patient's blood was drained through an incision (or incisions). The eighteenth-century apothecary closet contained a variety of remedies that promoted similarly bizarre (and now outmoded) therapies—vomiting, purging, and blistering among them—but others remain in use today.

Many herbal remedies used the active ingredients found in plants (synthetic chemical cures would come later). Some preparations were *tinctures,* in which the vegetative material (leaves, roots, or other plant parts) was crushed and immersed in alcohol (often whiskey), then sealed for a time, typically two weeks. Once the tincture was poured off, it was ready for use. *Infusions* were prepared by mixing the leaves, flowers, bark, or root of the plant with hot water (typically one-half ounce of the crude drug to a pint of liquid). When the medicament was boiled and simmered, it was termed a *decoction*. Topical *unguents* or *salves* were decoctions mixed with an oil and then boiled to the consistency of an ointment.

One group of infusions was the barks. Powdered bark would be mixed with water, wine, or brandy, often with spices such as ginger or cinnamon added. While the use of barks may seem quaint, drugs we continue to use, such as aspirin, quinine, and tamoxifen, were first isolated from the bark of the willow, the chinchona, and the Pacific yew. Valerian root was a widely used tincture that had been prescribed for centuries as a sleep aid, cough suppressant, and stimulant of the gastrointestinal tract.

A *poultice* is a warm, moist mass enclosed in cloth applied to the skin to warm or stimulate an aching part of the body. Some poultices were *blisters,* inflammatory agents intended to produced irritation (cantharides, a preparation made from a dried and crushed beetle also known as Spanish fly, was used as a blister by Washington's doctors in the hours before his death; see "The Death of Washington," page 269).

A few drops of a poisonous substance such as calomel (mercurous chloride) acted as a *purgative,* intended to induce vomiting or diarrhea and cleanse the system. Alexander Hamilton's mother, at age thirty-eight, came down with a raging fever, cause unknown. After a week it was unabated, so her St. Croix physician prescribed purgatives. The son, then age twelve, suffered similar symptoms, but the doctor chose bloodletting and an enema for his treatment. Alexander survived, but his mother was dead within forty-eight hours.

A loose classification of tonics made from various plants, bitters were bitter tasting when taken by mouth and often were used to soothe the stomach, though sometimes they were also applied topically. Teas made of various herbs were commonly used to treat slight fevers; brandy was prescribed as a sleeping draft; and coughs were treated with sugar- or herbal-based remedies. The tincture of opium laudanum had a range of uses, among them as a pain reliever (analgesic) and antidiarrheal. The Signer William Stockton's wife, Annis, following instructions from her son-in-law, the noted physician Benjamin Rush, dosed her "cholic" with "eighty drops of laudanum." Spirits of hartshorn, distilled from the hoofs and horns of oxen, has the strong smell of ammonia, making it useful as smelling salts. The preparation was administered to Alexander Hamilton after he had been mortally wounded in his duel with Aaron Burr. Peppermint water, an extract from the leaves and flowers of the plant of the same name, was thought to relieve digestive complaints, including flatulence. It is still in use for similar purposes, though its efficacy is uncertain.

Many, many more preparations were used in the eighteenth century, but perhaps the luckiest patients were those for whom their physicians chose to do nothing at all. *Vis medicatrix nature*—that is, the healing power of nature—was also memorialized in Hippocrates' advisory, "Do no harm."

The John Jay Homestead

For many years, Sarah Jay entertained the desire to withdraw from public life.

She and her husband, John, seemed the perfect couple when they married, in 1774 at Liberty Hall. The fourth daughter of the New Jersey Patriot William Livingston (see "William Livingston's Liberty Hall," page 228), Sarah was seventeen and a renowned beauty. John's family tree included prominent Dutch names such as Van Cortlandt and Philipse, and everyone knew the twenty-eight-year-old lawyer was well on his way to great things.

The couple were soon separated by his work when Jay, along with his father-in-law, rode to Philadelphia to serve in the Continental Congress. John and Sally's lives thereafter became peripatetic. Living in a war zone during the early years of the Revolution meant rapid moves to elude British troops ("Wherever I am," Sally wrote to her husband in 1777, "I think there are alarms"). Soon afterward she joined John on his diplomatic travels; the list of their children's birthplaces tells the tale. Peter was born in New Jersey (1776), Susan (1780) and Maria (1782) in Madrid, and Ann (1783)

When he became governor of New York, Jay shipped a set of twenty-four chairs (four with arms, the rest side chairs) to his home in Albany. A dozen of those chairs survive, some of them around this dining table. The mahogany table, too, belonged to Jay, along with the Chinese export china that bears the Jay monogram, the sideboard in the alcove, and the urn on top. The gilt overmantel mirror, at right, did not belong to Jay; in fact, he would probably have thought it ostentatious. As he once wrote, "Neatness + utility is all I ought or wish to aim at in Dress or Equipage."

John Jay settled into the life of an unpretentious and pious widower after his wife's death, in 1802. This portrait, dating from the previous decade, was executed by the painter and sometime diplomat John Trumbull.

JOHN JAY . . . SAGE AND CHIEF JUSTICE

John Jay left behind his judicial robes and the perquisites of some of the highest offices in the land when he retired. His son, William Jay, described his decades of retirement this way:

Although for many years filling stations which necessarily brought him into constant intercourse with the rich and fashionable, his dress, furniture and equipage were always as plain and frugal as propriety would permit. As a republican, he thought it became him to set an example of plainness and simplicity; as a Christian, he acknowledged the obligation to be "temperate in all things"; and as a parent, he shrunk from impoverishing his children by a vain and useless display, which, to use his own words, serves only to please other people's eyes, while it too often excites their envy. But his frugality had nothing in common with parsimony.

"A wise man," Jay said, "has money in his head, but not in his heart."

entered the world at Benjamin Franklin's house in Passy, France. William (1789) arrived in New York City, as did their last child, Sarah Louisa (1792).

Madrid proved an unhappy posting: "[B]ehold us in a country whose customs, language and religion are the very reverse of our own, without connections, without friends," Sally wrote to her mother. Paris was better ("I am very much pleased with France"), but after living in the world's cultural capital, Sally wished for a simpler life. "[N]othing could add more to my happiness than being mistress of a plentiful dairy and comfortable farm-house," she confided to one of her sisters.

After his father's death, Jay inherited a farm of 287 acres in Bedford, New York. Although he took title to the property in 1785, his diplomatic, judicial, and political careers occupied him for another sixteen years. Jay spent most of that time living in the nation's capitals (New York and Philadelphia) and New York's (Albany), but at last he resolved to retire to Bedford. He then embarked upon a renovation that made the modest farm manager's home more suitable for him, Sally, and their younger children. When Jay's second, three-year term as governor of New York ended, John Adams wished to reappoint him to the post of chief justice of the United States. But Jay wrote to the President in January 1801 to decline. Retirement beckoned, not least because his Sally was not well.

For Jay, retirement would prove to be of long duration. He spent three decades living the life a gentleman farmer in the mode of a Roman senator, tending his fields and orchards. But Sally was not so fortunate. After less than seven months in their "comfortable farm-house," she died there in May 1802. John never remarried.

JOHN JAY, A SUMMARY LIFE

Within his own family, he had been one of the lucky ones. Three of his siblings died in childhood, one had a crippling learning disability, and two others were blinded by smallpox. But John Jay (1745–1829) went about assembling the most diverse résumé of any of the Founding Fathers.

Although not initially an advocate for independence—he wished for reconciliation with Britain—he recognized in 1776 that

TOP: *The two armchairs in the Jay library came from Federal Hall in New York, where the U.S. Senate first convened.*

ABOVE: *Jay's desk was made about 1790 in New York of mahogany with birch veneer.*

John Jay and Manumission

In November 1786, John Jay asserted:

It is much to be wished that slavery be abolished. The honour of the States, as well as justice and humanity, in my opinion, loudly call upon them to emancipate these unhappy people. To contend for our liberty, and to deny that blessing to others, involves an inconsistency not to be excused.

While the noble sentiment rings true today, "liberty" proved to be a relative concept in the revolutionary era.

Few people then argued for complete and immediate emancipation. The prevailing belief held that the abolition of slavery would be an economic disaster for the agricultural economy of the Southern states and hardly a boon for many of the slaves themselves, given how few had trades or even rudimentary educations. But Jay had seen the slave trade at its ugliest when the ship on which he and Sally were traveling to Spain, dismasted and rudderless, had limped into port on Martinique in December 1779. There slaves on sugar plantations were literally worked to death.

For the rest of his political career, Jay sought to make gains in freeing the slaves—yet he also continued to purchase slaves. His gradualist approach involved manumission. "I purchase slaves and manumit them at proper ages and when their faithful services shall have afforded a reasonable retribution," he explained. As governor of New York, he oversaw passage of "An Act for the Gradual Abolition of Slavery." As of July 4, 1799, all male slaves were to be freed at age twenty-eight, females at age twenty-five, and all children born thereafter were free.

John Jay had been the first president of the New York Society for Promoting the Manumission of Slaves, an organization that he and other slaveholders had founded in 1785. He helped found the African Free School in New York. But it was to be Jay's son William Jay and grandson John Jay II who assumed leadership roles in the abolitionist movement before the Civil War. They campaigned against slavery in essays and pamphlets, as members and founders of antislavery societies, and in the courts.

LEFT: *The front parlor was in the original portion of the Jay Homestead. The portrait over the sofa was by John Trumbull. In 1844 it was purchased by John Jay's son William, who initiated what would be a multigenerational interest in conserving objects from the Signer's life.*

BELOW: *Conserving the past was indeed a family affair for the Jays: the curtained bed was John Jay's, and his descendants slept in it as late as the 1950s.*

The original cottage, as completed in 1790, was modest, consisting of just three bays (that is, three-fifths of the main mass of the existing house, including the center entrance and the two sets of windows to the left). When Jay enlarged the house in 1799–1801, he added the fourth and fifth bays to the right, the wings on either side of the main block, and the veranda.

How Much Is My House Worth?

Just as John Jay set about enlarging his country house, Congress passed the first direct federal tax. In order to assess the new tax, a baseline inventory of every dwelling, mill, barn, and wharf in the country was taken between 1798 and 1800. The wealth of some 433,000 landowners and the values of their 577,000 properties were determined. Much of the data collected survives; among the many intriguing findings were these:

✤ Some three thousand houses were valued at $1.00 or less, while only three were assessed at $30,000 or more.

✤ About a third of the properties had assessed values between $100 and $500.

✤ The average value of a house was $262.

✤ Values tended to be higher in urban than in nearby rural areas,

higher in eastern sections of states than in western ones, and greater in coastal states than in western ones.

✤ The total valuation of dwellings amounted to just over $151 million, with land values assessed at some three times that.

✤ The most expensive house belonged to a Salem, Massachusetts, merchant, Elias Haskett Derby. It was assessed at $37,500. At his death in 1799, Derby's estate of many ships, warehouses, cargoes, and other properties was estimated at roughly a million dollars, making him America's first millionaire. That was equivalent to approximately 16 *billion* twenty-first-century dollars.

A further analysis of the housing inventory and corollary data found that, as a rule of thumb, the value of an American's home appears to have been approximately equal to his yearly income.

independence was essential. He became president of the Continental Congress in 1778. Dispatched to Spain as the new nation's minister in 1779, he spent three years before moving on to France, where along with Benjamin Franklin and John Adams, he helped negotiate the Treaty of Paris. Upon returning to America in 1784, he learned that he had been appointed secretary of foreign affairs, the chief diplomatic office under the Articles of Confederation. He held that post for five years, during which he also attended the Constitutional Convention and campaigned for ratification, writing five of the essays published as *The Federalist,* which proved crucial to shaping public opinion. In 1789, President Washington appointed him the first chief justice of the United States, which he remained until he went abroad once more, to negotiate another treaty with Great Britain as America's minister plenipotentiary to England. The controversial Jay Treaty helped postpone war with England but contained little else of benefit to his country; it won Jay few plaudits and probably crushed whatever hopes he may have harbored for becoming president. On his return to America, he was elected governor of New York, a post in which he served from 1795 to 1801.

All those offices added up to twenty-seven consecutive years of public service. Perhaps it is no wonder that Jay declined President Adams's invitation to resume his seat on the Supreme Court in 1801 and instead retired to Bedford.

ABOVE: *During Jay's retirement, his son William and his family came to reside in the homestead. William's Jay bedroom reflects an early Victorian taste.*

RIGHT: *A shaving mirror that arrived at the Jay House compliments of a descendant in the nineteenth century.*

JOHN JAY, WIDOWER

Over the years, Jay added to the acreage he'd inherited. By the time it became his principal home, his holdings were up to 750 acres, including a nearby sawmill. He regarded the property not as a pleasure ground but as a working farm, with orchards, fields planted in grains, and pastures for grazing animals. He ordered the construction of two barns, a corncrib, a potato shed, and a wagon shed. When he decided to retire there, Jay commissioned a mason, a carpenter, and other workers to more than double the existing house. The staircase was moved and the roof raised.

When he took up residence in his enlarged home in May 1801, Jay arrived with his daughter Nancy, then eighteen. Sally Jay, her health steadily failing, remained with relatives a considerable distance away. "The noise and hurry of carpenters, masons, and labourers in and about the house are inconveniences to be submitted to," Jay wrote to his wife, "but not to be chosen by convalescents or invalids." At first Sally was accepting, but after a time she grew impatient. "Oh my Mr. Jay! The distance that separates us is too great." In October she arrived in Bedford, though the plasterers would still be at work in the dining room two months later.

The renovated dwelling was not the sort of country seat that Sarah's parents, uncles, and other wealthy relations inhabited; it also seemed modest in comparison with the town houses she and John had occupied in New York and Albany, where they had entertained lavishly, often welcoming large groups for dinner several times a week. Even so, compared with neighboring farmhouses, the Jays' twenty-four-room dwelling was large and comfortable, with ample space for John, Sally, and the three children who still lived with them, including Nancy, twelve-year-old William, and the youngest, Sarah Louisa, nine years old. Despite her continuing illness, Sally arrived with a sense of faith and hope. "In the country," she told John, "I feel ever sensible of an ever present deity dispensing light & life & cheerfulness around & my heart is animated with confidence & joy & love."

After Sally's death, in 1802, John rarely left Westchester County, preferring to remain at Bedford, then a two-day journey from New York City, where mail arrived only once a week. Although the kind of elaborate formal entertainments for which Sally had

James Sharples executed this pastel portrait of Sarah Livingston Jay and her two youngest children, William and Sarah Louisa, around 1798. He used an artistic conceit: the family has found a nest and two baby birds, which had fallen from a tree. One bird is still in the nest in Sarah's hand, while the other is fed berries by her daughter. The rescue of the birds is intended to be read as a metaphor for Sarah's nurturing love for her children.

been renowned were things of the past, the widower rarely lacked for company. For some years, he brought up his younger children; then in 1812, William returned with his bride, and they raised five children at the homestead. The presence of William's children inspired Jay to construct a schoolhouse behind the home. Other visitors—old Federalists and revolutionary veterans—came to enjoy his simple hospitality, his "company and sweet conversation."

Jay's health was always variable. Among the complaints from which he suffered over the years were rheumatism, piles, eye inflammation, and liver problems. When he became seriously ill in 1827, William assumed management of the farm; at his father's death two years later, the son inherited the property. The Jay family proved an enduring presence in the Bedford house, as ownership passed from William (1789–1858) to his son John (1817–1894), then to John Jay's great-grandson William (1841–1915), and finally to his great-great-granddaughter Eleanor Jay Iselin (1882–1953). Five generations of Jay ownership ended when the house went into the public trust. Since 1958 it has been owned by the State of New York, which operates it as a historic site.

Alexander Hamilton's The Grange

As he sat at his desk writing, Alexander Hamilton could hardly help but think of his eldest son, Philip, namesake of his wife's father, General Philip Schuyler (see "The Schuyler Mansion and Farm," page 156). Two years earlier, the nineteen-year-old boy had died in a duel—and now here his father was, putting pen to paper under the heading "Statement of the Impending Duel." Hamilton was readying for his own confrontation at dawn the following morning.

He expected an outcome quite different from what had befallen his son. Throughout his life, Hamilton had overcome great odds to succeed where other men might have failed. Not that he anticipated the fall of his challenger, the sitting vice president, Aaron Burr; in fact, as he wrote, "I have resolved . . . to *reserve* and *throw away* my first fire, and I *have thoughts* even of *reserving* my second fire."

Hamilton was forty-nine years old, and after years immersed in political controversies, he was out of government service. His old mentor George Washington was five years buried. His chief political nemesis, Thomas Jefferson, was ensconced in the President's House. And the Federalist party that Hamilton had helped establish seemed to be marching inexorably into irrelevance.

The parlor at the Grange was one of two public spaces of the house (the other being the dining room). Both are elongated octagons and originally they were connected by mirrored doors.

Hamilton reviled Burr and what he stood for. Or rather what he did *not* stand for, as Hamilton had been heard to observe that Burr was "unprincipled, both as a public and private man." It was a matter of honor for him to stand up to Burr, although viewed from a more modern perspective, it was a fool's errand, since Hamilton had nothing whatever to prove. His life had been filled with accomplishments. After success as General Washington's adjutant, he had won admiration for his bravery at the Battle of Yorktown. In civilian life he had served in the congress under the Articles of Confederation, then cowritten with James Madison and John Jay the essays in *The Federalist,* which were instrumental in winning ratification of the Constitution. As the first secretary of the treasury (1789–1795), he created a plan for a national economy, established a national bank, devised a means of funding the national debt, and secured credit for the government. Many people disliked Hamilton—his politics favored the rich, and he himself was vain and imperious, never suffered fools gladly, and had a dangerously sharp tongue—but no one questioned his intelligence or his commitment to the American cause.

But Hamilton wasn't writing about what he had done. His mind was on the impending duel and what he had to lose. "My wife and Children are extremely dear to me," he wrote, "and my life is of the utmost importance to them, in various views."

Hamilton's recent fade from public life had had two happy consequences. Now that he had time to devote to his law practice, his financial fortunes rose as his client list expanded, welcoming many of the most powerful people and institutions in New York. His private life had also taken a happy turn. Over the twenty-four years of his marriage, his wife, Betsy, had presented him with eight children, for whom she had assumed primary responsibility. But he had begun to appreciate anew the joys of family. Of late he had engaged in fewer extramarital distractions—some years before, one of his affairs had exploded in America's first great sex scandal. And he sought a new contentment at the Grange, the country estate he had completed two years before in Harlem Heights.

The events of the morning of July 11, 1804, changed all that. Contrary to his plan, Hamilton discharged his weapon; Burr also fired his. Hamilton's shot crashed into the branch of a cedar tree some six feet over Burr's head, but his opponent's aim was true. The Vice President's bullet penetrated Hamilton's abdomen on his right side, smashing a rib and passing through the liver before being halted by the spine. His lower body paralyzed, the dying man was taken to the mansion of a friend in lower Manhattan.

A message was dispatched to Betsy Hamilton (the gravity of her husband's injury was kept from her at first), and she hurried south from the Grange. The journey of nine miles required almost

FACING PAGE: *Even as the end of the nineteenth century approached, the Grange—true to its name—retained the feel of a farmhouse. Several of the thirteen gum trees that Hamilton planted as symbols of the colonies survived on the original site.*

RIGHT: *When we look at the Grange today, it is hard to imagine it once stood alone. Its relocation south changed more than its setting: The house was turned 90 degrees, its entrance porch removed, the front door shifted, and the interior stairs altered. Yet valuable historic fabric remains within.*

three hours, but with their seven surviving children, Betsy arrived in time to find she had been summoned to a death watch. His physician dosed him liberally with laudanum to dull the pain, but Hamilton survived only until the next afternoon when, at two o'clock, he breathed his last.

"A SWEET PROJECT"

A few years earlier, Alexander Hamilton (1757–1804) had embarked upon an architectural adventure. He determined that he would have a house—he had never owned one before—and that it would be in the countryside, a safe distance from the disease and inconvenience of the city. Northern Manhattan then was entirely rural, and Hamilton confided in Betsy, "I have formed a sweet project . . . in which I rely that you will cooperate with me cheerfully." His notion was to purchase property and build an idyllic retreat for them and their children.

The Hamiltons spent the following autumn in a rented home in Harlem Heights. Finding the area to his liking, Hamilton persuaded a friend to sell him a fifteen-acre tract nearby. The property rose gradually to a knoll that, at an altitude of two hundred feet, offered a panoramic vista of the Hudson River to the west, with complementary eastern views of the Harlem and East Rivers. In

1798 Hamilton purchased an adjacent twenty-acre parcel. After spending his adult life either at war or walking the streets of New York and Philadelphia as a politician, he contemplated the life of a country gentleman.

Hamilton had an architect in mind, a man who had worked for him in his Treasury Department days building lighthouses. A second-generation New York builder-designer, John J. McComb, Jr., had emerged as the city's leading architect, having just completed a mansion for the merchant Archibald Gracie (much later, it became the mayoral residence), and was a favorite in the design competition for a new City Hall (the following year, he was awarded the prize). He worked in what has come to be called the Federal style, a mode like the one Charles Bulfinch practiced in Boston, which also inspired George Washington's old military confidant Henry Knox at his home in Maine (see "General Knox's Montpelier," page 250). Like another great architectural avatar of the time, Thomas Jefferson, McComb favored unusual shapes, in particular octagonal rooms, of which there were two in his design for Hamilton. Though moderate in size, Hamilton's country house possessed grand details, in the distinctive and current neoclassical style, indebted to the Scots-English architects Robert and James Adam, whose book *The Works in Architecture of Robert and James Adam* was in his library.

McComb executed the drawings. Hamilton's father-in-law, General Schuyler, contributed the timber, shipping lumber and boards down the Hudson River from the sawmill on his Saratoga farm. The house was under construction by 1801; it was largely completed the following year, though Schuyler provided the paint for its finish in the spring of 1803. The carpenter was Ezra Wells, another known quantity; Hamilton had recently acted as his brother's legal counsel in a widely publicized murder trial.

Hamilton, always a meticulous administrator, took great pleasure in managing the construction, working with McComb on all manner of details, including chimney design and the Italian marble mantels. But during the building, his law practice periodically took him away, and Betsy helped managed construction.

Betsy and Alexander Hamilton planned their landscape with care. "A garden, you know, is a very usual refuge of a disappointed politician," he explained to a friend. Hamilton took special pride in the circular bed of tulips, hyacinths, and lilies. A stream meandered through the pretty property, and they planted wild roses, laurel, and dogwood trees for ornament, as well as strawberries, cabbages, and asparagus. The property featured outbuildings, too, including a springhouse (for keeping the milk cool), a barn, a shed, and a chicken house.

Establishing himself as a country squire offered Hamilton the opportunity to complete his reinvention. A man who had risen far above the expectations of his illegitimate birth (see "The Perfect Woman?" page 159), he chose in naming his country home to reference the status of his father's family, calling his new home after an ancestral estate in Ayrshire, Scotland. Hamiltons had resided there since the Middle Ages in the seaside town of Stevenston, and Alexander's grandfather had been the fourteenth laird of the Grange, residing in his manor house overlooking the Firth of Clyde. From the summit of his little hill, with its majestic view across the Hudson to the New Jersey Palisades, Hamilton attempted to settle himself back into the honorable line of the landed gentry.

ABOVE: *The coffee urn on the sideboard in the dining room belonged to Hamilton, as did the large silver piece on the table rimmed with the low gallery. Called a plateau, the flat stand was designed to reflect and enhance all available light, as were many dining room objects of silver, gilt, and cut glass in that candlelit age.*

FACING PAGE: *This was the room Hamilton used as his home office. He is said to have had a rolltop desk that he called "my secretary at home."*

DINNERTIME

A French aristocrat visiting America in 1780 described the experience of dining this way.

The dinner was served in the American, or if you will, in the English fashion; consisting of two courses, one including the entrées, roast, and warm side dishes; the other, the sweet pastries and preserves. When the second course is removed, the cloth is taken off, and apples, walnuts, and chestnuts are served; it is then that healths are drunk; the coffee which comes afterward serves as a signal to rise from table.

— *François Jean de Beauvoir, Marquis de Chastellux,* Travels in North America, in the Years 1780, 1781, and 1782

THE DINNER PARTY

The painting at right is a rare visual record of a dinner party. It does not portray a meal at the Grange (the artist lived in Boston, and the canvas was painted some years after Alexander Hamilton's death), but Henry Sargent's oil portrays a scene Hamilton and his Federalist friends would have recognized.

Hamilton prided himself on his entertainments. At the Grange in May 1804, he feted Napoleon's youngest brother, Jérôme Bonaparte. On July 3, 1804, the week before he sustained the gunshot wound that killed him, he held an elegant *fête champêtre*, a French-style garden party. His guests included Abigail Adams Smith, daughter of John and Abigail, and her husband; Thomas Jefferson's former secretary and protégé, William Short; and the painter-diplomat John Trumbull. With perhaps seventy others, they wandered through the Hamiltons' gardens and grounds. On that particular evening, a small musical ensemble had been secreted behind a copse of trees, so music seemed to waft out of the nearby woods.

A room dedicated to dining was an eighteenth-century innovation. Following French and English precedents, the dining room became the ultimate luxury (and often the largest room in the house) in the decades before and after the Revolution. Dining evolved into an experience calculated to be sumptuous and elegant. Chairs were comfortable, with cushioned seats. A fireplace helped warm the room. Good conversation was nurtured at table; servants were expected to be seen and heard as little as possible as they went about their duties. Plate warmers heated the china, and lead-lined wine coolers kept the vintage chilled.

Furniture in the eighteenth-century dining room was often left "at rest" between meals, meaning the chairs and tables were moved by the servants to the walls of the room. To prepare for a meal, the furniture was arranged on top of a crumb cloth spread on the floor; as its name suggests, the fabric protected the carpet beneath from crumbs and stains. It was removed and shaken after the meal.

Dinner, eaten between two and three o'clock, was often a prolonged affair, with two principal courses (the first of meats and warm side dishes, the second of sweets), after which the tablecloth was removed. The ladies usually withdrew to the parlor or "withdrawing" room (often shortened to drawing room), while the men remained for nuts and fruits, over which they might linger, drinking their Madeira and toasting one another.

Painted by Henry Sargent (1770–1845), The Dinner Party is one of the earliest surviving images to portray the rituals of American dining. Sargent carefully rendered the details: the textiles (the window hangings and the crumb cloth on the floor), the furniture (note the pier mirror between the windows and the sideboard), and the circumstances. In the painting, the fruit course has been served, the wine is in hand, the guests have assumed relaxed positions, and the servants are at the ready.

PHOTOGRAPH © MUSEUM OF FINE ARTS, BOSTON

After the Revolution, a few professional architects pioneered an alternative to the old Georgian style, named for the English kings whose governance the colonists had rejected. Their architectural experiments at the turn of the nineteenth century produced the Federal style.

The Federal house was a simplification of the English Georgian. The rectangular character and the symmetrical arrangement of windows and doors remained much the same, though with lower rooflines the newer houses looked less massive. Federal houses lacked the heavy decorative classical details common to Georgian houses, as bulky corner quoins disappeared and the pilasters and moldings thinned and flattened. These houses reflected the move from royal pretension to an appreciation of native materials, wood in particular.

The Federal style also evolved from the emerging field of archaeol-

ogy. Systematic excavations in Italy produced a new understanding of antiquity; architects such as the Scottish Adam brothers measured and recorded Roman ruins, adapting them for buildings in England (thus, one of the Federal style's alternate names, Adamesque). In America, designers such as Thomas Jefferson, Boston's Charles Bulfinch, and the émigré Englishman Benjamin Henry Latrobe melded these trends, creating the Federal style.

Federal floor plans reflected a sense of spatial experimentation. Rooms with curved walls or octagonal shapes broke the flat planes of exterior walls to accommodate elegant salons. Richly carved decorative swags, urns, rosettes, and festoons derived from ancient sources were applied to mantels, window frames, cornices, ceilings, and exteriors.

This Neoclassical design would be the dominant mode for a few aging Founding Fathers as well as the next generation of the American elite.

The Georgian and the Federal resemble each other—but the details differ. The Georgian Cliveden (left) seems more stolid and bold; in contrast, Charles Bulfinch's Federal mansion (right), as sketched in 1795, has an almost airy quality with its swags and elliptical curves.

LEFT: *A bronze Alexander Hamilton watches passersby on Convent Avenue. The house is larger than it looks, with eight fireplaces and six chambers on the second floor. The Grange was originally painted yellow, its trim a soft white.*

FACING PAGE, TOP: *In Hamilton's time, there was a tall Gilbert Stuart portrait of George Washington, the gift of a merchant friend.*

FACING PAGE, BOTTOM: *In this undated photograph, probably taken at the time the house was moved, the Grange looks like a ship run aground on a rocky shore.*

AFTER HAMILTON

Before Burr's bullet ended his life, Hamilton got to enjoy his country escape for two short years. His survivors, Betsy and their seven children, remained there much longer, but only through the intervention of her husband's old political allies.

Although a fiscal conservative who spent years preoccupied with the solvency of the country he had helped establish, Hamilton seems to have lost all discipline when it came to the Grange. The land had been expensive, and construction costs had gone beyond estimates by a third. At his death, Hamilton left his widow deeply in debt; unbeknownst to her, a subscription among his former Federalist colleagues established a secret eighty-thousand-dollar trust for her and their children. The Grange was purchased by Hamilton's executors for thirty thousand dollars, then sold back to Betsy for half that sum.

She managed to hold on at the Grange, and only after three full decades, during which she assured the education of her children and saw them off to pursue marriages and careers of their own, did she sell. She then lived in Washington, D.C., with her daughter Eliza. Betsy took with her the Gilbert Stuart portrait of George Washington that had greeted visitors to the Grange, but the house was sold out of the family.

In the coming years, it changed hands numerous times, and in 1889, the wooden structure was lifted off its foundations and rolled two city blocks south, leaving the old kitchen and service rooms behind. The boundaries of the once bucolic thirty-five-acre estate are long gone, a grid of streets and avenues having divided it into more than a dozen city blocks. Brownstones, schools, and commercial structures have risen where domesticated animals grazed and the Hamiltons laid out their landscape.

Like a misplaced book on a library shelf, the Grange survived in a narrow slot in the streetscape between a church and an apartment building. But the house is being relocated once again by the National Park Service, this time some three hundred feet to the south and east, to St. Nicholas Park. At this writing the restoration schedule is uncertain—the house is closed to the public and may not reopen until 2009 or after—but when the day comes, the promise is of a house that more nearly resembles the Grange that Alexander and Betsy knew, complete with porches and some semblance of countrified landscape around it.

Jefferson's Monticello

*On March 4, 1809, Thomas Jefferson de-*clined an invitation to sit in the presidential carriage. He thought the honor of the day should go to his old friend James Madison. Jefferson was retiring, and Madison was assuming the nation's highest office.

Under cloudy skies, Jefferson (1743–1826) rode his horse along muddy Pennsylvania Avenue, trailing the military escort. No servants attended him, so he hitched his own horse to a post outside the Capitol, making his way with the crowd into the House chamber to listen to President Madison's brief inaugural address. That afternoon he dined alone, save for his grandson and namesake, Thomas Jefferson Randolph, a lad of sixteen. In the evening, the former president went to the first-ever inaugural ball before retiring to the President's House to pack up the papers and personal property he had accumulated over eight years in office.

A week later, Jefferson departed Washington, trailing by two days the three wagons that carried his possessions (two were loaded with boxes of books, clothing, and miscellaneous items, the third with shrubbery from a nearby nursery). On March 15, he reached Charlottesville, having passed his wagons along the way. Whatever the rigors of the journey—one day swirling snow surrounded him for eight hours—he rode on. "Never did a prisoner, released from

The decoration of his dining room suggests Jefferson's taste for the Neoclassical. Note the urns and classical figures on both the mantel and the mirror above.

Like many great eighteenth-century villas, Monticello offers two countenances: the entry looks outward with its bold portico (opposite), while the garden façade features a flattened dome (above).

his chains, feel such relief as I [have] on shaking off the shackles of power," he remarked.

Upon reaching the top of his "little mountain," Jefferson was greeted by his only surviving child, his daughter Martha Randolph. She had written him a few weeks before on behalf of "the people of the County," asking whether he "would have any objection to their meeting you on the road and escorting you to Charlottesville. . . . They wish it as the last opportunity they can have of giving you a public testimony of their respect and affection." Jefferson had declined, uncertain of his schedule and more concerned with the future than with the past.

During his presidency, Martha had moved temporarily to her father's house whenever he returned from Washington, serving as housekeeper and hostess to the widower Jefferson. But this time she arrived for good: Monticello became, once again, her principal home (she was born there in 1772). She and her children, with their grandfather's happy acceptance, helped set the tone. The eldest, eighteen-year-old Anne Cary Randolph Bankhead, was already married, but seven others (as well as two babies to be born to Martha in the years to come) would be members of Jefferson's household, along with Martha's husband, Colonel Thomas Mann Randolph, Jr.

The Sage of Monticello had come home.

LEFT: *Jefferson actually had two visions of Monticello: one was the restored version we see today, the other an earlier, never-completed incarnation, as sketched here by Jefferson himself.*

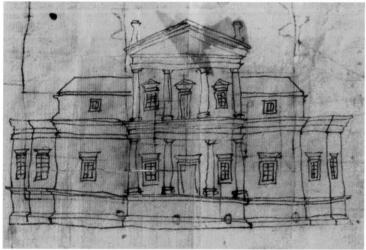

I look with infinite joy to the moment when I shall be ultimately moored in the midst of my affections, and free to follow the pursuits of my choice.

—*Thomas Jefferson, writing to his daughter Martha Randolph, February 27, 1809*

LIFE ON LITTLE MOUNTAIN

Less than a month later, Jefferson's feelings were bittersweet as he bade farewell to John Neilson and James Dinsmore. These men were not friends in the sense that Madison was; they certainly weren't family; both had emigrated from Ireland as adults not so many years earlier. But without them, Mr. Jefferson's Monticello might never have been finished.

Although the trunks of four tulip trees still supported the portico on the garden façade, the two departing carpenters had brought the interior of Monticello to near completion. Construction had been under way on the house for a staggering forty years, since work on the hilltop had begun with the digging of the foundation, brick making, the milling of chestnut boards, and Jefferson's purchase of glass and hardware before 1770. Still more years elapsed before the permanent columns of parged brick would replace the tulip trees in 1823, bringing the duration of Jefferson's pet project to a total of *fifty-four years.*

Dinsmore and Neilson had been latecomers to the project. The house they helped build bore little resemblance to Jefferson's original vision. Before the Revolution, he had adapted a plate in the

The front portico leads directly to the entrance hall, with its vast array of maps, sculpture, paintings, and Indian artifacts (thus, the alternative name Jefferson gave the space, the Indian Hall). The fortunate visitor in his time would be invited further into the home to Monticello's parlor.

The balcony on three sides (left) offers visual access to the space from the mezzanine level of the house. The hanging brass Argand lamp (right), with its central reservoir of oil, descended and ascended on pulleys. President Jefferson purchased it from a Philadelphia merchant in 1805, though it was probably manufactured in England.

ABOVE: *To Jefferson's delight, his daughters and granddaughters played the harpsichord. Late in life, he found comfort in a lolling chair like the one pictured here, which was also called a campeachey or siesta chair, after its apparently Spanish or Mexican origins. The walls of the parlor held some fifty-seven works of art, including thirty-five portraits of influential men.*

PAINTING HIS PICTURE

In March 1821, Thomas Sully arrived at Monticello to take Mr. Jefferson's picture. The superintendent at West Point had commissioned the work to commemorate the man who had established the U.S. Military Academy during his presidency. Jefferson expressed his doubts whether, at age seventy-eight, he was a

worthy subject, but spending twelve days at Monticello proved highly agreeable to Sully, who "left the place with the greatest reluctance."

The full-length portrait Sully completed in 1830 (he also executed several half-length versions, owned by Lafayette and James Monroe, among others) still hangs at West Point. Jefferson is posed beside the base and shaft of a Corinthian column in the House Chamber at the Capitol. The juxtaposition of the aging subject with an architectural element enhances the composition painting and reminds the viewer of Jefferson's insistence that America's public buildings be based upon "antient models."

The portrait was regarded in Jefferson's lifetime as an excellent likeness. The retired president remains dignified, with an expression that is at once serene and expectant. It is as if a thoughtful moment is about to pass, and momentarily, he will be on his way.

Four Books of Architecture by the Renaissance master Andrea Palladio (see "Andrea Palladio," page 131), and the house had been under construction for a dozen years when, in 1782, his wife died. Jefferson descended into deep mourning for his dear Martha, and progress at the work site effectively ceased for more than a decade. Only after Jefferson's years in Paris (1784–1789) as minister to France reinvigorated his passion for architecture and he completed his service as the nation's first secretary of state (1790–1793) did work on his house resume.

Some of the original structure was dismantled so the roofline could be lowered, giving the mansion the appearance of a one-story house (although the new envelope actually contained three levels with a basement below). It was a configuration Jefferson had admired on the streetscapes of Paris, where he watched the construction of new *hôtels* (town houses). His new design blended elements of French Neoclassical architecture, ancient Roman precedents, and his own taste for what he called "conveniences," innovations such as dumbwaiters, mechanical doors, and skylights.

The process had gained momentum when Jefferson hired Dinsmore in Philadelphia in 1798. The Ulsterman proved to be the first builder Jefferson trusted to carry out his wishes in his absence. John Neilson joined the team in 1804 and the two of them, as Jefferson noted in his *Farm Book,* proved to be "house joiners of the first order. They have done the whole of that work at my house, to which I can affirm there is nothing superior in the U.S."

But on April 18, 1809, he wished them well as they departed for their next job. "Dinsmore and Neilson are set out *yesterday* for Montpelier," he wrote to James Madison. Montpelier, in Orange County, Virginia, some thirty miles and a day's ride away, was Madison's plantation. There the two builders soon set to work remodeling and enlarging his dwelling into a mansion suited to the nation's chief executive.

THIS PAGE: *Adjacent to his bedroom suite, Jefferson had an indoor-outdoor piazza space that functioned as a greenhouse. He installed a pair of "Venetian enclosures" (above) on either side of the greenhouse. The shutters helped keep out the overheated summer air.*

FACING PAGE, LEFT: *His bedroom, with alcove bed, had a double-height ceiling. The ports high on the wall provided ventilation for a closet in which he stored his out of season clothing.*

FACING PAGE, RIGHT: *Monticello's garden façade.*

"A YOUNG GARDENER"

Jefferson's days quickly assumed a pattern. Recollections by family members, numerous visitors, and his own correspondence make it possible to trace the regime he followed in his retirement years.

Mr. Jefferson was an early riser. "The sun never found him in bed," according to his trusted overseer, Edmund Bacon. Upon climbing out of his alcove—he slept in a bed recessed into the partition between his bed chamber and study—he habitually made his own fire. A bell rang for the convenience of others at seven o'clock, but Jefferson remained in his quarters, reading and writing, until the second bell, at eight, drew the household to breakfast. Cold meats were served with hot breads of corn and wheat, along with tea and coffee. Silence rarely reigned at Jefferson's table, and guests remembered congenial talk at breakfast.

In good weather Jefferson visited his flower gardens. In planning for his retirement, he drafted a plan for twenty oval beds around the home to be planted with different species. Tulips were a favorite, as were poppies, carnations, hyacinths, peas, and lilies. Along with Wormley Hughes, a Monticello slave whose spade and hoe did most of the planting, two granddaughters were often on hand when roots and seeds arrived by mail from Philadelphia and elsewhere, labeled with names such as Marcus Aurelius, Psyche, and Roman Empress. After planting, each perennial was marked with a stick indicating its name.

On days when new varieties bloomed, Jefferson's granddaughter Ellen Wayles Randolph later remembered, "We were in ecstasies over the rich purple and crimson, or pure white, delicate lilac, or pale yellow of the blossoms." Jefferson himself observed happily to his old friend and fellow naturalist Charles Willson Peale in 1811, "But though I am an old man, I am but a young gardener."

Jefferson's slaves had flattened the top of the hill years before; there he established a manicured pleasure garden, a much larger canvas, on which the flower beds were mere splashes of color. There was a meandering walk around the hilltop, the Roundabout. The slope featured a variety of kitchen gardens, asparagus beds, orchards, vineyards, ornamental trees, and a hardwood grove. Jefferson's landscape spiraled away from the mansion, with a series of concentric roads that, like the lines of a topographic map, descended the mountain.

Jefferson's gaze was inevitably drawn beyond the immediate area to the grander landscape: the site offered a panoramic vista of the central Virginia countryside. One visitor in that first year of his retirement observed on a foggy morning that, from the eminence, the vista had "the appearance of an ocean . . . unbroken except when wood covered hills rose above the plain and looked like islands."

When the warmth of the day arrived, Jefferson retired to his private apartment, which consisted of a library, bed chamber, and study or cabinet. Closing and often locking the door after

Jefferson sometimes called the room below the dome the Sky Room. The stairs to the second floor were so narrow that the Dome Room never saw use as a public space. Instead it became a playroom, bed chamber, and under later owners, a billiard room.

"A Very Extra Workman": John Hemings, Slave

Jefferson kept about seventy adult slaves at Monticello, the most controversial of them being Sally Hemings, the enslaved woman with whom he probably had children. While the story of "Dusky Sally" has become an essential starting place for those who grapple with the moral contradictions of good men of the eighteenth century who were also slave owners, it was Sally's younger brother, John (1775–1830?), who performed essential roles in the building and finishing of both Monticello and Poplar Forest (see "Jefferson's Hermitage," page 308).

John was light-skinned, his grandmother and mother both having been mulatto (the first was the daughter of a ship's captain, the second of Jefferson's father-in-law, the slave trader John Wayles). Hemings's own father, Joseph Nelson, was also white, a sometime carpenter at Monticello.

John Hemings (whose surname was variously spelled) became a well-liked figure in the household, a favorite of Jefferson's grandchildren, who called him "Daddy" Hemings. Jefferson himself trusted "Johnny Hemmings" implicitly and even asked him to be his eyes and ears in managing other slaves during construction at Poplar Forest. Hemings also worked as joiner, wheelwright, and Jefferson's in-house millworker and cabinetmaker.

His workshop stood on Mulberry Row, the hillside avenue at Monticello where free and enslaved workmen lived and worked. He produced made-to-order picture frames, bookcases, tables, dumbwaiters, chairs, candlestands, and other pieces of utilitarian furniture, many of them designed by Jefferson. What survives is well made, typically of mahogany with local secondary woods. The result of Hemings's and Jefferson's collaboration was a range of household objects in familiar forms but unadorned, with a Shaker-like simplicity. Much of the later architectural joinery at both Jefferson's homes was also the work of John Hemings.

Hemings was freed by a codicil to Jefferson's will. "I also give to my good servants John Hemmings and [blacksmith] Joe Fosset their freedom at the end of one year after my death and to each of them respectively all the tools of their respective shops." Several other members of the Hemings clan were freed, including two of Sally's children. Sally herself was not among them.

An oculus or "bull's-eye" window in the Dome Room looking out on one of Monticello's ancient trees.

him—everyone in the household understood that Mr. Jefferson was not to be disturbed—he settled into his reading and writing. He read voraciously: his library at the time numbered some six thousand volumes, and all three rooms in his personal suite were lined floor to ceiling with books. Many were in foreign tongues (he spoke five languages, and read seven, including Latin and Greek). The subject matter ranged widely. Jefferson cataloged the entire collection, employing the principles of the Renaissance philosopher Francis Bacon. Human knowledge was divided into the three principal "faculties"—Memory (encompassing works of history), Reason (philosophical writings), and Imagination (books devoted to the fine arts). When he wasn't reading or thinking, Jefferson was often writing. It is estimated he wrote more than nineteen thousand personal letters, many of them in retirement as he corresponded with distant friends on politics, agriculture, and a hundred other matters.

When guests were at hand, Jefferson regularly offered his services as a tour guide. He might take the visitor to the room beneath the dome, which in the early days of his retirement remained empty (later his grandson Jeff and his wife would take up residence there,

though the space, the most dramatic in the house, would never assume a public purpose because the narrow staircases—"suppressed stairs," Jefferson called them—made access difficult). A privileged visitor might be shown the library.

One certainty was that Mr. Jefferson would excuse himself for his midday ride. At one o'clock each day, a horse was brought around for him, and he would don his overalls in preparation for riding out to inspect his plantations. A natural rider, he sat easily on his mount, tall in the saddle, always in control. He returned at three o'clock, drank a glass of water, and prepared for the main meal of the day. Dinner commenced at half past three.

Jefferson had a hearty appetite, consuming quantities of vegetables and fruits grown on his farms. He was a meat eater—favoring guinea hen, beef, and lamb—and his cooks used the "French method" of preparation because he found it made the meats more tender. The family ate together—often there were a dozen or more family members—and guests were usual. Conversation followed dessert, and visitors remembered Jefferson's inclination to listen and ask questions. His conversation was "easy, flowing, and full of anecdote." He disliked argument, so he rarely disputed the assertions of others. He never used tobacco or strong spirits but favored wine, often with water.

After dinner he might return to his rooms but reemerge later to enjoy the sunset or walk the lawn or the terrace, and he often played with the children. He liked to organize games and races for them. In the summertime he played chess with his favorite granddaughter, Ellen, under Monticello's great trees. For him, the children were an escape: "It is only with them," he told a friend, "that a grave man can play the fool."

The evenings he generally spent in company. By candlelight, he read amid a respectful silence or lay his book aside on a little round table or on his knee to talk with guests, his daughter Martha—Patsy, she was called—or as one grandchild remembered, "any child old enough to make one of the family-party." As a young man, Jefferson himself played the fiddle, but later Patsy regularly played the harpsichord he had purchased for her during his sojourn as minister to France.

An evening tea was served at nine and then a fruit course. Jefferson went off to bed before ten o'clock.

*This garden pavilion—a 1984 reconstruction based on archaeological findings and Jefferson's notes—
overlooks his agricultural experiments as well as a wider vista from his mountaintop aerie.*

BELOW: *Called the family sitting room, this space functioned as Martha Jefferson Randolph's sewing room, office, and schoolroom. Martha was Jefferson's oldest daughter and, upon his retirement, she became the lady of the house at Monticello. "Patsy," as she was familiarly known, was fifty-one when the portrait over the mantel was painted by itinerant Virginia portraitist James Westhall Ford in 1823.*

FACING PAGE, TOP LEFT: *Named Mr. Madison's Room for one of its frequent occupants, this octagonal bedroom has a built-in bed (called an alcove bed) and a reproduction of the original wallpaper with a trellis pattern, which Jefferson imported from Paris.* **TOP, CENTER:** *The sitting area in Jefferson's bedroom.* **TOP RIGHT:** *In Monticello's entrance hall, the visitor is met by, among other objects, a bust of Voltaire and a folding ladder made in the Monticello joinery.* **BOTTOM:** *The Tea Room with some of Jefferson's most admired friends along the walls, among them Washington and Franklin.*

ABOVE: *Jefferson adapted a French convention of the time, creating for himself within his bedroom suite a "cabinet." For him the space was less a dressing room than a study, where he read, wrote, and thought. Note the contraption on the table: called a polygraph, it simultaneously produced an original and a duplicate of a letter.*

LEFT: *In August 1825, Jefferson received as a gift a bust of John Adams, which, according to his thank-you note, he placed in his cabinet. Copied from an original marble sculpture, the plaster portrayed Jefferson's old friend as he looked in 1818.*

THE WORK OF A LIFETIME

Monticello is an autobiographical work. Yes, the property is a hill-top estate with a fine house at its acme; and, no, Monticello does not recount the particulars of Jefferson's long life in any literary way. Yet the house and its grounds embody the evolution, ideals, and passionate commitment of the man who imagined, inhabited, and supervised their creation.

The curiosity of his mind is everywhere evident. Jefferson kept his own greenhouse, workbench, and telescope close at hand. Today's restored gardens reflect his experiments. Despite its debt to Palladio, the other books in his library, and the sites he saw in Europe, the architecture is uniquely his, an amalgam of his imagination and his enthusiasms. He built the house at the peak of a small mountain—something no one else was doing in his time. He taught

Monticello's parlor, with its array of portraits, furniture, mirrors, and a terra-cotta cast of Jean-Antoine Houdon's masterly bust of Jefferson (right).

himself architectural drafting in an age when most houses were constructed on the basis of an engraving in a book or one rudely drawn sheet. During his retirement years, he created the University of Virginia, establishing its curriculum, hiring its faculty, and designing the "Academical Village" itself (his trusted carpenters, Dinsmore and Neilson, built much of it).

Yet the idyll he lived in retirement can be viewed from other, less sanguine angles, too. The serious student of Jefferson's life and of Monticello encounters slavery, a practice he denounced as a young man but managed to conscience into old age. When Jefferson died, he left his heirs with so much debt that his daughter Martha and favorite grandson, Jeff Randolph, were forced to auction Monticello's contents six months later. The proceeds fell far short of satisfying his creditors—he owed more than $100,000, and the

auction netted less than a third of that—so Monticello itself was soon on the market. Nearly a century would pass before the house was acquired by the Thomas Jefferson Memorial Foundation for restoration as a museum.

After Jefferson's retirement, he lived another seventeen years. Not once during that time did he cross the boundaries of Virginia. Several times a year, when the many visitors at Monticello became too much, he escaped to his other home, Poplar Forest (see "Jefferson's Hermitage," page 308), and he visited Madison at Montpelier. He helped transform Charlottesville, the courthouse town where his brainchild, the University of Virginia, came to life. But after his presidency, Jefferson's world was Monticello. It was the world as he would have it.

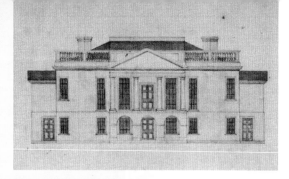

A careful rendering of Jefferson's home away from home, Poplar Forest, executed by one of the builders he helped train, John Neilson.

JEFFERSON'S HERMITAGE

During his second term as president, Thomas Jefferson built a second home. The site was the profitable plantation called Poplar Forest, three days' journey from Monticello. He wished to be there to supervise farming operations at the property he called "the most valuable of my possessions," but another motive probably ranked higher.

The house he began in 1806 became his retreat from the admirers knocking on his door in Charlottesville. His respites at Poplar Forest in the first decade of his retirement—he often went there for several weeks—allowed him, as he put it, "to pass my time . . . in a tranquility and retirement much adapted to my age and indolence."

He chose for company his favorite grandchildren, one of whom, Ellen Wayles Randolph, described her interludes at Poplar Forest many years later:

> My grandfather was very happy during these sojourns in a comparatively simple and secluded district—far from noise and news—of both of which he got too much at Monticello; and we, his grand-daughters, were very happy too. . . . We saw more of our dear grandfather at those times than at any other. He was most desirous that we should find congenial occupations, and we had books, drawing materials, embroidery, and never felt time heavy on our hands. He interested himself in all we did, thought, or read. He would talk to us about his own youth and early friends, and tell us stories of former days.

Like Monticello, Poplar Forest was a prototypical villa, both a farmhouse and a grand home, although on a smaller scale than Monticello. Jefferson based his plan on plates in his library books, but he made the project a geometric experiment. The footprint of the house is an octagon; the dining room at its center is a twenty-foot cube. He surrounded the house with a carefully contoured and elaborately planted landscape that featured flanking mounds of earth in the shape of cones.

The connections to Monticello are numerous—Jefferson's longtime carpenter James Dinsmore probably made the original windows and doors for Poplar Forest at his Monticello shop, and the slave John Hemings executed most of the finished woodwork—but Poplar Forest is a unique site. A mid-nineteenth-century remodeling has been undone, and in an ongoing restoration program the house is reemerging as the place where, as Jefferson himself remarked, he sought "the solitude of a hermit."

FACING PAGE, LEFT: *The sunlight pours into the parlor from the tall windows (Jefferson always sought ways to welcome volumes of natural light into his buildings); when he wished to bask more directly in the sunlight, he had only to walk out of his private chambers onto the terrace outside (below), defined by the elegant geometry of the Chinese Chippendale railings.*

FACING PAGE, RIGHT: *Jefferson liked his "contrivances," and one of them was the perspective glass standing on the table in the parlor, also known as a* vue d'optique, *it was used to examine prints or maps that were placed on the table for magnified viewing through the device's lens.*

The Owens-Thomas House

Although born to a noble French family,
Marie-Joseph-Paul-Yves-Roch-Gilbert du Motier was certifiably a Founding Father. All Americans seemed to understand that instinctively: after not having set foot on American soil for forty years, "the friend of Washington" received a great outpouring of popular sentiment upon his arrival late in the summer of 1824. Day after day, the sixty-seven-year-old Frenchman met with a universal welcome of speeches, parades, endless toasts, banquets, and cheering crowds.

The Marquis de la Fayette (1757–1834) arrived in America as a nineteen-year-old volunteer (de la Fayette officially became Lafayette after a 1790 French decree abolishing titles). The young man had been a captain in the French dragoons when he embraced the cause of the American revolt, in 1775. Drawing upon his inherited wealth, he purchased and outfitted a ship, *La Victoire,* which landed him in South Carolina in 1777. A month later he met George Washington, and the two men established an immediate and enduring bond.

The Frenchman was wounded at the Battle of Brandywine and experienced the harsh winter of 1777–78 at Valley Forge. After a respite in France, where he helped persuade his government to recognize the new nation and provide military aid, he returned to America in 1780 and played a hero's role at Yorktown, in the war's

Upstairs at the Owens-Thomas is this remarkable "bridge," which leaps over the run of stairs that climbs to the second floor, connecting the front and rear portions of the upper level.

deciding battle. Back in Europe after the close of the war, he was imprisoned in the wake of his country's revolution, but his American connections remained important to him. During Lafayette's incarceration, the wife of the American minister to France, Mrs. James Monroe, arrived at the La Force prison in Paris in the official carriage of the U.S. Legation, demanding—and obtaining—the release of Madame Lafayette.

Much later, Lafayette welcomed the letter from James Monroe. "The whole nation," wrote the President on February 24, 1824, "ardently desire[s] to see you again." Lafayette accepted Monroe's invitation. Instructions were issued by Congress that General Lafayette should expend not one cent on his tour (much of his wealth had been confiscated during the French Revolution). A stop he made in Savannah reflected the kind of celebration he met with. In three days he was feted by the city's leaders, dedicated two monuments, and stayed in one of the city's most elegant homes.

THE THIRTEENTH COLONY

Savannah became Georgia's first settlement when James Oglethorpe arrived in 1733 with 120 other travelers. They founded the city on a bluff overlooking the river of the same name.

The grid Oglethorpe laid out produced a city of squares, with lots designated for public buildings on the east and west sides, along with smaller plots for private properties on the north and south. By the time of Lafayette's arrival, Savannah had expanded from Oglethorpe's original six wards, with fine town houses lining the streets. The city's fortunes had risen in the preceding three decades, the burgeoning wealth based upon Sea Island cotton. Some seven thousand people called Savannah home; more than half of them were white. Slavery had contributed to the city's prosperity, as did the invention of the cotton gin at nearby Mulberry Grove (see "Three Yankees Who Went Down to Georgia," opposite).

FACING PAGE: *William Jay's Neoclassical design for the cotton merchant Richard Richardson overlooks Oglethorpe Square, a fine—and rare—American example of English Regency architecture. The walling is stucco, tooled to resemble stone.*

BELOW: *Gentle, elliptical curves were essential to William Jay's design vocabulary, as seen here on the entrance porch and window arches, as well as throughout the interior.*

On his arrival in the port of Savannah on March 18, 1825, Lafayette was greeted with the firing of cannons and a string of speeches. Next came a procession of politicians, clergy, military men (including a carriage of elderly revolutionary officers), and fraternal organizations that accompanied him into the city. The ceremony and the short journey required two and a half hours; as Lafayette's landau, drawn by four gray horses, brought him to his lodgings in Oglethorpe Square, the panoply continued. Observers filled every doorway and window as the general was saluted by marching troops, ladies waving handkerchiefs, and the firing of more guns.

As the sun went down, the travelers—Lafayette was accompanied by his son, George Washington Lafayette, among others—finally entered Mrs. Mary Maxwell's boardinghouse. Her establishment, Lafayette's quarters for his Savannah stay, was far from the average accommodation.

THREE YANKEES WHO WENT DOWN TO GEORGIA

During Lafayette's stopover in Savannah, he dedicated a monument to another of Washington's most trusted generals, Nathanael Greene (1742–1786). When the war had begun in 1775, the big-boned Rhode Islander with a pronounced limp ran a family ironworks but could claim no military experience. He won George Washington's trust while serving in Boston and New York. Later he was quartermaster general of the Continental Army, then commander in the South, where his troops harassed General Cornwallis and his troops in the months before the decisive Battle of Yorktown.

Having personally guaranteed large sums to purchase supplies for his troops, Greene was heavily in debt to Charleston merchants after the war. He moved his family to Mulberry Grove, a rice plantation of 2,141 acres on the Savannah River granted him by the Georgia legislature in appreciation of his military service. There Greene attempted to rebuild his fortune, but he died suddenly of sunstroke at age forty-three.

His widow, Catherine Littlefield Greene, affectionately known as Caty, was fourteen years younger. During the Revolution, Caty and her children were among the families who joined the army in winter encampments. Young, pretty, and vivacious, she was a great favorite of George Washington, who once famously danced with her for "upward of three hours" (reported her husband).

Caty eventually remarried, but the presence of another man at Mulberry Grove proved to have much greater historical significance. In 1792, she befriended the Yale-educated Eli Whitney. Whitney planned to read law, but he was so good at fixing things that Mrs. Greene challenged him to devise a means of separating the seeds from cotton fibers. In ten days, as the story goes, he produced at Mulberry Grove the first workable cotton gin (*gin* is short for *engine*).

The invention had broad economic and social implications. Almost overnight, cultivating cotton became immensely profitable; but the economic model also depended upon inexpensive slave labor. Slavery, which had shown signs of decline, suddenly became essential to getting rich quickly by growing King Cotton. One consequence of slavery's economic importance was the Civil War; another was the torching of Mulberry Grove by the Union general William Tecumseh Sherman's army in 1865.

Catherine Littlefield Greene.

To use a tin wash pan like this one, the bather remained standing (a child might sit) and washed with a sponge. The design kept water splashed on the floor to a minimum and allowed for bathing the entire body, a new concept to most Americans.

Which Way to the Bathroom, Please?

Toilet facilities as we know them were nonexistent in the eighteenth century. The outdoor privy was the warm-weather and daytime option; the alternative was the chamber pot, stowed under a bed or in the lower cupboard of a washstand. Chamber pots were also built into chairs, camouflaged by hinged seats. When clean and not in use, chamber pots were typically stored in the kitchen.

Personal cleanliness was taking on new importance. The individual returning from the privy or stables would usually find a container of cold water and a towel near the back door. Cleaning equipment grew larger and more usual as the century ended, with washstands becoming fixtures in the bedroom or, in fancier houses, the dressing room. The stands were equipped with washbasins and water bottles called flasketts.

The washing of hands, arms, and sometimes feet was a regular ritual for many. As the century drew to a close, the Saturday night bath became more common, generally in a shallow, portable tub. Still, a washing vessel larger than a washstand was unknown to a majority of the population.

Designated rooms for bathing appeared early in the nineteenth century, but running water came later. None of the Founding Fathers encountered a room we would call a bathroom, though Lafayette—both in France and during his brief stay in Savannah—experienced the first wave of new facilities in the fanciest of houses, where some permanent fixtures had begun to be attached to supplies of running water.

WILLIAM JAY, ARCHITECT

Another sometime visitor to America designed the mansion Lafayette visited, known today as the Owens-Thomas House.

Handsome, cultured, and talented, William Jay also met with a warm—if less effusive—welcome in Savannah. Born in Bath, then England's second city, he grew up walking its elegant streets, many of them lined with buildings decorated with great stone pilasters, columns, and cornices carved in a Classical manner. Though only twenty-four, Jay arrived on the American scene in 1817 with a cultivated architectural sensibility, having served an apprenticeship with a noted London architect and exhibited his designs at London's Royal Academy. Savannahians flush with the profits from selling cotton and possessed of a taste for English style and culture soon hired William Jay, Architect, to build them fashionable mansions. He remained in America for seven years before returning to England; during that span, he put an unmistakable architectural imprint on the place, constructing half a dozen mansions, the customhouse, a school, a bank, and the Savannah Theatre.

The Savannah banker and merchant Richard Richardson gave Jay his first American commission. The house for Richardson consisted of two main stories atop a raised basement. The floor plan was roughly square, with a dramatic central hall and staircase. The house is pure Regency, the English style that got its name from the King's status at the time (George III had gone permanently insane and in 1811 Parliament authorized the Prince of Wales—and future King George IV—to rule as Prince Regent until his father's death). Built upon a double lot 60 feet wide and 180 feet deep, Richardson's house overlooked Oglethorpe Square. To the rear, Jay laid out a formal walled garden and a service building that served as a carriage house and slave quarter.

The builders used local materials, beginning with a foundation of tabby, a masonry conglomerate of oyster shells, lime, sand, and water used in a manner not unlike modern poured concrete. The structural walls of the upper floors were of a limestone called coquina, formed of shells and coral. But Jay also specified the use of iron in the structure, the first time the material was given large-scale use in America.

LEFT: *One of the most striking features of the house is the cast-iron balcony on the south side. Jay ordered it from fabricators in England, and its installation represents one of the first uses of structural cast iron in America. This balcony may also have been the site of one of Lafayette's addresses to an adoring crowd in March 1825. According to Savannah legend, he delivered his words twice, once in English, once in French.*

RIGHT: *The rear porch surveys a formal parterre garden enclosed by walls and, at the far boundary of the property, a dependency that once served as a carriage house and slave quarter.*

I am happy, sir, to enjoy the long wished-for gratification of a visit to this interesting and classic city, where you so kindly welcome me.

—*General Lafayette, in response to a welcoming address in Savannah, March 9, 1825*

The William Scarborough house, with its crisp geometric character, overlooks its garden to the rear (left); the main façade surveys today's Martin Luther King Jr. Boulevard (right).

A Visitor to Scarborough House

Before Lafayette's visit, another Founding Father embarked upon a national tour. Inspired by George Washington's presidential journey a generation earlier, the popular and personable James Monroe (1758–1831) sought to smooth over the scars of recent partisan battles. A Boston paper captured the spirit nicely, suggesting that the fifth president's Boston visit signaled the beginning of an "era of good feelings."

On May 8, 1819, Monroe arrived in Savannah. He inspected the steamship *Savannah,* which was soon to depart for Liverpool, making it the first steamship to cross the Atlantic (actually, it was a hybrid sail-and-steam-powered vessel). The ship's owner, William Scarborough, made wealthy in the cotton trade, welcomed Monroe into his home.

By some accounts, Scarborough's house was the finest in Savannah. Its architect was William Jay, who had designed Mr. Richardson's house a few blocks away. It featured more Grecian elements, such as burly Doric columns, but resembled Jay's other Savannah work in its size and grandeur.

The hero Lafayette, painted in 1825 during his visit to the United States.

Along with Benjamin Henry Latrobe (see "America's First Professional Architect," page 264), Jay represented a watershed in American building. He arrived as no dilettante but as a trained professional familiar with the newest technological advances. He, too, helped separate the design and planning phase from the construction of a house; he was a professional architect in a city where none had ever worked before. And he brought with him modern notions such as indoor plumbing. For Mr. Richardson's house, he specified rain-fed cisterns built into the attic and ceilings that powered flushing water closets, basins, bathing tubs, and even a shower in the cellar.

By the time of Lafayette's arrival, Richardson's financial fortunes had plummeted and title to the property was held by the Bank of the United States, from which Mary Maxwell leased it for her boardinghouse. But the house remained a showplace, a quite suitable site for the Nation's Guest.

FACING PAGE: *A grand space at Scarborough House (top left), illuminated by an elliptical window; and two upstairs chambers at the Owens-Thomas House. One was probably a family space but the other (below), called the Lafayette Bedroom, is believed to have served as the Frenchman's accommodation in 1824.*

LEFT: *The parlor is a grand, tall room—but its ceiling makes it spectacular. The ceiling appears to be a dome, an illusion enhanced by the plasterwork in the corners, which looks like pleated fabric.*

ABOVE: *The* **D***-shaped dining room has its innovations, too, including a sinuous wall that contains a built-in marble-top sideboard lit by an amber window overlaid with a Greek key design.*

WELCOMING THE NATION'S GUEST

Lafayette resembled no one else among America's Founders. During the Revolutionary War, he held the highest rank among the foreign officers who served with the Continental Army. In the colonies, he underwrote military expenses from his own pocket; back in France, his was a crucial voice in making the case to King Louis XVI and his ministers for supporting the American cause. Later still, he played a role as a revolutionary in his homeland, emulating the man to whom he had become a surrogate son, General George Washington.

By 1824–25, Washington had been in his grave nearly a quarter century. But Lafayette's widely publicized arrival prompted Americans to look back on the founding of their nation. Among the stops on the tour was the new Federal City, Washington, D.C. There on New Year's Day 1825, James Monroe received Lafayette at the President's House, and both men attended a congressional dinner. Lafayette participated in a two-day commemoration of the Battle of Yorktown in Virginia and laid the cornerstone at the Bunker Hill

Monument in Massachusetts. A private stop took him to Mount Vernon, where Lafayette's son, George, had resided for five years during his father's imprisonment. Greeted by members of Washington's family, Lafayette visited the general's tomb. According to his secretary's memoir, he "descended alone into the vault, and a few minutes after re-appeared, his eyes overflowing with tears."

Layfayette's tour amounted to a celebration of the nation's origins and an unusual pause in the American quest for growth and progress. It was a retrospective moment, during which the press, politicians, patricians, and hoi polloi alike honored the one man who had remained untainted by politics (even Washington had taken his share of criticism from opponents of the Federalist party). Lafayette's long tour—the journey took thirteen months, traveling to all twenty-four states—produced an outpouring perhaps unique in the nation's history. The Nation's Guest, a man of conscience whose commitment to two revolutions cost him dearly, stood above petty disagreements.

The staircase is pure look-at-me!
architecture. As if the details—
the Corinthian columns, the inlaid
brass, the faux grain painting and
marbleizing—were insufficient, the
design seems to say, "Look what I can
do!" The stairs divide at a landing,
with two matching flights continuing
to the second floor. The lavish
decoration and daring design speak
for the wealth of Savannah's merchant
princes in the antebellum age. For the
second-floor landing, see page 311.

John Adams's "Old House"

*By the mid-1820s, the revolutionary gener-*ation was largely gone. Benjamin Franklin and George Washington were many years dead, as was just about everyone from the New England delegations, including Stephen Hopkins, the elderly Quaker from Rhode Island who had so amused John Adams at the Continental Congress. Aside from Charles Carroll of Maryland, who was nearly ninety and had been out of federal politics for thirty-five years, only two of the fifty-six Signers still lived.

After a hiatus, John Adams and Thomas Jefferson had resumed their friendship in 1812. Their personal histories had been entwined since their meeting in May 1775, when Jefferson, eight years Adams's junior, showed the older man due deference. In Philadelphia the two discovered shared passions for books, the law, and the revolutionary cause. Later, during their service in Paris after the war, they became intimate friends; later still, the friendship devolved to political rivalry—and bitter resentment— in the wake of the campaigns of 1796 and 1800, when they took turns winning the presidency. But after years of silence, the two, both happily retired from public life, had established an epistolary friendship unlike any other in American history.

In hundreds of letters written between 1812 and 1826, the men rarely revisited old battle lines; philosophy rather than politics

Remodeled by Charles Francis Adams in the 1850s, the dining rooms reflects Victorian era tastes.

The elderly and almost sightless John Adams spent his last years in his upstairs study, but the contents of the room today were accumulated by four generations of Adams men. The French empire ormolu mantel clock (below, left) belonged to John's son, John Quincy Adams, while great-grandson Henry Adams, the historian and author of The Education of Henry Adams, worked at the desk at the center of the room in his Paris apartment. Adams himself purchased the Louis XVI secretary (left) in France in 1783, and while seated at it resumed his memorable correspondence with Thomas Jefferson in 1814.

dominated their shared ruminations. Law and government, literature (especially Classical authors), and theology (particularly for Adams) were favored topics, as were old friends, their families, and, inevitably the various physical complaints of two men growing old. Arching over all of it was the historical epoch the two men shared and had shaped. Both knew that this correspondence, though apparently no more than the written conversation of two aging actors, would help frame posterity's perception of the drama.

By 1825, Adams knew his months were numbered. Although largely confined to his second-floor study, the widower—his life mate and most valued counselor, Abigail, had died in 1818—still welcomed visitors. He had shared reminiscences with Lafayette. Gilbert Stuart had come to paint his picture once more. His son, John Quincy Adams, who six months earlier had been sworn in as

the sixth president of the United States, spent a few days with his father that October.

While Jefferson, burdened with his own poor health, could not contemplate a visit to his old friend, his favorite granddaughter proved to be his proxy. Ellen Wayles Randolph Coolidge, the new bride of Joseph Coolidge of Boston, arrived in Quincy in December 1825 bearing a letter from her grandfather. But it is the letter this devoted granddaughter wrote back to Jefferson following her afternoon with Adams that best tells the tale.

> We found the old gentleman . . . afflicted with bodily infirmities, lame, and almost blind but as far as his mind is concerned as full of life as he could have been fifty years ago; not only does he seem to have preserved the full vigor of his intellect but all the sprightliness of his fancy, all the vivacity of his thoughts and opinions. . . . He is surrounded by grandchildren exceedingly attached to him, and watching over him with great care and tenderness, and altogether presented an image so venerable, so august even amid the decay of his bodily powers, as sent us away penetrated with respect and admiration for the noble ruin which time-worn and shattered looks still so grand in comparison with what is offered to us by present times.

The two patriarchs held on a few months longer, before dying within hours of each other on July 4, 1826, the fiftieth anniversary of the day on which they presented what Jefferson liked to call "the great Charter of our Independence."

TOP: *In 1823, John Quincy Adams prevailed upon his father to pose once more for Gilbert Stuart. Both painter and sitter were aged and ill, and Stuart himself died in 1828, at which point his daughter, Jane, took up where he had left off. The canvas pictured here is a Jane Stuart copy of her father's original portrait. It hangs at the Old House in Quincy over the dining room mantelpiece.*

BOTTOM: *This 1798 painting of the Old House predates the substantial extension John and Abigail Adams added in 1800. According to a handwritten note left by John's grandson Charles Francis Adams, "This is a representation of the Mansion at Braintree as it was when conveyed in September 1787 by Leonard Vassall Borland to John Adams."*

MONTIZILLO?

Adams joked he might call the property Montizillo after Jefferson's far grander estate. For a time he considered calling it Peacefield, but consistent with their distinctly earthbound New England ways, John and Abigail Adams's house came to be known to them as "the Old House."

The name distinguishes the home from the humbler homestead in Braintree where their five children (four of whom lived to adulthood) had been born. When away from it, Adams always spoke of that farmhouse with affection, but as he and Abigail contemplated their return from England, where John served as minister to the Court of Saint James's in the mid-1780s, the low-ceilinged, cramped saltbox—the main story consisted of four small rooms crowded around a massive center chimney—had begun to seem ill-suited to a man of his station. And as Abigail's sister, Mary Smith Cranch, pointed out, it was also impracticable. "You can never live in that house . . . it is not large enough. You cannot crowd your sons with a little bed by the side of yours now."

Even from London, Adams knew what he wanted. He held an image in his mind of a substantial house a short walk from his birthplace, one that he had admired in childhood. Built in 1731 as the summer home for Leonard Vassall, a wealthy sugar planter with holdings in the West Indies, the manse stood empty, the Vassalls' Royalist daughter having fled to England in 1775. Through an intermediary—the Adamses remained in London—they purchased the house and seventy-five acres of land for 600 pounds. They took title on September 23, 1787.

When the *Lucretia* dropped anchor in Boston Harbor the following spring, the Adamses occupied their new house. They found that the work they had commissioned from afar remained incomplete. Abigail reported the house "a swarm of carpenters [and]

FACING PAGE: *John and Abigail doubled the size of the Old House (it's nearly eighty feet long). They added the large section fronted by the three sets of openings in the foreground. Beneath the vine-covered porch (below) are two entrances, the one on the left to the 1731 hall, the other to the Long Hall of the 1800 addition.*

RIGHT: *John and Abigail opened windows in the end wall of the original house to gain a view of the garden from the parlor.*

LEFT: *The garden, the Old House, and the stone library (rear, center) added by John Adams's grandson Charles Francis Adams in 1870 to contain more than twelve thousand volumes and three generations of family papers. Collecting books was indeed a family affair; John Adams himself owned about four thousand.*

RIGHT: *John Adams's birthplace in Braintree, Massachusetts.*

APPLE CIDER ANYONE?

From his days as a fifteen-year-old at Harvard, John Adams enjoyed a spot of cider each morning. "I shall never forget, how refreshing and salubrious we found it, hard as it often was." In the eighteenth century, water quality was unreliable, so cider, along with small beer (a weak variety of the familiar fermented beverage), was often consumed.

Upon moving to the Old House, the Adamses constructed a cider house and barn on the estate. It was probably a single large building, some fifty-six feet by twenty, and it was known to produce fifty barrels of cider in a year (perhaps only a fifth of which was kept for household consumption, the balance sold). The raw materials—native apples—were abundant and when mature were put through a mechanical mill and then into a press that crushed them to a pulp, releasing the juices. The acids in the juice produced fermentation in the barrels or casks.

Adams retained a taste for a gill (one-fourth of a pint) of cider all his life. "I drank this Morning and Yesterday Morning," he confided in his diary in 1799, "about a Jill of Cyder. It seems to do me good, by diluting and dissolving the Phlegm or the Bile in the Stomach."

masons," and worse yet, after her years in a generous London house, the place seemed small. To her, the house resembled a "wren's nest" with all the comfort of a "barracks." The couple added a kitchen ell to the rear, painted the dark mahogany paneling in the parlor white, wallpapered several rooms, and inserted two windows to overlook the garden. But just as they started to settle in, John was elected to the vice presidency. He served eight years (1789–1797) in that office and four more as the nation's second president (1797–1801), during which time he and his wife resided in New York, Philadelphia, and, briefly, as the first occupants of the President's House in the Federal City of Washington. For the most part, the Old House stood empty.

Contemplating once again a return to Massachusetts, John and Abigail decided to enlarge their house. The original façade consisted of a center entrance flanked by pairs of first-floor windows; the addition made during Adams's last year as president contained a second entrance and another pair of windows. The footprint of the house nearly doubled, with the deep, two-and-a-half-story addition enclosing a grander entrance hall than the simple dogleg stairway of the original house. Alongside the Long Hall was a large reception room, and over the Long Room was a spacious study for the soon-to-be-retired President Adams.

The much larger house was to accommodate the extended Adams family, and various children and grandchildren came and went, for months and even years at a time. A staff consisting of a

cook and three or four maids or manservants attended their needs. The Old House property and the numerous other farms and parcels in the Adamses' real estate portfolio were all working farms, some operated by tenant farmers, some run by Adams himself.

The Old House shared its site with a new woodshed to the north. An existing building on the property, a smaller farmhouse, served as a library and a place for the processing of milk and cheese. In retirement, the farmer-attorney turned politician and president kept farm animals, so there was a stable and cart sheds, along with other purpose-built farm and utility buildings, including a corncrib and a cider house. Even when residing in New York and Philadelphia, Abigail had written home requesting that Russet apples or Germain pears be posted from their farms. Late in life, John continued to boast to correspondents about the volume of hay his fields produced or his healthy stand of corn.

TOP LEFT: *A bust of John Adams surveys the generous Long Hall.*

ABOVE: *John Adams purchased twelve Louis XV armchairs in Paris, which he subsequently used at the President's House before bringing them back to Quincy and installing them in the Long Room. The circular ottoman (at center) was the property of grandson Charles Francis Adams. The unfinished portrait over the mantel (top right) painted by John Singleton Copley, portrays the Adamses's friend and family physician, Joseph Warren, who was killed at the Battle of Bunker Hill.*

A DYNASTY IN QUINCY

John Adams (1735–1826) served his country in a variety of roles. The former schoolteacher and lawyer came to prominence during the trial of the British soldiers responsible for the Boston Massacre (1770); though he was a fervent Patriot, his principled defense of the hapless soldiers won the respect of his fellow citizens, who soon elected him to the Massachusetts legislature. By 1774 he was a delegate to the Continental Congress; in 1775 he proposed George

As portrayed in an 1849 painting, the Adams homesteads in Braintree were at the heart of a hardscrabble New England farm. The houses still stand today, but the orchards and fields that once surrounded the dwellings have become a densely packed streetscape.

Two Adams Birthplaces

Both small saltbox houses were within walking distance of the Old House. They sit at the base of Penn's Hill; in John's absence in 1775, John Quincy and his mother climbed to its summit to watch the smoke and hear the reports of the guns at the Battle of Bunker Hill.

Before buying the Old House, John and Abigail—at times, Abigail alone—ran the farm. Later, their son Thomas lived in the adjacent house where his father had been born. But both homes were modest: their frames of oak, the walls filled with brick nogging for insulation, the heart of each an immense masonry chimney mass with multiple fireplaces that held the heat, in winter and summer alike. The acres around were planted with vegetables, berries, and fruit and nut trees, the fields with hay and grains.

The Adams homesteads provided little more than a subsistence life based on the output of the soil and the hard labor of the inhabitants. The comforts were few, the furnishings plain and practical. In short, the move to the Old House represented a step up in style, society, and comfort.

Yet the two seventeenth-century farmhouses, one not more than a hundred feet from the other, produced two presidents. The home of "Deacon John" Adams was the site of John Adams's birth in 1735; the other, then home to John and Abigail, was the birthplace of John Quincy Adams in 1767.

Washington for commander in chief of the Continental Army; and in 1776 he served on the Committee of Five charged with drafting the Declaration of Independence. While Thomas Jefferson was the document's principal author, Adams's ringing defense on the floor of Congress led to its adoption.

After General Burgoyne's surrender at Saratoga, Adams traveled to France to seek that nation's cooperation in the war; with French support assured, he returned to Boston in 1780 to draft a new constitution for Massachusetts. He then went back to Europe, secured Dutch recognition of the new nation, and with John Jay and Ben Franklin helped negotiate the Treaty of Paris (1783). After his time in England as the American minister and his executive days, he retired to Quincy (in 1792, the northern portion of his native Braintree had been incorporated as a separate town).

Adams's long retirement was marked by losses—several grandchildren, his daughter Nabby (Abigail) to breast cancer, and hardest of all, his wife. He did live to see his son John Quincy Adams (1767–1848) emerge as a brilliant scholar, diplomat, and politician. As a ten-year-old, John Quincy had traveled to France with his father; he studied in Holland and at Harvard, served as minister to the Netherlands, Portugal, Prussia, and Russia, then as a U.S. senator and secretary of state before becoming president in the disputed election of 1824.

At his father's death, John Quincy Adams purchased title to the Old House from the estate, along with the bulk of the house's contents. He returned to Congress after his presidency, but he summered at the Old House, until his death in the capital. After his parents' deaths (John Quincy's widow died in 1852), Charles Francis Adams made various improvements to the house, incorporating running water and, a few years later, gas illumination. Charles Francis would serve as minister to Great Britain during the Civil War, but he also had a passion for the history of his family. He collected, conserved, and edited the papers left by John, Abigail, and John Quincy Adams before his death in 1886. Two of John Adams's great-grandsons, the antiquarian Brooks Adams and the writer and historian Henry Adams, also resided in the home; it was Brooks who remained there the longest, becoming its principal caretaker until his death, in 1927. Then the surviving heirs formed the Adams

Memorial Society, which opened the house to public. Finally, in 1947, it became a property of the National Park Service, which administers it today as a National Historic Site.

While much remains as it did when John and Abigail resided there, the house reflects a variety of changes made by the ensuing three generations of Adams owners. John Quincy added a passage to the rear to ease flow to the kitchen. Charles Francis had the white paint removed from the mahogany paneling in the west parlor, and the moldings and other woodwork in the dining room were redone in a Victorian taste. The result is a house that reflects four generations of Adamses, all of whom played roles in their nation's history.

FOUR FATHERS

To close this book with John Adams seems appropriate: along with George Washington, Thomas Jefferson, and Benjamin Franklin, Adams is an American cornerstone. At different times in his long public career, he stood shoulder to shoulder with each of them—at the Continental Congress with Jefferson, in France with Franklin, as Washington's vice president.

The four of them make a varied lineup. Washington stands tall and big-boned, the strong and silent type, the man of action. Jefferson is the intellectual, the well-mannered philosopher, pale-complected, tall and slim, with a mane of red hair. The stooped and portly Franklin, older than the rest, is a self-made man full of wry wit, charm, and profound insights.

Enter John Adams: amiable, curious, short, and squat, but hardened by physical work on the farm he loved. Honest to a fault, he was loquacious and fiery in his public life, known among his friends and family as gentle, passionate, and possessed of a gift for friendship. He could be querulous, impatient, and thin-skinned, but he was never overcome by a lust for power or money. An American Everyman, he found his greatest joys in his marriage, his family (especially his son John Quincy), his books, his garden, his faith, and most of all, in his nation. He died confident in the success of the experiment he and his fellow Founding Fathers had helped launch.

John Adams purchased the bed in Holland while abroad tending to diplomatic matters. He slept in this bed chamber, as did Abigail until she died here in 1818 of typhoid fever.

Visitor Information

Amstel House, New Castle, Delaware.

Adams National Historical Park
FOUNDING FATHER: John Adams
OWNER/ADMINISTRATOR: National Park Service, U.S. Department of the Interior
ADDRESS: 135 Adams Street, Quincy, MA 02169
WEB ADDRESS: http://www.nps.gov/adam/
PHONE: 617-773-1177
HOURS: April 19 through November 10: Daily, 9:00 A.M. to 5:00 P.M. November 11 through April 18: Daily, 10:00 A.M. to 4:00 P.M.

Alexander Hamilton's The Grange
FOUNDING FATHER: Alexander Hamilton
OWNER/ADMINISTRATOR: National Park Service, U.S. Department of the Interior
ADDRESS: 287 Convent Avenue, at 141st Street, New York, NY 10031
WEB ADDRESS: http://www.nps.gov/hagr/index.htm
PHONE: 212-283-5154
HOURS: The Grange is closed for restoration and relocation

Amstel House
FOUNDING FATHER: Nicholas Van Dyke
OWNER/ADMINISTRATOR: New Castle Historical Society
ADDRESS: 2 East Fourth Street, New Castle, DE 19720
WEB ADDRESS: http://www.newcastlehistory.org/houses/amstel.html
PHONE: 302-322-2794
HOURS: April through December: Wednesday through Saturday, 11:00 A.M. to 4:00 P.M.; Sunday, 1:00 to 4:00 P.M.

Chase-Lloyd House
FOUNDING FATHERS: Samuel Chase and Edward Lloyd
OWNER/ADMINISTRATOR: The Chase Home, Inc.
ADDRESS: 22 Maryland Avenue, Annapolis, MD 21401
PHONE: 410-263-2723
HOURS: March through December: Tuesday through Saturday, 2:00 to 4:00 P.M.

Cliveden
FOUNDING FATHER: Benjamin Chew
OWNER/ADMINISTRATOR: National Trust for Historic Preservation
ADDRESS: 6401 Germantown Avenue, Germantown, PA 19144
WEB ADDRESS: http://www.cliveden.org/
PHONE: 215-848-1777
HOURS: April through December: Thursday through Sunday, 12:00 noon to 4:00 P.M.

Deshler-Morris House
FOUNDING FATHER: George Washington
OWNER/ADMINISTRATOR: National Park Service, U.S. Department of the Interior
ADDRESS: 5542 Germantown Avenue, Germantown, PA 19144
WEB ADDRESS: http://www.nps.gov/demo/index.htm
PHONE: 215-596-1748
HOURS: April through mid-December: Friday, Saturday, and Sunday, 1:00 to 4:00 P.M.

Drayton Hall
FOUNDING FATHER: William Henry Drayton
OWNER/ADMINISTRATOR: National Trust for Historic Preservation
ADDRESS: 3380 Ashley River Road, Charleston, SC 29414
WEB ADDRESS: http://www.draytonhall.org/
PHONE: 843-769-2600
HOURS: March through October: Daily, 9:30 A.M. to 4:00 P.M. November through February: Daily, 9:30 A.M. to 3:00 P.M.

Ford Mansion
FOUNDING FATHER: George Washington
OWNER/ADMINISTRATOR: National Park Service, U.S. Department of the Interior
ADDRESS: 30 Washington Place, Morristown, NJ 07960
WEB ADDRESS: http://www.nps.gov/morr
PHONE: 908-766-8215
HOURS: Daily, 9:00 A.M. to 5:00 P.M.

Franklin Court
FOUNDING FATHER: Benjamin Franklin
OWNER/ADMINISTRATOR: National Park Service, U.S. Department of the Interior
ADDRESS: Market Street, between Third and Fourth Streets, Philadelphia, PA 19106
WEB ADDRESS: http://www.nps.gov/inde/franklin-court.html
PHONE: 215-965-2305
HOURS: The courtyard is open to the street; the underground museum is open daily, 11:00 A.M. to 5:00 P.M.

General Philip Schuyler House Saratoga National Historical Park
FOUNDING FATHER: Philip Schuyler
OWNER/ADMINISTRATOR: National Park Service, U.S. Department of the Interior
ADDRESS: Route 4, Schuylerville, NY 12871
WEB ADDRESS: http://www.nps.gov/sara/pphtml/facilities.html
PHONE: 518-664-9821, ext. 224
HOURS: May 28 through September 5: Wednesday through Sunday, 9:30 A.M. to 4:30 P.M.

George Washington's Mount Vernon
FOUNDING FATHER: George Washington
OWNER/ADMINISTRATOR: Mount Vernon Ladies' Association
ADDRESS: P.O. Box 110, Mount Vernon, VA 22121
WEB ADDRESS: http://www.mountvernon.org/
PHONE: 703-780-2000

HOURS: April through August: Daily, 8:00 A.M. to 5:00 P.M. March, September, and October: Daily, 9:00 A.M. to 5:00 P.M. November through February: Daily, 9:00 A.M. to 4:00 P.M.

The George Wythe House
FOUNDING FATHER: George Wythe
OWNER/ADMINISTRATOR: Colonial Williamsburg Foundation
ADDRESS: P.O. Box 1776, Williamsburg, VA 23187
WEB ADDRESS: http://history.org/
PHONE: 757-229-1000
HOURS: Vary with the season

The Governor John Langdon Mansion Memorial
FOUNDING FATHER: John Langdon
OWNER/ADMINISTRATOR: Historic New England
ADDRESS: 143 Pleasant Street, Portsmouth, NH 03801
WEB ADDRESS: http://www.spnea.org/visit/homes/langdon.htm
PHONE: 603-436-3204
HOURS: June through October 15: Friday through Sunday, 11:00 A.M. to 4:00 P.M.

Governor's House Inn
FOUNDING FATHER: Edward Rutledge
OWNER/ADMINISTRATOR: Governor's House Inn
ADDRESS: 117 Broad Street, Charleston, SC 29401
WEB ADDRESS: http://www.governorshouse.com/
PHONE: 800-720-9812
HOURS: Not a museum, but like John Rutledge's house across the street (see "John Rutledge House Inn"), Edward's home has become an inn

Gunston Hall
FOUNDING FATHER: George Mason
OWNER/ADMINISTRATOR: Commonwealth of Virginia/Gunston Hall Board of Regents, National Society of Colonial Dames of America
ADDRESS: 10709 Gunston Road, Mason Neck, VA 22079

WEB ADDRESS: http://www.gunstonhall.org/
PHONE: 703-550-9220
HOURS: Daily, 9:30 A.M. to 5:00 P.M.; except Thanksgiving, Christmas, and New Year's Day

Hammond-Harwood House
FOUNDING FATHER: Matthias Hammond
OWNER/ADMINISTRATOR: Hammond-Harwood House Association
ADDRESS: 19 Maryland Avenue, Annapolis, MD 21401
WEB ADDRESS: http://www.hammondharwoodhouse.org/
PHONE: 410-263-4683
HOURS: April through October: Tuesday through Sunday, 12:00 to 5:00 P.M.

The Heyward-Washington House
FOUNDING FATHER: Thomas Heyward, Jr.
OWNER/ADMINISTRATOR: Charleston Museum
ADDRESS: 87 Church Street, Charleston, SC 29403
WEB ADDRESS: http://www.charlestonmuseum.org
PHONE: 843-722-0354
HOURS: Monday through Saturday, 10:00 A.M. to 5:00 P.M.; Sunday, 1:00 to 5:00 P.M.

Hopsewee
FOUNDING FATHERS: Thomas Lynch, Sr., and Thomas Lynch, Jr.
OWNERS/ADMINISTRATORS: Frank and Raejean Beattie
ADDRESS: 494 Hopsewee Road, Georgetown, SC 29440
WEB ADDRESS: http://www.hopsewee.com/
PHONE: 843-546-7891
HOURS: March through October: Monday through Friday, 10:00 A.M. to 4:00 P.M. November through February: Thursday and Friday, 10:00 A.M. to 4:00 P.M.

John Adams's Old House, Quincy, Massachusetts.

Iredell House
FOUNDING FATHER: James Iredell
OWNER/ADMINISTRATOR: Historic Edenton State Historic Site/North Carolina Department of Cultural Resources
ADDRESS: 108 North Broad Street, P.O. Box 474, Edenton, NC 27932
WEB ADDRESS: http://www.edenton.nchistoricsites.org
PHONE: 252-482-2637
HOURS: April through October: Monday through Saturday, 9:00 A.M. to 5:00 P.M.; Sunday, 1:00 to 4:00 P.M. November through March: Monday through Saturday, 10:00 A.M. to 4:00 P.M.; Sunday, 1:00 to 4:00 P.M. Closed most major state holidays

The entrance hall at Monticello.

THE JEREMIAH LEE MANSION
FOUNDING FATHER: Jeremiah Lee
OWNER/ADMINISTRATOR: Marblehead Museum and Historical Society
ADDRESS: 161 Washington Street, Marblehead, MA 01945
WEB ADDRESS: http://www.marbleheadmuseum.org/LeeMansion.htm
PHONE: 781-631-1768
HOURS: June through October: Tuesday through Saturday, 10:00 A.M. to 4:00 P.M.

THE JOHN DICKINSON PLANTATION
FOUNDING FATHER: John Dickinson
OWNER/ADMINISTRATOR: State of Delaware, Division of Historical and Cultural Affairs
ADDRESS: 340 Kitts Hummock Road, Dover, DE 19901
WEB ADDRESS: http://history.delaware.gov/museums/jdp/jdp_main.shtml
PHONE: 302-739-3277
HOURS: March through December: Tuesday through Saturday, 10:00 A.M. to 3:30 P.M.; Sunday, 1:30 to 4:30 P.M. January and February: closed Sundays

JOHN JAY HOMESTEAD
FOUNDING FATHER: John Jay
OWNER/ADMINISTRATOR: New York State Office of Parks, Recreation and Historic Preservation
ADDRESS: Box 832, Katonah, NY 10536
WEB ADDRESS: http://nysparks.com/sites/info.asp?siteID=14
PHONE: 914-232-5651
HOURS: April through October: Tuesday through Saturday, 10:00 A.M. to 4:00 P.M.; Sunday, 11:00 A.M. to 4:00 P.M. November: Tuesday through Saturday, 10:00 A.M. to 3:00 P.M.; Sunday, 11:00 A.M. to 3:00 P.M.

JOHN RUTLEDGE HOUSE INN
FOUNDING FATHER: John Rutledge
OWNER/ADMINISTRATOR: Charming Inns, Inc.
ADDRESS: 116 Broad Street, Charleston, SC 29401
WEB ADDRESS: http://www.johnrutledgehouseinn.com/
PHONE: 866-720-2609
HOURS: Not a museum but like Edward Rutledge's house across the street (see "Governor's House Inn"), this home has become an inn

LIBERTY HALL
FOUNDING FATHER: William Livingston
OWNER/ADMINISTRATOR: Liberty Hall Foundation
ADDRESS: 1003 Morris Avenue, Union, NJ 07083
WEB ADDRESS: http://www.libertyhallnj.org
PHONE: 908-527-0400
HOURS: April through December: Wednesday through Saturday, 10:00 A.M. to 4:00 P.M.; Sunday, 12:00 noon to 4:00 P.M.

LONGFELLOW NATIONAL HISTORIC SITE
FOUNDING FATHER: George Washington
OWNER/ADMINISTRATOR: National Park Service, U.S. Department of the Interior
ADDRESS: 105 Brattle Street, Cambridge, MA 02138
WEB ADDRESS: http://www.nps.gov/long/
PHONE: 617-876-4491
HOURS: April through May: Tuesday through Saturday, 10:00 A.M. to 4:30 P.M. May through October: Wednesday through Sunday, 10:00 A.M. to 4:30 P.M. Winter: closed

MIDDLETON PLACE
FOUNDING FATHERS: Henry Middleton and Arthur Middleton
OWNER/ADMINISTRATOR: Middleton Place Foundation
ADDRESS: 4300 Ashley River Road, Charleston, SC 29414
WEB ADDRESS: http://www.middletonplace.org
PHONE: 843-556-6020; 800-782-3608
HOURS: Daily, 9:00 A.M. to 4:30 P.M.

MOFFATT-LADD HOUSE AND GARDEN
FOUNDING FATHER: William Whipple
OWNER/ADMINISTRATOR: The National Society of the Colonial Dames of America in the State of New Hampshire
ADDRESS: 154 Market Street, Portsmouth, NH 03801
WEB ADDRESS: http://www.moffatt/add.org
PHONE: 603-436-8221
HOURS: Mid-June through mid-October: Monday through Saturday, 11:00 A.M. to 5:00 P.M.; Sunday, 1:00 to 5:00 P.M.

MONTICELLO
FOUNDING FATHER: Thomas Jefferson
OWNER/ADMINISTRATOR: Thomas Jefferson Foundation, Inc.
ADDRESS: P.O. Box 316, Charlottesville, VA 22902
WEB ADDRESS: http://www.monticello.org
PHONE: 434-984-9822
HOURS: March through October: Daily, 8:00 A.M. to 5:00 P.M. November through February: Daily, 9:00 A.M. to 4:30 P.M. Closed Christmas Day

MONTPELIER/THE GENERAL HENRY KNOX MUSEUM
FOUNDING FATHER: Henry Knox
OWNER/ADMINISTRATOR: Friends of Montpelier
ADDRESS: U.S. Route 1 and Maine Route 131, P.O. Box 326, Thomaston, ME 04861
WEB ADDRESS: http://www.generalknoxmuseum.org
PHONE: 207-354-8062
HOURS: Memorial Day through Columbus Day: Tuesday through Saturday, 10:00 A.M. to 3:00 P.M.

MORVEN MUSEUM AND GARDEN
FOUNDING FATHER: Richard Stockton
OWNER/ADMINISTRATOR: Historic Morven, Inc.
ADDRESS: 55 Stockton Street, Princeton, NJ 08540
WEB ADDRESS: http://www.morven.org
PHONE: 609-924-8144
HOURS: Wednesday through Friday, 11:00 A.M. to 3:00 P.M.; Saturday and Sunday, 12:00 noon to 4:00 P.M.

OWENS-THOMAS HOUSE MUSEUM
FOUNDING FATHER: General Lafayette
OWNER/ADMINISTRATOR: Telfair Museum of Art
ADDRESS: 124 Abercorn Street, Savannah, GA 31401
WEB ADDRESS: http://www.telfair.org/buildings/ot_house.asp
PHONE: 912-233-9743
HOURS: Sunday, 1:00 to 5:00 P.M.; Monday, 12:00 noon to 5:00 P.M.; Tuesday through Saturday, 10:00 A.M. to 5:00 P.M. Closed some holidays

THE PEYTON RANDOLPH HOUSE
FOUNDING FATHER: Peyton Randolph
OWNER/ADMINISTRATOR: Colonial Williamsburg Foundation
ADDRESS: P. O. Box 1776, Williamsburg, VA 23187
WEB ADDRESS: http://history.org
PHONE: 757-229-1000
HOURS: Vary with the season

POPLAR FOREST
FOUNDING FATHER: Thomas Jefferson
OWNER/ADMINISTRATOR: The Corporation for Jefferson's Poplar Forest
ADDRESS: P.O. Box 419, Forest, VA 24551
WEB ADDRESS: http://www.poplarforest.org
PHONE: 434-525-1806
HOURS: April through November: Wednesday through Monday, 10:00 A.M. to 4:00 P.M. Closed Thanksgiving

SCHUYLER MANSION
FOUNDING FATHER: Philip Schuyler
OWNER/ADMINISTRATOR: New York State Office of Parks, Recreation and Historic Preservation
ADDRESS: 32 Catherine Street, Albany, NY 12202
WEB ADDRESS: http://nysparks.state.ny.us/sites/info.asp?siteID=25
PHONE: 518-434-0834
HOURS: Mid-April through October: Wednesday through Sunday, 11:00 A.M. to 5:00 P.M.

STEPHEN HOPKINS HOUSE
FOUNDING FATHER: Stephen Hopkins
OWNER/ADMINISTRATOR: National Society of the Colonial Dames of America of Rhode Island
ADDRESS: 15 Hopkins Street, Providence, RI 02903
WEB ADDRESS: http://www.nscda.org/museums/rhodeisland.htm
PHONE: 401-247-4755
HOURS: April through November: Wednesday and Saturday, 1:00 P.M. to 4:00 P.M.

STRATFORD
FOUNDING FATHERS: Richard Henry Lee and Francis Lightfoot Lee
OWNER/ADMINISTRATOR: Robert E. Lee Memorial Foundation, Inc.
ADDRESS: 483 Great House Road, Stratford, VA 22558

WEB ADDRESS: http://www.stratfordhall.org
PHONE: 804-493-8038
HOURS: Daily, 9:30 A.M. to 4:00 P.M.

WEBB-DEANE-STEVENS MUSEUM
FOUNDING FATHER: Silas Deane
OWNER/ADMINISTRATOR: National Society of the Colonial Dames of America in the State of Connecticut
ADDRESS: 211 Main Street, Wethersfield, CT 06109
WEB ADDRESS: http://www.webb-deane-stevens.org/
PHONE: 860-529-0612
HOURS: May through October: Wednesday through Monday, 10:00 A.M. to 4:00 P.M. November through April: Saturday and Sunday, 10:00 A.M. to 4:00 P.M.

THE WILLIAM PACA HOUSE AND GARDEN
FOUNDING FATHER: William Paca
OWNER/ADMINISTRATOR: Historic Annapolis Foundation
ADDRESS: 186 Prince George Street, Annapolis, MD 21401
WEB ADDRESS: http://www.annapolis.org
PHONE: 410-267-7619
HOURS: January through March: Friday through Sunday, 12:00 noon to 5:00 P.M. April through December: Daily, 10:00 A.M. to 5:00 P.M.

WILLIAM SCARBOROUGH HOUSE
FOUNDING FATHER: James Monroe
OWNER/ADMINISTRATOR: Ships of the Sea Maritime Museum
ADDRESS: 41 Martin Luther King Boulevard, Savannah, GA 31401
WEB ADDRESS: www.shipsofthesea.org
PHONE: 912-232-1511
HOURS: Tuesday through Sunday, 10:00 A.M. to 5:00 P.M.

Glossary

ARCHITRAVE: In Classical architecture, the lowest portion of the *entablature,* set immediately on the columns or *pilasters* (originally, the architrave was the structural beam spanning the distance between columns). See also *cornice* and *frieze.*

ASHLAR: Building stone that has been squared and finished.

BALUSTRADE: Series of balusters capped by a handrail.

BASEBOARD: Interior, horizontal molding fastened at the base of the wall. Also called a skirting board in Great Britain.

BAY: Unit of space between the principal vertical framing members.

The John Langdon House, Portsmouth, New Hampshire.

CHAMBER: In the eighteenth century, a room generally for sleeping.

CHAMFER: Bevel of approximately forty-five degrees put on a previously square-cut corner of a beam or other wooden member.

CHATTEL: Tangible property, except for real estate, including *slaves.*

CLASSICISM: The architectural style of the buildings of ancient Rome and Greece, characterized by use of the *orders.* See also *Neoclassicism.*

COLONNADE: Row of columns supporting an *entablature.*

CORINTHIAN: *Order* of architecture characterized by capitals decorated with carved acanthus leaves.

CORNICE: Band at the top of the Classical *entablature* that projects at the crown of a wall. See also *architrave* and *frieze.*

COURSE: Horizontal row of bricks, shingles, stones, or other building material.

DEPENDENCIES: Secondary buildings containing support functions, including summer kitchen, dairy, barns, stables, or carriage houses near the principal structure.

DORIC: *Order* of architecture characterized by simple capitals without the carved acanthus leaves of the *Corinthian* or the scrolls of the *Ionic.*

DOUBLE-PILE: Plan in which the house is two rooms deep.

DRAWING ROOM: Formal entertaining space; short for withdrawing room.

ELEVATION: Architectural drawing indicating how completed interior or exterior walls will look; the point of view is that of an observer from a horizontal vantage. Also the wall surface represented in such a drawing.

ELL: Rear extension to a building at right angles to the main section.

ENTABLATURE: In the *orders* of Cassical architecture, the assemblage of the horizontal bands of the *cornice, frieze,* and *architrave,* the elements immediately above (and supported by) the columns and capitals.

FABRIC: Physical material of a building; the implication is of the interweaving among the various materials.

FANLIGHT: Semicircular or half-elliptical window sash, often over a doorway.

FESTOON: Chain of flowers suspended in a curve between two points. See also *swag.*

FIVE-PART PLAN: Architectural design pioneered by the Italian Renaissance architect Andrea Palladio that incorporates a large central block flanked by matching support structures to either side consisting of pavilions and connecting passageways.

FLANKER: One of a symmetrical pair of *dependencies,* often a kitchen, washhouse, or slave quarter.

FLOOR PLAN: Top-view drawing in section that indicates outside walls, interior room configurations, and wall openings (windows and doors).

FOOTPRINT: In architectural terms, the exterior perimeter of a structure where it meets the ground.

FRAME HOUSE: House in which the structural parts are wood or depend upon a wood frame for support.

The Vassall-Craigie-Longfellow House, Cambridge, Massachusetts.

Frieze: Horizontal band between the *cornice* and the *architrave* in the *entablature* in classical architecture.

Gable: End wall of a building formed by the eave line of a double-sloped roof in the shape of an inverted **V**.

Gentry: Upper class in early America, consisting of lawyers, doctors, clergy, and wealthy farmers or merchants; gentlemen.

Header: Brick laid with its end outward.

Hip roof: Gable roof with the ends shortened to form sloping triangular surfaces.

Housewright: Tradesman skilled in building with wood; carpenter.

Indenture: Contract by which a person, often an apprentice, is bound to service.

Ionic: Order of architecture identifiable by the carved volutes (scrolls) of its capitals.

Jamb: Side or head lining of a window, door, or other opening.

Joiner: Craftsman skilled in making objects by joining pieces of wood.

Lath: Strips of wood nailed to the frame of a building to support plaster or shingles.

Looking glass: Large mirror, typically framed and often mounted over a mantel.

Mantel: Decorative frame around the fireplace made of wood or stone. Also called mantelpiece.

Manumission: Legal act of release from slavery.

Masonry: Brick, concrete, stone, or other materials bonded together with mortar to form walls, piers, buttresses, or other *mass.*

Mass: Collective external form of a structure. See also *volume.*

Material culture: Interdisciplinary study of artifacts as a means of understanding culture.

Middling sort: Eighteenth-century term to describe middle-class artisans, farmers, and merchants.

Modillion: Ornamental blocks or brackets applied in series to the soffit, the underside of a *cornice.*

Moldings: Strips of wood used for finish or decoration with regular channels or projections, which provide transitions from one surface or material to another (e.g., *baseboard, chair rail,* or *cornice* moldings).

Necessary: Freestanding structure containing a latrine; outhouse.

Neoclassicism: Architectural style that revived the principles of *Classicism;* in the eighteenth century, a range of designers—among them Thomas Jefferson, Benjamin Henry Latrobe, and Charles Bulfinch—shaped the American Neoclassical style.

Newel: Large post at the top, bottom, turn, or landing of a stairway.

Ogee: Molding consisting of a double curve.

Orangery: Gallery or building with large windows in which plants are cultivated; also orangerie.

Orders: The combinations of vertical (columns or *pilasters*) and horizontal elements *(entablature)* that distinguish the structure of a Classical building. See also *Corinthian, Doric, Ionic, Classicism,* and *Neoclassicism.*

Palladian window: Three-part window consisting of a taller center window, usually with an arched top, flanked by two shorter windows. Named after the sixteenth-century architect Andrea Palladio, it is also known as a Venetian window.

Paneling: Wall surface consisting of panels set within a framework of vertical stiles and horizontal rails.

Paperhangings: Eighteenth-century term for wallpaper.

The garden at Scarborough House, Savannah, Georgia.

Parlor: Formal sitting room used for entertaining.

Parterre: Ornamental garden that incorporates, flowers, shrubs, grass, and gravel walks into geometric patterns.

Passage: In eighteenth-century American houses, the space, usually extending from front to back, that provided access to the rooms. See also *chamber* and *parlor*.

Pediment: Shallow, triangular area formed at the gable end of a roof by the two rooflines, echoing the temple end of a Classical structure. Pedimented headpieces are sometimes found over doors and windows.

Pilaster: Flattened column affixed to a wall and projecting only slightly from it.

Planter: Person who owned a plantation and was of an elevated social class; or one who derived his principal income from growing crops.

Pleasure garden: The immediate landscape surrounding a house or other building planted and maintained for beauty and amusement. Also termed pleasure ground.

Portico: In Classical architecture, a covered entry porch supported by columns.

Quoin: Decorative projecting stone (or wooden element carved to resemble stone) at the corner of a building.

Rafter: One of a series of inclined structural members that support the roof, running from the exterior wall to the ridge.

Rotunda: In Classical architecture, a circular domed building or space.

Rustication: Masonry walling in which cut blocks of stone are emphasized by deeply recessed joints.

Sash: Single, light frame that holds the glass in a window unit and is designed to slide vertically in a track.

Scantling: Small-dimension lumber used in framing a building.

Sidelight: One of a pair of windows flanking a door.

Siding: Finished surface of exterior walls.

Stretcher: Brick laid lengthwise.

String course: Projecting, horizontal molding distinguishing levels of a building, typically in *masonry* construction.

Swag: Length of fabric suspended in a curve between two points. See also *festoon*.

Tabby: Aggregate of oyster shells, lime, sand, and water used as concrete.

Topography: Rendering on a map of the natural and man-made features of a place or region.

Undertaker: In the eighteenth century, a builder or contractor; one who *undertakes* the construction of a building.

Vernacular: Guileless, unpretentious buildings erected with local materials and labor guided by local tradition rather than national or international trends.

Volume: The internal space of a structure. See also *mass*.

Notes and Acknowledgments

This book exists because of the caretakers, the men and women who have restored and operate the houses in its pages. Given the breadth of the subject—all of the colonies are represented by the nearly forty sites visited—my debt to the directors, curators, site managers, researchers, librarians, educators, docents, and others is incalculable. Thus, my first and foremost thanks must go to my guides, who without exception served as welcoming gatekeepers while I visited and learned of their sites.

Next must come the scholars and writers who have recorded the life histories of the Founding Fathers. In assembling this book, I have relied upon many primary sources (including diaries, journals, letters, and other documents). Because this book consists of dozens of mini-biographies, as many architectural appraisals, and an array of dramatic stories, mini-essays on social history, and other elements, I am indebted to shelf after shelf of secondary sources, including books, historic structure reports, articles, guidebooks, furnishings plans, pamphlets, monographs, obituaries, Web sites, and a vast array of other printed materials. To the authors who have gone before, my appreciation. My thanks, too, to the librarians and archivists who helped me at the New York Public Library, the Massachusetts Historical Society, the Boston Public Library, the New-York Historical Society, the Sterling and Francine Clark Art Institute Library in Williamstown, Massachusetts, the Sawyer Library at Williams College, the Library of Congress, and my local libraries, the Chatham Library in Chatham, New York, and the Lenox Library Association in Lenox, Massachusetts.

This book was the brainchild of the publisher Peter Workman; photographer Roger Straus III and I are indebted to him for launching this venture, and to our editor, Ann Bramson, for seeing it through with patience and enthusiasm. The rest of the Artisan staff worked tirelessly on our behalf. Trent Duffy's ability to juggle all the pieces at once—while maintaining a remarkable sense of the book's nuances *and* his equanimity—leaves us especially in his debt. We owe our appreciation to Nick Caruso and Vivian Ghazarian for their design, and Jan Derevjanik for art direction; to Nancy Murray for production; to Susan M. S. Brown for copy editing; to Nicki Clendening and Jaime Harder for publicity; and to Anna Berns for tending to untold details.

My thanks, as always, to my friend and agent, Gail Hochman, whose sage publishing counsel and guidance I value most. Many people pointed me in useful directions—among them were Robin Bodo, Allan Gurganus, Bernard Herman, Charles Lyle, Travis McDonald, Marc Mappen, John I. Mesick, Brian Pfeiffer, Daves Rossell, Peter Sandbeck, and Reid Thomas.

A bibliography of the principal books consulted follows, but first I wish to acknowledge, in the order that their sites appear, the people who guided me in writing this book and the most essential sources for individual chapters.

THE GEORGE WYTHE HOUSE. For the Wythe House in particular, my thanks to Robert Leath, Emily Roberts, William Graham, Kevin Kelly, and Carl R. Lounsbury; for lessons about Colonial Williamsburg in general, I thank Edward A. Chappell, Peter Sandbeck, and Mark R. Wenger; and for easing my access, my thanks to Joseph Roundtree and Julie Watson. The most detailed telling of George Wythe's demise is to be found in *The Murder of George Wythe* by Julian P. Boyd and W. Edwin Hemphill. For matters architectural, the reader may wish to consult *The Eighteenth-Century Houses of Williamsburg* by Marcus Whiffin or my own *Colonial Houses*.

THE JOHN DICKINSON PLANTATION. My appreciation to Gloria Henry for her thorough introduction to the site and its history. The most valuable source for Dickinson's life history is Milton E. Flower's biography, *John Dickinson, Conservative Reactionary*. My thanks as well to Professor Bernard Herman for his guidance on Delaware.

THE WILLIAM PACA HOUSE AND GARDEN. Glenn E. Campbell of the Historic Annapolis Foundation at the Paca House guided my examination of the property and my research into its past; I owe particular thanks to Glenn and his colleague Alexandra Deutsch for their investigations into the illness of Henrietta Maria Dorsey and her caregiver, the slave girl Bett. For more general information regarding the house and garden restoration, I am indebted to various interpretive materials prepared by the staff at the Historic Annapolis Foundation, while for life facts, my debt is to Gregory A. Stiverson and Phebe R. Jacobsen and their biography, *William Paca*.

IREDELL HOUSE. My thanks to Linda Jordan Eure at the Historic Edenton State Historic Site for her good offices, and to D. Ross Inglis and Frances Inglis for their orientation to their beloved town. In examining the streetscapes and houses of Edenton, Thomas R. Butchko's *Edenton: An Architectural Portrait* proved a valuable reference; for the man himself, Willis P. Whichard's biography, *Justice James Iredell*, is the essential source.

THE JEREMIAH LEE MANSION. I owe a large debt to the generous and studious Judy Anderson, curator of the Jeremiah Lee Mansion, a property of the Marblehead Historical Society; her thorough researches into Lee, his house, and his town provided much of the raw material for this chapter. In writing of John Singleton Copley, I made reference to the thorough *John Singleton Copley in America*, by Carrie Rebora and Paul Staiti et al.

PEYTON RANDOLPH HOUSE. A restoration remarkable for its thoroughness was recently completed at the Randolph House (few organizations other than Colonial Williamsburg could muster such an array of archaeologists, architectural historians, curators, and conservators). For their research, writings, and installations, a debt is owed to Edward Chappell, William

Graham, Mark R. Wenger, Ronald L. Hurst, Robert Leath, Margaret Beck Pritchard, and Tanya Wilson. In writing this chapter, I drew in particular on the essays that appeared in *The Colonial Williamsburg Interpreter,* vol. 3, 1999. For the details of Randolph's life, the basic reference is John J. Reardon's *Peyton Randolph, 1721–1775: One Who Presided.*

THE VASSALL-CRAIGIE-LONGFELLOW HOUSE. James M. Shea, site manager at the Longfellow National Historic Site, proved an excellent guide, wise in the ways of the Washingtons and Longfellows alike. For her help in assembling the period images, thanks to Anita Israel. This chapter owes no small debt to various numbers of the *Longfellow House Bulletin,* as well as to the monograph *The Longfellow House* by Henry Wadsworth Longfellow Dana, grandson of the antiquarian poet. The biographical reference of choice is Charles C. Calhoun's *Longfellow: A Rediscovered Life.*

STRATFORD. Judith S. Hynson at Stratford was invaluable, as was the site's thorough yet cogent visitors' handbook, *A Guide to Stratford Hall Plantation and the Lees of Virginia.* The examinations of the late Paul Buchanan and his partner, Charles Phillips, explicated this unique house as even Fiske Kimball had been unable to do (their findings are enumerated in Paul Buchanan's *Stratford Hall and Other Architectural Studies*). The Richard Henry Lee letter to Hannah is in the Stratford archive, as is documentation of the Payne family's role at Stratford. Robert Leith also offered insights into the Walker family of builders and furniture makers who helped make Stratford the showplace it became.

STEPHEN HOPKINS HOUSE. Alice Walsh provided us entrée to the Hopkins House, which is owned by the state of Rhode Island but administered by the National Society of Colonial Dames, and to the Hopkins House research files. Other key sources in writing the chapter were William E. Foster's biography, *Stephen Hopkins: A Rhode Island Statesman,* Antoinette Forrester Downing's *Early Homes of Rhode Island,* and *Early Rhode Island Houses* by Norman M. Islam and Albert F. Brown.

MORVEN MUSEUM AND GARDEN. First thanks go to Martha Leigh Wolfe, executive director at Morven, for her overview. For the details, the essential source is the thorough *Morven: Memory, Myth and Reality* by Constance M. Greiff and Wanda S. Gunning. Annis Boudinot's story was memorialized early by Elizabeth Ellet in *The Women of the American Revolution.*

CLIVEDEN. My thanks to Phillip R. Seitz at the Chew house for his introduction to the place, for fielding my questions, and for providing me with two essential sources, both by Nancy E. Richards. They are two histories, *The Chew Mansion in Germantown* and *The City Home of Benjamin Chew, Sr., and His Family: A Case Study of the Textures of Life* (Philadelphia: Cliveden of

the National Trust, 1993 and 1996, respectively). I also drew on Thomas J. McGuire's *The Surprise of Germantown, or, the Battle of Cliveden: October 4th, 1777,* and Burton Alva Konkle's biography, *Benjamin Chew: 1722–1810.*

DRAYTON HALL. My excellent guide was Craig Hadley, former director of education at Drayton; my thanks as well to Vera Ford and to Diane Miller, who guided my research into the Bowens family, pointing me to Damon Fordham's essay, "Slavery at Drayton Hall: A Study in Ambiguity." Regarding the landscape, Barbara Orsolits's essay "The History of Landscape and Gardens for Drayton Hall" at www.draytonhall.org/ makes fascinating reading. For biographical matters, a key source was Keith Krawczynski, *William Henry Drayton: South Carolina Revolutionary Patriot.*

FORD MANSION. National Park Service Ranger Jude Pfister was my most agreeable guide at the Ford Mansion, the architectural centerpiece of the Morristown National Historical Park. The modest guidebook *Morristown National Historical Park,* edited by Christine Retz (Washington Association of New Jersey, 1982), was a valuable source, and several Washington biographies were also essential, in particular Douglas Southall Freeman's *George Washington: Victory with the Help of France.* Helen Bryan's *Martha Washington: First Lady of Liberty* filled in many details about what Washington called "the softer domestic virtues." The basic text on the events surrounding the Battle of Trenton is David Hackett Fischer's *Washington's Crossing.*

THE HEYWARD-WASHINGTON HOUSE. Neil E. Nohrden was my guide to the contents of the house; Jonathan H. Poston told me its architectural story. The numerous references on the houses of Charleston range from romantic recollections such as *Charleston: Historic City of Gardens* by William Oliver Stevens to Poston's authoritative *The Buildings of Charleston.* Washington's *Diaries* (Donald Jackson and Dorothy Twohig, eds.) were one source of information regarding his visit; another was Archibald Henderson's *Washington's Southern Tour, 1791.* For material on the two Rutledge houses, I am indebted to Linn Lesensne and Richard T. Widman at Charming Inns, as well as the archives at the South Carolina Historical Society.

GENERAL PHILIP SCHUYLER HOUSE/SARATOGA NATIONAL HISTORICAL PARK. At the Schuyler mansion, a New York State Historic Site administered by the Office of Parks, Recreation and Historic Preservation, Darlene Rogers and Heidi Hill were my guides to the house; Chris Robinson at Saratoga directed my examination of the National Park Service National Historical Park. Further research sources included Ron Chernow's *Alexander Hamilton;* John H. G. Pell's essay "Philip Schuyler: The General as Aristocrat" in George Athan Billias, ed., *George Washington's Generals;* and various documents prepared for the National Park Service, including the historic structure and furnishings reports for the Schuyler House at

Saratoga. Period sources included the Marquis de Chastellux's *Travels in North America* and Mrs. Anne Grant's *Memoirs of an American Lady.*

WEBB-DEANE-STEVENS MUSEUM. At the Silas Deane and Joseph Webb Houses in Wethersfield, Connecticut, Donna Keith Baron was essential to my research, into both the house itself and the surviving documentation and the research conducted into the site. The Webb-Deane-Stevens Museum Web site was helpful for its transcriptions of miscellaneous Deane papers (see http://www.silasdeaneonline.org). Juliana Smith's Thanksgiving account appeared in *Colonial Days & Ways* by Helen Evertson Smith.

HAMMOND-HARWOOD HOUSE. In revisiting Annapolis, I am indebted to Carter Lively and his associate Lisa Mason-Chaney at Hammond-Harwood House and to Toni Fearer at the Chase Home (better known in the architectural literature as the Chase-Lloyd House). In researching this chapter, I drew upon not only the self-titled Hammond-Harwood House guidebooks, but also a vast literature on William Buckland. Perhaps the wisest commentator over the years has been William H. Pierson, Jr., in his *The Colonial and Neoclassical Styles,* but I also drew upon the insights of other writers, including Rosamond Randall Beirne in *William Buckland, 1734–1774: Architect of Virginia and Maryland* and Luke Beckerdite in his essays "William Buckland and William Bernard Sears: The Design and the Carver" (in *Museum of Early Southern Decorative Arts,* vol. 8, November 1982) and "Architect-Designed Furniture in Eighteenth-Century Virginia: The Work of William Buckland and William Bernard Sears" (in *American Furniture: 1994*). For the data in "Imagining Mother Hammond," I am particularly indebted to Mary Beth Norton's *Liberty's Daughters: The Revolution Experience of American Women, 1750–1800.*

GOVERNOR JOHN LANGDON MANSION MEMORIAL and the MOFFATT-LADD HOUSE AND GARDEN. The indefatigable Peter Michaud was of immense help in enabling me to tell the story of the Langdon Mansion in particular and Portsmouth in general. Barbara Ann Cleary's "The Governor John Langdon Mansion Memorial: New Perspective in Interpretation" (*Old-Time New England,* vol. 69, 1976) remains the basic reference for the house's history. At Moffatt-Ladd, my debt is to Barbara Ward. I learned the stories of Oney Judge and Cyrus deBruce from Peter Michaud, once again, and found more materials in *Black Portsmouth: Three Centuries of African-American Heritage* by Mark J. Sammons and Valerie Cunningham, and in Henry Wiencek's remarkable *An Imperfect God.* The work of the fine craftsmen of Portsmouth's greatest days is given detailed treatment in Brock Jobe's handsome *Portsmouth Furniture.*

AMSTEL HOUSE. For information on Amstel House, my thanks to Bruce Dalleo, New Castle Historical Society; regarding the town, my apprecia-

tion to Charles Lyle, several incarnations ago, as director of the Delaware Historical Society.

MIDDLETON PLACE. First, thanks go to the welcoming and voluble Charles Duell, who seems to embody his family's passion for the place; next, my appreciation to M. Tracey Todd for giving me the tour and permission to use the stereopticon view and the Benjamin West portrait; and finally, to Barbara Doyle for her research help, in particular relating to the untimely demise of Arthur Middleton.

GUNSTON HALL. Susan Borchardt, then Gunston's assistant director, and Kevin Shupe, archivist, made my time at Gunston Hall both agreeable and productive. In assembling this chapter, I have drawn upon a wide range of sources, among them Kate Mason Rowlands's *Life,* Peter B. Enriques's essay "An Uneven Friendship," and Peter Wallenstein's "Flawed Keepers of the Flame." The latter two appeared in *The Virginia Magazine of History and Biography* (vol. 97, no. 2, and vol. 102, no. 2, respectively). Useful in assembling the architectural story was Bennie Brown's exhibition catalog *William Buckland: Master Builder of the 18th Century* (Mason's Neck, Va.: Board of Regents of Gunston Hall, 1977).

LIBERTY HALL. Bill Schroh, Jr., and Fran Sullivan introduced me to the rich history of the Livingstons and Keans at Liberty Hall. Bill guided my research, pointing me to a range of sources including *As We Were* by Theodore Thayer and *A Memoir of the Life of William Livingston* by Theodore Sedgwick, Jr. The story of Susan Livingston and Colonel Sterling seems to have been told first by Mrs. Ellet in *The Queens of American Society.*

THE GERMANTOWN WHITE HOUSE. My thanks to Bernard Enright at the Deshler-Morris House for his tour of the site and insights into Washington's time in residence, and to Coxey Toogood for sharing her broad knowledge of the house. Essential sources regarding Germantown include Harry M. Tinkcom and Margaret B. Tinkcom et al., *Historic Germantown: From the Founding to the Early Part of the Nineteenth Century,* and several works by the local historian Charles Francis Jenkins, including *The Guidebook to Historic Germantown, Jefferson's Germantown Letters,* and *Washington in Germantown.* As with all things Washington, I am also indebted to James Thomas Flexner, specifically *George Washington and the New Nation, 1783–1793,* and *George Washington, Anguish and Farewell, 1793–1799.*

MONTPELIER/THE GENERAL HENRY KNOX MUSEUM. Ellen Dyer provided me with much essential research, not least her collections catalog *Montpelier: This Spot So Sacred to a Name So Great.* Other sources included the military historian North Callahan's *Henry Knox: General Washington's General;* it is the essential source for the facts of Harry Knox's life. For Montpelier's story, I drew upon Thomas Morgan Griffiths's *Major General Henry Knox and the Last Heirs to Montpelier;* the unpublished historic structures report by Sheila McDonald found in the archives at Montpelier; and *General Knox and His Home in Maine, Montpelier* by his descendant Henry Thatcher Fowler. Various stories of Lucy Knox are found in Mrs. Ellet's *The Women of the American Revolution,* Sally Smith Booth's *The Women of '76,* and Cokie Roberts's *Founding Mothers.*

MOUNT VERNON. My thanks to Melissa Wood for her goodwill and Mary V. Thompson for her vast knowledge of Mount Vernon. The best book on the house itself is *George Washington's Mount Vernon: At Home in Revolutionary America* by Robert E. Dalzell, Jr., and Lee Baldwin Dalzell. Of the many biographical works I consulted, the most useful were those of Douglas Southall Freeman, James Thomas Flexner, and Joseph J. Ellis. The official guidebook, *George Washington's Mount Vernon,* also offers a sound overview of the plantation, its structures, history, and people. The source for the Latrobe visit is the Englishman's own *Virginia Journals,* Edward C. Carter II, ed. Martha Washington is also a key figure in books by Mrs. Ellet, Sally Smith Booth, and Cokie Roberts.

JOHN JAY HOMESTEAD. I am indebted to Allan Weinreb for providing access to the house and the assemblage of research in the site's archives. Other useful sources in writing this chapter were two monographs, Herbert Alan Johnson's *John Jay, 1745–1829* and Jennifer P. McLean's *The Jays of Bedford.* A mid-nineteenth-century description of the house by William S. Thayer appears in *Homes of American Statesmen* (1854). A valuable source for life facts is Walter Stahr's recent biography, *John Jay: Founding Father.* As with other Founding Mothers, the material on Sarah Jay appears in variant forms in books by Mrs. Ellet, Sally Smith Booth, and Cokie Roberts. The research for "How Much Is My House Worth?" is found in the summary and insightful analysis of the 1798 inventory *Distribution of Wealth and Incomes in the United States in 1798* by Lee Soltow.

THE GRANGE. At Alexander and Betsy Hamilton's Harlem Heights home, the Grange, I owe particular thanks to my various tour guides—Charles Kahlstrom, Ed Mucci, and Doug Massenburg, and especially Steve Laise, at the Hamilton Grange National Memorial, National Park Service, U.S. Department of the Interior. A nineteenth-century account of the house by James C. Carter appeared in *Homes of American Statesmen.* Ron Chernow's vast and valuable *Alexander Hamilton* is an essential source regarding the life. I also drew upon Eric Sloane and Edward Anthony's eccentric but intriguing *Mr. Daniels and the Grange* and consulted the drawings and papers of the builder John J. McComb, Jr., at the New-York Historical Society. Joseph J. Ellis's detailed consideration of the Burr-Hamilton duel in *Founding Brothers* makes for most stimulating reading.

MONTICELLO. My Monticello debts are numerous after my having invested several years of my life researching Jefferson and his architectural works for two other books, *Thomas Jefferson, Architect,* and *Dr. Kimball and Mr. Jefferson.* In this particular context, I must thank Wayne Mogielnicki at Monticello for his continued goodwill and Travis Macdonald at Poplar Forest for his passionate pursuit of the Jeffersonian essence. In considering Jefferson's architecture, I drew upon my own *Thomas Jefferson, Architect,* and Jack McLaughlin's *Jefferson and Monticello,* although my most essential touchstone, always, in considering Jefferson's architecture must be Dr. Kimball's *Thomas Jefferson, Architect.* For the recounting of Jefferson's daily regimen, the primary sources were his granddaughter Ellen Coolidge's recollections as reprinted in Sarah N. Randolph's *Domestic Life;* Thomas Jefferson Randolph's in Francis Coleman Rosenberger's *Jefferson Reader;* and Mrs. Smith's *The First Forty Years.* In considering the vast array of Jefferson objects, the reference of choice is Susan R. Stein's *The World of Thomas Jefferson at Monticello.* The biographical references are too numerous to name, but among my favorites are Andrew Burstein's *Jefferson's Secrets: Death and Desire at Monticello,* Joseph J. Ellis's *American Sphinx: The Character of Thomas Jefferson,* and Dumas Malone's majestic six-volume *Jefferson.*

OWENS-THOMAS HOUSE MUSEUM and WILLIAM SCARBOROUGH HOUSE. For Lafayette's visit, I drew upon the contemporary report published as "An Account of the Reception of Gen. Lafayette in Savannah" (Savannah: W. T. Williams, 1825). My guides at the Owens-Thomas House were Cyndi Sommers, site manager, and her associate David Zeleski. A useful resource regarding the Owens-Thomas House was Carol Hunt Chamberlain's essay "The Owens-Thomas House Past and Present," in *Collection Highlights: Telfair Museum of Art* (Savannah, 2005). In appreciating the transformation at William Jay's house on Martin Luther King Boulevard, I drew upon the monograph *Mr. Scarborough's House: History and Restoration* (Savannah: Ships of the Sea Maritime Museum, 1998) as well as the good guidance of Tony Pizzo, executive director of the Ships of the Sea Maritime Museum.

ADAMS NATIONAL HISTORICAL PARK. Kelly Cobble and Patty Smith of the National Park Service guided me through not only the house but also the Adams archive; in the latter, I found useful sources such as Charles E. Peterson's reconnaissance report, *The Adams Mansion* (National Park Service, 1963); and Helen Nelson Skeen's *Documentary Narrative of Buildings Shown of Historic Base Map of the Adams National Historic Site* (National Park Service, 1965). Among many other more general sources—the engaging characters and extensive correspondence of John and Abigail have attracted more than a few scholars—is David McCullough's recent and highly readable *John Adams.* Adams papers—John's, Abigail's, and John Quincy's—have been published; more than a few are easily accessed at the Massachusetts Historical Society Web site, www.masshist.org.

Bibliography

Montpelier, Thomaston, Maine.

ARCHITECTURE

Beirne, Rosamond Randall, and John Henry Scarff. *William Buckland, 1734–1774: Architect of Virginia and Maryland*. Baltimore: Maryland Historical Society, 1958.

Bennett, George Fletcher. *Early Architecture of Delaware*. New York: Bonanza Books, 1932.

Bill, Alfred Hoyt, and Walter E. Edge. *A House Called Morven*. Princeton, N.J.: Princeton University Press, 1954, 1978.

Brownell, Charles F., Calder Loth, William M. S. Rasmussen, and Richard Guy Wilson. *The Making of Virginia Architecture*. Richmond: Virginia Museum of Fine Arts, 1992.

Buchanan, Paul. *Stratford Hall and Other Architectural Studies*. Stratford, Va.: Robert E. Lee Memorial Association, 1998.

Butchko, Thomas R. *Edenton: An Architectural Portrait*. Edenton, N.C.: Edenton Woman's Club, 1992.

Carpenter, Ralph E., Jr. *The Fifty Best Historic American Houses: Colonial and Federal*. New York: E. P. Dutton, 1955.

Carter, Edward C., II, ed. *The Virginia Journals of Henry Latrobe, 1795–1798*, vol. 1. New Haven: Yale University Press, 1977.

Chamber, S. Allen, Jr. *Poplar Forest and Thomas Jefferson*. Forest, Va.: Corporation for Jefferson's Poplar Forest, 1993.

Dalzell, Robert E., Jr., and Lee Baldwin Dalzell. *George Washington's Mount Vernon: At Home in Revolutionary America*. New York: Oxford University Press, 1998.

Davis, Deering. *Annapolis Houses*. New York: Bonanza Books, 1947.

Downing, Antoinette Forrester. *Early Homes of Rhode Island*. Richmond, Va.: Garrett and Massie, 1937.

Fairhurst, Janet Perry. *Homes of the Signers of the Declaration*. New York: Hartt Publications, 1976.

Greenspan, Anders. *Creating Colonial Williamsburg*. Washington, D.C.: Smithsonian Institution Press, 2002.

Greiff, Constance M., and Wanda S. Gunning. *Morven: Memory, Myth and Reality*. Princeton, N.J.: Historic Morven, 2004.

Hafertepe, Kenneth, and James F. O'Gorman. *American Architects and Their Books to 1848*. Amherst: University of Massachusetts Press, 2001.

Herman, Bernard L. *Town House: Architecture and Material Life in the Early American City, 1780–1830*. Chapel Hill: University of North Carolina Press, 2005.

Hosmer, Charles B., Jr. *Presence of the Past: A History of the Preservation Movement in the United States Before Williamsburg*. New York: G. P. Putnam's Sons, 1965.

———. *Preservation Comes of Age: From Williamsburg to the National Trust,* vol. 2. Charlottesville: University Press of Virginia, 1980.

Howard, Hugh. *Colonial Houses*. New York: Harry N. Abrams, 2004.

———. *Dr. Kimball and Mr. Jefferson*. New York: Bloomsbury U.S.A., 2006.

———. *Thomas Jefferson, Architect*. New York: Rizzoli International Publications, 2003.

Howells, John Mead. *The Architectural Heritage of the Piscataqua*. New York: Architectural Book Publishing Company, 1937.

Isham, Norman M., and Albert F. Brown. *Early Connecticut Houses: An Historical and Architectural Study*. Providence, R.I.: Preston & Rounds, 1900.

———. *Early Rhode Island Houses: An Historical and Architectural Study*. Providence, R.I.: Preston & Rounds, 1895.

Kimball, Fiske. *Domestic Architecture of the American Colonies and of the Early Republic*. New York: Charles Scribner's Sons, 1922.

———. *Thomas Jefferson, Architect*. New York: Da Capo Press, 1968.

Lathorp, Elise. *Historic Houses of Early America*. New York: Tudor Publishing Co., 1927, 1941.

Lossing, Benson J. *The Home of Washington*. Hartford: A.S. Hale, 1871. This book has been republished as *George Washington's Mount Vernon*.

Lounsbury, Carl R., ed. *An Illustrated Glossary of Early Southern Architecture and Landscape*. Charlottesville: University Press of Virginia, 1994.

McLaughlin, Jack. *Jefferson and Monticello: The Biography of a Builder*. New York: Henry Holt, 1988.

Morrison, Hugh. *Early American Architecture, From the First Colonial Settlements to the National Period*. New York: Oxford University Press, 1952.

Olmert, Michael. *Official Guide to Colonial Williamsburg*. Williamsburg, Va.: Colonial Williamsburg Foundation, 1998.

Pierson, William H., Jr. *The Colonial and Neoclassical Styles*. New York: Oxford University Press, 1970.

Poston, Jonathan H. *The Buildings of Charleston: A Guide to the City's Architecture*. Columbia: University of South Carolina Press, 1997.

Sloane, Eric, and Edward Anthony. *Mr. Daniels and the Grange*. New York: Funk & Wagnalls, 1968.

The Moffatt-Ladd House, Portsmouth, New Hampshire.

Stevens, William Oliver. *Charleston: Historic City of Gardens.* New York: Dodd, Mead & Company, 1939.

Summerson, John. *Architecture in Britain: 1530–1830.* London: Penguin Books, 1953.

Tinkcom, Harry M., and Margaret B. Tinkcom et al. *Historic Germantown: From the Founding to the Early Part of the Nineteenth Century.* Philadelphia: American Philosophical Society, 1955.

Unrau, Harlan D. *Here Was the Revolution: Historic Sites of the War for American Independence.* Washington, D.C.: National Park Service, U.S. Department of the Interior, 1976.

Waterman ,Thomas T. *The Mansions of Virginia.* Chapel Hill: University of North Carolina Press, 1946.

Whiffin, Marcus. *American Architecture, 1607–1860.* Cambridge, Mass.: MIT Press, 1981.

———. *The Eighteenth-Century Houses of Williamsburg.* Williamsburg, Va.: Colonial Williamsburg Foundation, 1960.

Whitehead, Russell F., and Frank Chouteau Brown, eds. *The White Pine Series of Architectural Monographs.* St. Paul, Minn.: White Pine Bureau, 1915–1940.

Yetter, George Humphrey. *Williamsburg Before and After: The Rebirth of Virginia's Colonial Capital.* Williamsburg, Va.: Colonial Williamsburg Foundation, 1988.

Revolutionary Ladies, Life, and Culture

Ball, Edward. *Slaves in the Family.* New York: Farrar, Straus & Giroux, 1998.

Beckerdite, Luke. *American Furniture: 1994.* Hanover, N.H.: University Press of New England with the Chipstone Foundation, 1994.

Berkin, Carol. *First Generations: Women in Colonial America.* New York: Hill and Wang, 1996.

———. *Revolutionary Mothers.* New York: Alfred A. Knopf, 2005.

Booth, Sally Smith. *The Women of '76.* New York: Hastings House, 1973.

Bryan, Helen. *Martha Washington: First Lady of Liberty.* New York: John Wiley & Sons, 2002.

Bushman, Richard L. *The Refinement of America.* New York: Alfred A. Knopf, 1992.

Calhoun, Charles C. *Longfellow: A Rediscovered Life.* Boston: Beacon Press, 2004.

Chastellux, Marquis de (François Jean de Beauvoir). *Travels in North America, in the Years 1780, 1781, and 1782.* 2 vols. Edited by Howard C. Rice, Jr. Chapel Hill: University of North Carolina Press, 1963.

Delaware Federal Writers' Project. *New Castle on the Delaware.* New Castle, Del.: New Castle Historical Society, 1973.

Dyer, Ellen S. *Montpelier: This Spot So Sacred to a Name So Great.* Thomaston, Maine: Friends of Montpelier, 2004.

Ellet, Mrs. [Elizabeth Fries]. *The Queens of American Society.* New York: Charles Scribner, 1867.

Ellet, E[lizabeth] F[ries]. *The Women of the American Revolution.* 3 vols. New York: Baker and Scribners, 1848–1850.

Fithian, Philip Vickers. *Journal and Letters of Philip Vickers Fithian: A Plantation Tutor of the Old Dominion, 1773–1774.* Charlottesville: University of Virginia Press, 1968.

Flexner, James T. *Doctors on Horseback: Pioneers of American Medicine.* New York: The Viking Press, 1937.

Fraser, Walter J. *Charleston! Charleston!* Columbia: University of South Carolina Press, 1989.

Garrett, Elisabeth Donaghy. *At Home: The American Family, 1750–1870.* New York: Harry N. Abrams, 1990.

Grant, Anne. *Memoirs of an American Lady.* 2 vols. Dodd, Mead and Company, 1901.

Hoffman, Ronald, and Peter J. Albert. *Women in the Age of the American Revolution.* Charlottesville: University of Virginia Press, 1989.

Hofstadter, Richard. *America at 1750: A Social Portrait.* New York: Alfred A. Knopf, 1971.

Isaac, Rhys. *The Transformation of Virginia, 1740–1790.* Chapel Hill: University of North Carolina Press, 1982.

Jenkins, Charles Francis. *The Guidebook to Historic Germantown.* Germantown, Pa.: Site and Relic Society, 1904.

The James Iredell House, Edenton, North Carolina.

Jobe, Brock, ed. *Portsmouth Furniture: Masterworks from the New Hampshire Seacoast*. Boston: Society for the Preservation of New England Antiquities, 1993.

Larkin, Jack. *The Reshaping of Everyday Life, 1790–1840*. New York: Harper & Row, 1988.

Miller, Lillian B., and David C. Ward, eds. *New Perspectives on Charles Willson Peale*. Washington, D.C., and Pittsburgh: Published for the Smithsonian Institution by the University of Pittsburgh Press, 1991.

Murphy, Jim. *An American Plague: The True and Terrifying Story of the Yellow Fever Epidemic of 1793*. New York: Clarion Books, 2003.

Norton, Mary Beth. *Liberty's Daughters: The Revolutionary Experience of American Women, 1750–1800*. Boston: Little, Brown, 1980.

Nylander, Jane C. *Our Own Snug Fireside: Images of the New England Home, 1760–1860*. New York: Alfred A. Knopf, 1994.

Randolph, Sarah N. *The Domestic Life of Thomas Jefferson*. New York: Harper & Brothers, 1871.

Rebora, Carrie, Paul Staiti et al. *John Singleton Copley in America*. New York: Metropolitan Museum of Art, 1995.

Richardson, Edgar P., et al. *Charles Willson Peale and His World*. New York: Harry N. Abrams, 1983.

Roberts, Cokie. *Founding Mothers: The Women Who Raised Our Nation*. New York: William Morrow, 2004.

Sammons, Mark J., and Valerie Cunningham. *Black Portsmouth: Three Centuries of African-American Heritage*. Durham: University of New Hampshire Press, 2004.

Smith, Helen Evertson. *Colonial Days and Ways as Gathered from Family Papers*. New York: Century Company, 1901.

Smith, Mrs. Samuel Harrison [Margaret Bayard]. *The First Forty Years of Washington Society*. New York: Charles Scribner's Sons, 1906.

Soltow, Lee. *Distribution of Wealth and Incomes in the United States in 1798*. Pittsburgh: University of Pittsburgh Press, 1989.

Thayer, Theodore. *As We Were: The Story of Old Elizabethtown*. Elizabeth, N.J.: New Jersey Historical Society, 1964.

Upton, Dell. *Holy Things and Profane: Anglican Parish Churches in Colonial Virginia*. New Haven: Yale University Press, 1986.

Wolf, Stephanie Grauman. *As Various as Their Land: The Everyday Lives of Eighteenth-Century Americans*. New York: HarperCollins, 1993.

Zimmerman, Philip D. *Seeing Things Differently*. Winterthur, Del.: Henry Francis du Pont Winterthur Museum, 1992.

BOOKS ON THE FOUNDERS

Bailyn, Bernard. *To Begin the World Anew: The Genius and Ambiguities of the American Founders*. New York: Alfred A. Knopf, 2003.

Billias, George Athan, ed. *George Washington's Generals*. New York: William Morrow, 1964.

Boyd, Julian P., and W. Edwin Hemphill. *The Murder of George Wythe*. Williamsburg, Va.: Institute of Early American History and Culture, 1955.

Burstein, Andrew. *Jefferson's Secrets: Death and Desire at Monticello*. New York: Basic Books, 2005.

Callahan, North. *Henry Knox: General Washington's General*. New York: Rinehart & Company, 1958.

Chernow, Ron. *Alexander Hamilton*. New York: Penguin Press, 2004.

Cooper, Helen A. *John Trumbull: The Hand and Spirit of a Painter*. New Haven: Yale University Art Gallery, 1982.

Custis, George Washington Parke. *Recollections and Private Memoirs of Washington*. New York: Derby & Jackson, 1860.

Ellis, Joseph J. *American Sphinx: The Character of Thomas Jefferson*. New York: Alfred A. Knopf, 1996.

———. *Founding Brothers: The Revolutionary Generation*. New York: Alfred A. Knopf, 2000.

———. *His Excellency George Washington*. New York: Alfred A. Knopf, 2004.

Fischer, David Hackett. *Washington's Crossing*. New York: Oxford University Press, 2004.

Flexner, James Thomas. *George Washington*. 4 vols. Boston: Little, Brown, 1965–1972.

Flower, Milton E. *John Dickinson, Conservative Reactionary*. Charlottesville: University of Virginia Press, 1983.

Foster, William E. *Stephen Hopkins: A Rhode Island Statesman*. Providence, R.I.: Sidney S. Rider, 1884.

Fowler, Henry Thatcher. *General Knox and His Home in Maine, Montpelier*. Thomaston, Maine: Knox Memorial Association, 1931.

Monticello (left) in 1802 as recorded by houseguest Anna Maria Thornton, wife of architect of the Capitol, William Thornton. Behind the cabinet door in the dining room mantel (right) Jefferson hid a dumbwaiter to the basement for delivering wine from the cellar.

Freeman, Douglas Southall. *George Washington*. 7 vols. New York: Charles Scribner's Sons, 1948–1957.

Griffiths, Thomas Morgan. *Major General Henry Knox and the Last Heirs to Montpelier*. Monmouth, Maine: Monmouth Press, 1965.

Hamilton, Allan Maclane. *The Intimate Life of Alexander Hamilton*. New York: Charles Scribner's Sons, 1910.

Henderson, Archibald. Washington's Southern Tour, 1791. Boston: Houghton Mifflin, 1923.

Jenkins, Charles Francis. *Jefferson's Germantown Letters*. Philadelphia: William J. Campbell, 1906.

———. *Washington in Germantown*. Philadelphia: William J. Campbell, 1905.

Johnson, Herbert Alan. *John Jay, 1745–1829*. Third ed. Albany: University of the State of New York/State Education Department, 1970.

Judson, L. Carroll. *A Biography of the Signers of the Declaration of the Independence and of Washington and Patrick Henry*. Philadelphia: J. Dobson, and Thomas, Cowperthwait & Co., 1839.

Kirkland, C. M., C. F. Briggs, et al. *Homes of American Statesmen: With Anecdotal, Personal, and Descriptive Sketches*. New York: Alfred W. Upham, 1858.

Konkle, Burton Alva. *Benjamin Chew: 1722–1810*. Philadelphia: University of Pennsylvania Press, 1932.

Krawczynski, Keith. *William Henry Drayton: South Carolina Revolutionary Patriot*. Baton Rouge: Louisiana State University Press, 2001.

Langguth, A.J. Patriots: *The Men Who Started the American Revolution*. New York: Simon & Schuster, 1988.

Lee, Richard Henry. *The Letters of Richard Henry Lee*. New York: Macmillan Company, 1911–1914.

Lossing, Benson J. *Biographical Sketches of the Signers of the Declaration*. New York: George F. Cooledge and Brother, 1858.

McCullough, David. *1776*. New York: Simon & Schuster, 2005.

———. *John Adams*. New York: Simon & Schuster, 2001.

MacIntire, Jane Bacon. *Lafayette, the Guest of the Nation*. Newton, Mas.: Anthony J. Simone Press, 1967.

McLean, Jennifer P. *The Jays of Bedford*. Katonah, N.Y.: Friends of John Jay Homestead, 1984.

Malone, Dumas. *Jefferson and His Time*. 6 vols. Boston: Little, Brown, 1948–1981.

Mayo, Lawrence Shaw. *John Langdon of New Hampshire*. Concord, N.H.: Rumford Press, 1937.

Reardon, John J. *Peyton Randolph, 1721–1775: One Who Presided*. Durham, N.C.: Carolina Academic Press, 1982.

Rosenberger, Francis Coleman. *Jefferson Reader: A Treasury of Writing About Thomas Jefferson*. New York: E. P. Dutton, 1953.

Rowland, Kate Mason. *The Life of George Mason*. New York: Russell & Russell, 1964.

Sedgwick, Theodore, Jr. *A Memoir of the Life of William Livingston*. New York: J. & J. Harper, 1833.

Stahr, Walter. *John Jay: Founding Father*. New York: Hambledon and London, 2005.

Stein, Susan R. *The Worlds of Thomas Jefferson at Monticello*. New York: Harry N. Abrams, 1993.

Stiverson, Gregory A., and Phebe R. Jacobsen. *William Paca, A Biography*. Baltimore: Maryland Historical Society, 1776.

Whichard, Willis P. *Justice James Iredell*. Durham, N.C.: Carolina Academic Press, 2000.

Wiencek, Henry. *An Imperfect God: George Washington, His Slaves, and the Creation of America*. New York: Farrar, Straus & Giroux, 2003.

Wood, Gordon. *The American Revolution: A History*. New York: Random House, 2002.

———. *The Americanization of Benjamin Franklin*. New York: Penguin Press, 2004.

Index

The Schuyler Mansion, Albany, New York.

The homes of Silas Deane (left) and Joseph Webb, Wethersfield, Connecticut.

LEFT: *Stephen Hopkins of Rhode Island.* RIGHT: *George Read of Delaware.*

Gunston Hall, Mason's Neck, Virginia.